Dave knows firsthand the difference between living a life of brokenness or fully living a renewed life of redemption. In his book, Addition By Subtraction, Dave guides you through that same journey so your pain no longer holds you back from what God has in store!

Kyle Idleman
Senior Pastor, Southeast Christian Church
Author of not a fan and Don't Give Up

At last, a book that helps readers understand the real struggles of the heart, the honest cries of the soul and the unending kindness and mercy of a God that heals and restores. Dr. Dave is a master at taking you on a journey in order to bring wholeness to every piece of your broken heart. Help is here!

Bill and Lisa Roitsch
Founders, Power of His Love Ministries
Authors of Shame, Let's Break Up

Dr. Dave tackles an issue at the core of every human being's life; identity, and the shame that steals a healthy identity! God created us with a healthy identity by creating us in His Image. Unfortunately, the wounds of the sin nature within us and others muddle that. In his book, Dr. Dave is not just reminding us of our God-given identity, but he is taking us on a journey with God to heal our hearts and restore our true identity and the joy that comes from God in it!!

Dr. Lisa Winchell
Founder, HisImage.me and In His Image Institute of Counseling & Training

Addition by Subtraction offers you the opportunity to be honest with your-self about how to make meaningful changes that will transform your life. Bottom line, you can become free from what holds you back, and find true meaning and hope for your heart. Dr. Ralston masterfully assembled the roadmap so that we can all enjoy the journey!

Rev. Steven M. Baran
President, National Christian Counselors Assc

In his book, Addition by Subtraction, Dave reveals his heart for teaching people the reality of how God sees them. Through stories, experiences, and explanations, he shares how Christ can lead us out of our misinterpretations of identity, shame, dependence, and the lies we've learned and believed. And he provides us clear direction into the truth of Jesus' soul healing love. In his book, Dr. Ralston weaves together the beautiful harmony between Biblical truth and clinical understanding to lay out a pathway to restoration. This book is overdue, but Dave brings it to us masterfully.

Katie Englert
Founder & President, Compass Counseling

Broken pieces of our lives are often covered up, denied, or completely misunderstood. Addition by Subtraction uncovers the beauty of brokenness, how to embrace our brokenness, and the Biblical purpose to brokenness. Learn how our broken pieces, redeemed by Jesus, make us whole. The Master + our broken pieces = MASTERPIECES! Thank you, Dr. Dave.

Denny Stevenson
Care & Shepherding Director, Crossroads Christian Church

Addition By Subtraction:

GOD TURNS OUR BROKEN PIECES INTO MASTERPIECES

*How to Let Go of Your Past and Discover
Lasting Hope for the Future*

DAVID RALSTON, PHD

WESTBOW
PRESS®
A DIVISION OF THOMAS NELSON
& ZONDERVAN

WestBow Press books may be ordered through booksellers or by contacting:

WestBow Press
A Division of Thomas Nelson & Zondervan
1663 Liberty Drive
Bloomington, IN 47403
www.westbowpress.com
844-714-3454

ISBN: 978-1-6642-3716-2 (sc)
ISBN: 978-1-6642-3717-9 (hc)
ISBN: 978-1-6642-3715-5 (e)

Library of Congress Control Number: 2021911657

Print information available on the last page.

WestBow Press rev. date: 11/12/2021

DEDICATION

Dedicated to my wonderful wife Ann, who has been the most amazing partner, encourager, and fan I could ever hope for. And to our four amazing kids – Becky, Sean, Mike, and Seth – and each of their beautiful families. Each of you entered into my journey at different times, yet at exactly the right times. When my days on this earth are finished, my hope and prayer is that you will say of me that your life was more full, your journey was more hopeful, your heart was more whole, and Jesus was more real to you because I was in your life.

CONTENTS

SECTION 2: THE ROADMAP

Piece 5: TURN: *I'm A New Creation!*

"Broken pieces become Masterpieces."

Dr. Dave Ralston

Trust Me, I've Been There

When my personal journey from my broken past began, I was a 26-year-old husband, father, professional, and young "Christian." I put the word Christian in quotations, because for me to call myself a Christian at that point was literally more of a label than it was anything deep or authentic. Five years earlier, I had "given my life to Jesus" the best I knew how. Yet very little had changed in me or in my life aside from my having a greater assurance of going to heaven when that day would someday come (not that that alone is any small thing). Besides that, I was pretty much the same ol' Dave living with the same persistent inner struggles, thought patterns, false beliefs, compulsions, and emptiness that had become familiar through a good bit of my life.

Most people had no trouble believing I was a Christian though. I had cleaned up most of the bad behaviors and habits developed in college and grad school. I was very responsible in my roles both at home and at work. My young family and I were in church every time the doors were opened. And we were involved in the lives of others. So, why not think Dave was everything a Christian – let alone a good man, husband, and father – was supposed to be? How could inner peace be something I lacked?

Just a couple years earlier, I had earned my master's degree from the University of Michigan and became the first person through all of the generations of my family to receive a master's degree. While in graduate school, I had the amazing opportunity to serve as an assistant athletic trainer for the Michigan Wolverines football team and became personally acquainted with high-profile folks like legendary coach Bo Schembechler, and current coach Jim Harbaugh.

What more could a guy want than to have a great career, a loving family, and a newly discovered Christian faith. Sounds like the American dream. Honestly it had also been <u>my</u> dream since childhood. But as the dream on the inside of me began to becme reality on the outside, I still felt just as empty and confused as before. But empty of what? And confused about what? I really had no idea how to answer those questions. I just knew something wasn't right.

For several years, I had tirelessly hoped and prayed and searched for something – anything – that might take away the obscure pain that smoldered deep in my soul. I had tried to placate it with success, approval, prestige, degrees, marriage, religion. These didn't make it go away. And neither did pornography or masturbation or alcohol. These just seemed to make the pain even worse. It was a gnawing that not only could I not explain; but when I attempted to speak about it with others, they just looked at me with a strange look, kind of like my Cavalier King Charles Spaniel, Astro, does when I ask him if he's cute. Head cocked to the side. Eyes half glazed over. Totally perplexed.

It was then that a lifelong friend gave me a book – just out of nowhere – and she suggested I read it… soon. No apparent reason. No specific instructions. She just believed that it could be something I might want to read. To be honest, I had never spent much time reading just for leisure. So, I politely accepted her gift, but with no real intention of doing anything with it.

Hope Became Within Reach

Oh my! While holding my 6-month-old, very-premature, very small son Sean in my lap one evening, I began reading the book that had begun to gather dust on my nightstand. And I read. And underlined. And read some more. And marked with circles and asterisks and double underlines. And kept on reading. At some point, after putting Sean in his crib, I just kept on reading well into the night. Until I had read the entire book. All 240 pages of it!

You're probably thinking that the book was a classic, like *Mere Christianity* by C.S. Lewis. Or maybe *The Hiding Place* by Corrie Ten

Boom. Or possibly a best-selling book by Dr. James Dobson or Pastor Bill Hybels. Nope, it wasn't one of those.

The title of the book was *Bradshaw On: The Family*, by bestselling author John Bradshaw. In the 1980s this wasn't a book you would find at the local Christian bookstore. Or even on the shelf in your church library. Today you can though, through numerous online Christian book distributors. It was a personal growth book written by a very experienced professional counselor. And I have no idea where my friend had even found it. But it was a gift that God had sent directly to me right when I needed it the most!

I had never heard of this guy Bradshaw. But as I read intently through the pages of his book, I literally felt like he knew me more completely than anyone else in my life, maybe even myself. He was telling my story. He was speaking of the emotions I had long felt but could not articulate. He described the family I had grown up in as if he had been our next-door neighbor. It was surreal. Many times, even painful. But miraculously, it was very healing. What I read in this book began to create a bridge – a connection for the very first time – between my wounded soul and the life I knew that God had prepared for me. Up to this point in my life, those were two parallel roads. Now there was a glimmer of hope!

The author spoke of things like toxic shame and dysfunctional family roles and codependency and frozen feelings and compulsiveness and on and on. The validation and hope I experienced in reading and reflecting on that book literally changed the trajectory of my life from that moment forward!

Something Had to Change

Maybe you're thinking or feeling similar to how I was thirty or so years ago. I knew something wasn't right within me. I knew that by growing up in the family system that I had, there were parts of my inner person that in some ways had been underdeveloped, and in other ways even damaged. But I had no idea what all that meant, or how to do anything about it. I just knew something wasn't right. And I didn't want to spend the rest of my life feeling that way, believing I had to strive to prove that I was enough, seeking others' approval to know that I was accepted, and believing that something about me made me different than other people, especially other men. Something had to change!

This was long before some of the trendy sayings like "broken to be made whole" even began to enter the Christian landscape. Long before personal self-care was talked about at any level beyond just eating right and exercising. Long before the Christian community, let alone the church, began to allow "imperfect" people to enter through their doors. Long before society began to accept that being human was actually an okay thing.

In those early days of my journey, it was a pretty lonely road. It seemed that, at age 27, I was watching an amazing, life-changing movie that hadn't even been released to the public yet. I loved it and craved more of it. Every scene resonated deep within me. But no one I talked to about it could even begin to understand. They seemed to either pity me for being so emotionally undone. Or they tried to fix me because my newly discovered vulnerability caused them to feel really uncomfortable. Or they related to me as though my real life was a poor representation of my claim to be a Christian.

But, as I look back on the many years that I've been on this journey, it has become very evident that through this season of aloneness, I learned to need Jesus more desperately, to love Him more intimately, and to trust Him more fully. Each time I took the risk to be more honest with myself, more vulnerable before others, and more trusting in Him for my hope and my future, I seemed to grow closer to Jesus. I took the risks. God did the rest.

The Road Has Been Narrow and Rough at Times

Despite any resistance I encountered – real or imagined, within me or around me – God has given me the stamina to continue on this amazing adventure with Him, for decades now. If I'm totally honest and transparent, the most persistent obstacle along the path has been me. Sometimes I felt like I had no more energy, no more motivation, and no more hope to keep pushing the ball forward. Yet, other times, when things seemed to be going well for me, my attentiveness to my inner journey would just get placed on a shelf in my mind. But God was always faithful to draw me back onto the path and to breathe new vigor into my soul. And forward movement would resume.

Similar to the process of breathing, the journey of transformation in Christ includes amazing, refreshing periods where we breathe in God's love, mercy, and renewing hope. But there will also be just as many seasons where we exhale a deep sigh, honestly not sure we have the energy (or the desire for that matter) to continue onward.

Paradox Became My New Normal

On the mountaintops, as well as in the darkest, driest valleys along this path, I've never doubted that God has been with me. Whether I have been breathing in His love or breathing out my shame, He has remained steadfast in moving me forward on the path He had laid out for me. Therein lies the paradox that gave me the clarity to write this book – my sin, shame, and brokenness made whole only in Jesus. This seeming contradiction is a wonderful reminder that all that I am is found in Him!

> **Because of the sin living in me** — shame, sarcasm, dishonesty, self-righteousness, sexual immorality, criticism, retaliation, selfishness, privilege, giving up, anger, abandonment, unforgiveness, envy, pretentiousness, recklessness, pride – I do the evil I do not want to do. [from Romans 7:15-20]

> **Because of Jesus,** I am completely forgiven and fully pleasing to God, and I no longer have to fear failure. Because of Jesus, I am totally accepted by God, and I no longer have to fear rejection. Because of Jesus, I am deeply loved by God, and I no longer have to fear punishment, nor do I have to punish others. And because of Jesus, I have been made brand new, complete in Christ, and I no

longer need to experience the pain of shame. [From *The Search For Significance*]

In innumerable ways, both subtle and profound, God continues to turn my darkness into light, my story into His, and my brokenness into a Masterpiece.

- Obstacles become redirects
- Conflicts become opportunities
- Codependence becomes compassion
- Sadness becomes empathy
- Control becomes influence
- Worry becomes meditation
- Loneliness becomes solitude
- Perfectionism becomes attentiveness
- Unforgiveness becomes mercy
- Failure becomes grace
- Hopelessness becomes purpose

"Consider it pure joy, my brothers and sisters, whenever you face **trials** of many kinds, because you know that the testing of your faith produces perseverance. Let **perseverance** finish its work so that you may be **mature** and complete, not lacking anything" (James 1:2-4 NIV).

Come with Me on A Journey

"We can make our plans, but the Lord determines our steps" (Proverbs 16:9 NLT).

"If the path before you is clear, you're probably on someone else's." (Joseph Campbell)

"If you are able to see further than others, it is because you are standing upon the shoulders of giants." (Sir Isaac Newton)

My entire adult life I've been fortunate to stand on the shoulders of many wonderful, trustworthy men and women, and have journeyed along the paths they have cleared before me. I invite you to do the same.

In the words of the apostle Paul, "Follow my example, as I follow the example of Christ" (1 Corinthians 11:1 NIV). Stand on my shoulders. Sojourn a few steps behind me on the path. Trust that where God has led me, He will lead you as well. **Get ready for an amazing, life changing journey!**

SECTION 1

THE JOURNEY

PIECE 1

Identity: *Who Am I?*

"But to all who believed Him and accepted Him, He gave the right to become children of God."

John 1:12 NLT

CHAPTER 1

I Don't Even Know
Who I Am

From the moment the concept of writing this book came to my mind, my hope has been to provide a clearly illuminated pathway upon which hurting people can move from a place of inner pain and brokenness to a future filled with hope and purpose.

Unknowingly, the person each of us has become is externally defined by the unhealthy life experiences and the false narratives we've held onto for as long as we can remember. The inescapable effect of this is a loss of identity – lack of a clear concept of who we are. Regardless our story, if we experienced any form of hurt, rejection, abandonment, or loss during childhood, we continue to battle something inside us that we wish we could fix.

The thread that connects every one of us reading this book is that our identity has been adversely defined by the actions or inactions of others. We're all byproducts of shame-based, emotionally unhealthy family systems, functioning within a fallen world. This can occur regardless of our age, gender, race, nationality, or generation. And in twenty-first century America, this is not limited only to the family, but now underlies the culture of our churches, workplaces, communities, and society as a whole.

A New Life Has Begun

I've found that within some Christian circles, a discussion of soul health often seems to be awkward, off limits, or even taboo. Many well-meaning church folks strongly believe that when an individual placed their faith in Jesus Christ, every part of their being became "new" – spirit, soul, and body. In 2 Corinthians 5:17 (NLT), the apostle Paul states:

> "This means that anyone who belongs to Christ has become a new person. The old life is gone; a new life has begun!"

The blood of Christ makes us new from that moment forward. Jesus remarkably sent His spirit to live within the heart of every believer so that we might experience His intimate presence moment by moment, forever and ever. Jesus knew that Him living in the hearts of His disciples was more significant than Him walking beside them. This process of being made new is referred to as "justification." Jesus took upon Himself the sin of every human being that will ever live (mercy) and placed within us His righteous standing with God the Father (grace).

> "For God made Christ, who never sinned, to be the offering for our sin, so that we could be made right with God through Christ" (2 Corinthians 5:21 NLT).

All who have placed their faith in Jesus Christ alone are promised to live in His presence for all eternity in a place called heaven (see John 3:16, John 5:24, Ephesians 2:8-9, Romans 10:13).

At the moment we are justified, God's spirit within us commences an unceasing transformation of our soul – mind, will, and emotions – into the very nature of Jesus Christ. The lifelong journey of becoming more like Jesus unfolds through the remainder of our life on earth (see Galatians 2:20, 1 Thessalonians 5:23, Romans 12:2, Philippians 1:6, Matthew 16:24). The Bible calls this transformational process "sanctification." Dying to self. Being transformed into the very nature and character of Jesus.

Please don't miss this, okay? Justification saves you to be <u>with</u> Jesus. Sanctification transforms you to be more <u>like</u> Jesus. The two are interdependent, yet very distinct. Your Christian life will seem hollow and lacking if one of these two is developed disproportionately to the other. **The maturity of a person's spirit will not exceed the health of their soul!**

Who (Or What) Have I Given Power to Define Me?

In a very simplistic sense, "identity" is as fundamental as how a person perceives themselves. It addresses the deep question, "Who am I?" Through childhood, how we learned to see ourselves was a result of the imperfect people we were surrounded by and the fallen world we grew up in. Because we were impressionable young children, we believed that everything we learned from these sources was true and right. And in many ways, we still do! Regardless of the best of their intentions or abilities, we gave the power to define who we were to people who were just as human, immature, or lacking as ourselves. Our entire life picture began to be painted upon that very canvas. And we carried that self-portrait into adulthood without even being aware.

Finding My True Identity in Christ

Peter Scazzero, in his book entitled *Emotionally Healthy Spirituality: It's Impossible to Be Spiritually Mature, While Remaining Emotionally Immature*, claims, "The vast majority of us go to our graves without knowing who we are."

Our relationship with Jesus provides us a **new identity**. Our true identity. His identity! We are no longer merely a collection of messages the world has defined us by, nor are we defined by the pain and shame of our past. Today, our identity is found in Jesus and lived in relationship with Jesus!

The lies propagated in our heart (both passively and actively) through childhood experiences of shame and codependence are what gave rise to our "false identity." God wants us as His children to be set free from our shame-based identity, and to walk daily in the "true identity" He uniquely knit together within each of us.

> "For you created my inmost being. You knit me together in my mother's womb. I praise you because I am fearfully and wonderfully made. Your works are wonderful, I know that full well" (Psalm 139:13-14 NIV).

3

Truth Lies within the Paradox

Something about me has always had a need for deeper explanations, answers, reasons, and solutions for things. I've never been one to just accept things at face value. I don't really think it's an issue of trust, though. Maybe I just have an inborn hunger for details. Or possibly a compulsive need to solve things. Who knows?

All I know is that I'm magnetically drawn to enigmas like mysteries, puzzles, riddles, cryptograms, spot-the-difference pictures, oxymorons, and pretty much anything that's counterintuitive or not as it appears. But my very favorite – **paradoxes**.

Very Few Answers Are Actually Black-and-White

According to Merriam-Webster's Collegiate Dictionary, a "paradox" is defined as: "a logically self-contradictory statement, or a statement that runs contrary to one's expectation. It is a statement that, despite apparently valid reasoning from true premises, leads to a seemingly self-contradictory or a logically unacceptable conclusion. A paradox usually involves **contradictory-yet-interrelated elements that exist simultaneously and persist over time.**"

Human nature seems to be drawn to what is often referred to as "black-and-white" thinking -- good vs. bad; right vs. wrong; true vs. false. So, the inherent nature of a paradox only adds to the confusion that many of us concrete thinkers already have when it comes to understanding God and His teachings. Further, as we'll discuss at great length throughout this book, internalized brokenness and shame from our past only heighten our demand for absolutes. Anything less arouses fear and insecurity within us, which quickly translates into some familiar pattern of control, compulsivity, or perfectionism.

In stark contrast, King Solomon, known in the Bible as "the wisest man who ever lived," says in Ecclesiastes 7:18 (NLT), "Pay attention to these instructions, for anyone who fears God will avoid both extremes."

From the vantage point of paradox, we might deduce that the best and most important answers are neither black nor white. But rather, a synthesis of both, that, fortunately or unfortunately, cannot be fully comprehended by our human minds. Unlike the two opposite extremes that we are somewhat able to predict or control, the elusive space in the middle can only be navigated through **faith**.

Addition by Subtraction

Prior to the amazing opportunity God has given me to be a Christian counselor, pastor, teacher, and author, I was very fortunate to experience a twenty-five-year career as a certified athletic trainer in Division 1 college athletics. The pinnacle of those years was the opportunity I had to be the lead athletic trainer for the University of Michigan men's basketball team during the historic "Fab Five" era -- Chris, Jalen, Juwan, Jimmy, and Ray. Sounds almost like how someone might describe the Beatles, huh? Paul, John, George, and Ringo.

Well, these guys literally were the "Beatles of Basketball." Droves of people of all ages would line up for hours just to get a picture taken with them, or hopefully to have them scribble an autograph on their game program or t-shirt. At the peak of this amazing ride, we actually had to sneak the entire team out the back doors of some hotels just so they could get to the team bus. At tournament time, when we would stay several days in another city, security would be hired just to contain the crowds of fans that were willing to do almost anything just to get a glimpse. Five eighteen-year-old true freshmen. Two back-to-back national championship games. Unprecedented, and still unduplicated. Go Blue!

My Favorite Paradox Ever

As you might imagine, doing life through those years with these guys and these teams was an amazing ride. Everywhere they went, I was there with them -- every practice, locker room, bus trip, airplane, airport, hotel, restaurant, and game, as well as traversing more states and countries than I could ever make a list of. As a team, we together experienced many of the highest of highs... and a few of the lowest of lows that big time sports had to offer.

I became very good friends with head coach Steve Fisher and his family during my years on his staff. He was a wonderful man, husband, father, and coach, and he exemplified faith, class, character, integrity, and so much more in the way he conducted himself. It was a great privilege to walk alongside him during my time in Ann Arbor.

One particular memory of Steve that I hold dearly is when he had called the team together on short notice for an important meeting in the locker room at Crisler Arena. I assumed something big must have been going on for a meeting of this nature to have been called. When there was a meeting, all team personnel were there. And that included me.

I've slept too many nights since then to remember all that Coach Fisher said in that meeting. But the one statement he said that I will never forget: **"addition by subtraction."** I absolutely loved it!

It was his respectful, yet honest, way of saying that a teammate had made the decision to transfer to another NCAA Division 1 institution. And apparently Coach felt that the chemistry of the team would be better without him. Basically, he was saying, **"Something was gained by something being lost."** The perfect paradox!

First in A Series

Addition by Subtraction is the first in a series of books I'll be authoring, each one continuing the paradox theme. I have come to believe that many of us struggle to make sense of our faith because we cannot get God's paradigms to fit into the realm of our logical human understanding and reason.

If we consider what we read about God and His ways as finite and explainable enough to fully comprehend, there's a good chance we're diminishing the amazing truth held within it. It's only by faith that we can even begin to appreciate the depth and breadth of His nature and His ways. And these cannot be found in the extremes. Honestly, the extremes tend to leave little room for true faith, as they compel us to greater levels of human understanding, expectation, and control.

> "'For my thoughts are not your thoughts, neither are your ways my ways," declares the Lord. 'As the heavens

are higher than the earth, so are my ways higher than your ways and my thoughts than your thoughts'" (Isaiah 55:8-9 NIV).

God's Paradoxes

Years ago, there was a beloved Christian preacher and publisher named Henry Clay Trumbull who wrote an entire book about the profound difference in our ways from the ways of God. Trumbull stated,

> It stands to reason that if there is a God in heaven, He would look at things differently from us, from a different vantage and perspective. That results in paradoxes – statements that appear to be contradictory but are actually more true than we can even comprehend. The law of the Christian life is, in itself, a paradox. It is made up of seeming contradictions. All its teachings are contrary to the common opinions of man. According to this law, giving is getting; scattering is gaining; holding is losing; having nothing is possessing all things; dying is living; it is he who is weak who is strong; happiness is found when it is no longer sought; the clearest sight is of the invisible; and things which are not bring about things which are.

I've been a born-again Christian since I was twenty-one years old. During that entire time, I have been intrigued by the truths of the Bible that land somewhere inexplicably between the opposites. Through the decades, those have been the lessons that have most meaningfully convicted my heart, grown my faith, and deepened my relationship with Jesus.

- **To be whole, we must be broken** (from Psalm 51:17)
- **To really live, we must die** (from Galatians 2:20).
- **To save our life, we must lose it** (from Luke 17:33)
- **To be wise, we must become fools** (from 1 Corinthians 3:18)
- **To reign, we must serve** (from Matthew 25:21)
- **To be exalted, we must become humble** (from Matthew 23:12)

- **To be first, we must be last** (from Matthew 20:16)
- **To bear fruit, we must first die** (from John 12:24)
- **To be strong, we must become weak** (from 2 Corinthians 12:10)
- **To have, we must freely give** (from Acts 20:35)
- **To be free, we must submit** (from Romans 6:18)
- **To gain, we must lose** (from Philippians 3:7-8)
- **To possess, we must accept having nothing** (from 2 Corinthians 6:10)
- **To find happiness, we must stop seeking it** (from Matthew 5:3-10)
- **To be more like Jesus, we must die to ourselves** (from Matthew 16:24)

From Broken Pieces to Masterpieces

There is no greater example of this book's title – Addition *by Subtraction* (something being gained by something being lost) – than God's promise to turn the broken pieces of our lives into masterpieces! That is an incredible paradox – a perfect masterpiece created entirely from broken pieces?

Kintsugi = Precious Recreation

Kintsugi is the centuries-old Japanese art of giving new life to broken pottery. Rather than rejoin ceramic pieces with an invisible adhesive, the Kintsugi technique employed a special tree sap lacquer dusted with powdered gold. Once completed, beautiful seams of gold glint in the conspicuous cracks of ceramic wares, gave a distinctive appearance to each "re-created" piece.

This unique method celebrated each item's unique history by emphasizing its fractures and breaks instead of hiding or disguising them. In fact, Kintsugi often makes the repaired piece even more precious and valuable than the original, remaking it with a new look and giving it a new life.

While Kintsugi's origins aren't entirely clear, historians believe that it dates back to the late fifteenth century. According to legend, the craft commenced when Japanese shogun Ashikaga Yoshimasa sent a precious cracked tea bowl back to China to undergo repair. To esteem the one who owned the item, craftsmen sought to employ an aesthetically pleasing method of restoring, and Kintsugi was born.

I Am God's Masterpiece

The most remarkable element of the word "masterpiece" is **master**. Regardless the nature of the piece itself – art, writing, music, design – it isn't precious because of what it is. No, the greatness of the piece is because of the one who created it! The master.

> "For we are God's masterpiece. He has created us anew
> in Christ Jesus, so we can do the good things He planned
> for us long ago" (Ephesians 2:10 NLT).

You and I no longer need to wonder or worry about the "why's" in life. Why did this happen? Why didn't that happen? Why was God not there? Why did He not answer my prayers? Why? Why? Why?

When we allow ourselves to fully trust <u>the Master</u>, we can find rest in knowing that He loves us fully and without conditions. He has a plan and purpose for our lives that cannot be disrupted, derailed, or denied by our own doing, or by that of others whose lives have been interwoven into ours. And He knows how to assemble all of the broken pieces into something greater than we could have ever imagined.

> "'For I know the plans *and* thoughts that I have for you,'
> says the Lord, 'plans for peace *and* well-being and not
> for disaster, to give you a future and a hope'" (Jeremiah
> 29:11 AMP)

As I've contemplated the peaks and valleys of my own life, I've learned a better, much more fruitful question than asking God "why?" I try to ask Him, "What now, God?"

In this question, He constantly reassures my heart that He loves me and cherishes me; He is with me amid every moment of my past, present, and future; He is fully aware of my current circumstances; and He is at work, intricately unfolding the one-of-a-kind story of my life – **a Masterpiece.**

Questions from Dr. Dave

For personal reflection or group discussion of Chapter 1

In this chapter I made the statement, "The maturity of a person's spirit will not exceed the authenticity of their soul." Assuming this to be true, is the person you present to others an accurate and authentic reflection of the inner person that only you and God fully know? What may be the reasons you are reluctant to reveal the "real" you?

Jesus teaches that to truly follow Him we must die to our flesh nature so that we might become more like Him. Is your personal journey with Jesus marked with times along the path where more of you died, and you became a little more like Jesus? If not, what would indicate to others that you are a follower of Jesus?

I've made a pretty strong case that a life in Christ is not defined by choosing good over bad and right over wrong, but rather in the paradox of the two opposites. As you read and pondered God's paradoxes in this chapter, in what ways did this cause you to rethink your current views of God and His word? Is it easier for you to live in a dichotomous world, or in the paradox of the two opposites?

"It's impossible to be spiritually mature while remaining emotionally immature."

Peter Scazzero

CHAPTER 2

Being Made Whole

For centuries, mankind has tried to create an improved version of ourselves. There seems to be a widespread assumption that in order to find ultimate fulfillment in life, we must find a way to become "better." Self-help books are flying off the shelves like never before. Researchers have discovered that today's younger generations are far more spiritually curious than their forefathers, although much less interested in organized religion. New churches are springing up every week, promising innovative methods to help their members find health and happiness. And for some, the promise of change is founded on the development of their human potential.

Despite all of this momentum toward self-improvement, the prevalence of anxiety, depression, and hopelessness in American culture has reached an all-time high. In fact, a study conducted by *US News and World Report* found the United States to be "one of the most depressed countries in the world." So, what's the disconnect? Are all the churches and preachers and teachers and books and podcasts all getting it wrong? Or could there possibly be an underlying flaw in the way we as civilized, intelligent human beings believe "wholeness" is found?

Only Jesus Can Make Us Whole

The Bible teaches that, in the words of the apostle Paul, a new life is the result of "belonging" to Jesus Christ.

"This means that anyone who belongs to Christ has become a new person. The old life is gone; a new life has begun!" (2 Corinthians 5:17 NLT).

Many, many Christians, let alone numerous churches and doctrinal perspectives, have fallen prey to the false belief that when a person makes the decision to believe in Jesus, God then does all the work from that point forward. All we have to do is simply say "yes" to Jesus and everything about us becomes new and different! And He assures us health, abundance, and happiness in our lives.

My longtime friend Kevin once told me: "Following Jesus is simple; it's just not easy." In other words, he was telling his young, newly saved friend that to follow Jesus was not complicated. But it would be a challenging journey that would span a lifetime.

My pastor and virtual mentor, Kyle Idleman, wrote in his book *not a fan*, "There **is** no way to follow Jesus without Him interfering in your life. Following Jesus will cost you something. Following Jesus always costs you something."

Why is it that way? Well, I've learned that in order to follow Jesus – to be His disciple and to experience authentic life change – there is one huge obstacle I must get past. ME. It took me many years to accept the fact that I don't possess the solution to my problems. I am my problem! And since becoming aware of this painful yet freeing reality, my life has discovered a genuine faith and love and grace and hope and purpose that I never knew were possible.

Couldn't God have chosen to just deliver us from the hurts of our past, and save us from the pain of having to work through them? Absolutely He could have. And in some people's lives He probably has. But I don't believe that's His typical MO. His greater desire is to use all of the experiences of our life to progressively mold us into the character and nature of Jesus. This transformation requires a process. A journey. Turning from the brokenness of life. Turning toward wholeness in Christ.

I Thought I Was a Christian

I can't even begin to tell you the number of counseling clients I've met over the past decade or so who have sincerely said to me something like this:

"I've always thought I was a Christian. But, if I really am, why do I still struggle with so much shame and doubt deep inside me? I thought God was supposed to take that away, wasn't He?"

Unfortunately, this widespread assumption, coupled with generations of pretentiousness among average American churchgoers, has caused countless individuals to go "underground" with their real-life inner struggles. Assuming the church doesn't care about their hurts. Or being dissuaded from trusting their relationship with Jesus, on the grounds "if I'm really saved, I shouldn't have these struggles."

Maybe we're battling loneliness we've felt since a parent passed away prematurely. Or feelings of unworthiness stemming from the emotional or physical absence of our father during childhood. Or the shame of having been addicted or incarcerated or divorced. Or maybe an overall inability to feel feelings at all, which is causing issues with intimacy in our marriage. Or shame-based perfectionism that blankets every part of our life. Or the compulsive need to be in control, even of the uncontrollable.

Without an emotionally safe, accepting environment where our deep, honest feelings can be expressed and validated, these become isolating "secrets" that we vow to never tell anyone. False beliefs – our beliefs that have no basis in truth – begin to sprout like weeds in our mind. They convince us it's not safe to expose the "real" us, for fear others will reject us or not like us, or not love us, or not approve us, or not accept us anymore. And that would feel worse than death itself.

As Claudia Black presents in her book *It Will Never Happen to Me*, these predictable responses are referred to as the "three dysfunctional family rules."

- **Don't talk.** "There's no way I could ever talk about what's really going on in my life. I have to pretend like everything is fine. That way everyone will think I'm fine. Because I know if I was really honest with people, they would just reject me."
- **Don't trust.** "People can't be trusted. If I ask them for anything, they'll either not care, be emotionally absent, or break their promises. So, it's safer to just not trust."
- **Don't feel.** "I refuse to acknowledge my feelings, because if I do, they will either be ignored, or who I express them to will become

angry, place blame on me, or shame me for being weak. So, it's safer to just to stuff feelings down. That way no one else can hurt me."

Connecting the Dots

John Bradshaw (along with several other authors, teachers, and pastors) laid out a path for me. Not the answer. Not a guru. But a path that would connect the unhealthiness of my soul with the presence of the spirit of Christ within me. Prior to that, these had been two parallel roads that seemed to have no hope of ever intersecting. That was 1988. I'm still on that journey today – yet countless miles further along the path. My sincere hope is to illuminate that path for you through the chapters of this book, so that you may have a roadmap of sorts to nudge you forward.

So, what's the destination this transformational pathway leads to? Surely, it's perfection, right? Or complete healing of the human soul? Or deliverance from anything that's painful? Or the erasing of uncomfortable memories from the past? Nope. **The journey is the goal!** It's much less about where the path is leading, and more about who I'm becoming while on that path. As Peter Scazzero put it in his book *Emotionally Healthy Spirituality,* "The critical issue on the journey with God is not "Am I happy?" but "Am I free?""

God's intention is for us to be transformed from the unhealthy effects and unrealistic expectations of our past to the life He has created for each of us – a life that is "pleasing and perfect." He offers us true inner joy, acceptance, hope, and purpose. His purpose!

> "And so, dear brothers and sisters, I plead with you to give yourselves fully to God because of all He has done for you. Let this be a living and holy sacrifice—the kind He will find acceptable. This is truly the way to worship Him. Don't copy the behavior and customs of this world, but let God transform you into a new person by changing the way you think. Then you will learn to know God's will for you, which is good and pleasing and perfect" (Romans 12:1-2 NLT).

Spirit and Soul Must Intersect

What I had been feeling all those years was that my spirit person and my soul person were running parallel. I knew many of the relevant truths and principles of the Bible. But what I came to learn about God and Jesus and grace and forgiveness and hope would just not travel the eighteen inches from my head to my heart. I so badly wanted to experience them for myself.

It was almost as though something was blocking the way for Jesus to move from my head (knowing about Jesus and the Bible) to my heart (knowing Jesus personally and intimately). I literally felt myself becoming out of balance and top heavy. Almost like a tall building with too small of a foundation. Or a huge corporation with a poorly developed infrastructure. Growing in my knowledge and understanding of the Christian way, but stagnant in my implementation of what I was learning at a level beyond just "behavior modification." I had become a pretender. A counterfeit Christian. The person I really was and the person that people perceived me to be just didn't line up. And I knew it.

In my counseling practice today, I have at least one client every single day tell me they are facing a similar dilemma. "Why can I not experience all that I know God has for me? What am I missing? What am I doing wrong?"

I repeatedly thank God for walking with me through the pain of my past, and for giving me the opportunity to know more of His love in the midst of each experience.

Author Troy Dobbs in his book, *The Blessed Life That No One Really Wants*, illuminates what I'm saying in his unpacking of the story of Joseph (son of Jacob) in the Old Testament: "Through a series of providentially painful events – false accusations, unjust imprisonment, and being forgotten to name a few – God eventually positioned Joseph (for the ultimate purpose He had created for Joseph)."

Providentially Painful Events

I did an online search for a relevant definition of the word "providential." Here is what I found: "Having foresight to make provision beforehand."

Hmm… so God knew in advance that Joseph needed to go through each and every one of the difficult aspects of his personal life journey in order to be fully equipped for the greater purpose God had planned for him at a point later in his future? Through numerous unexpected, undesirable events in Joseph's life, God "positioned" Joseph, so that – at exactly the right time – he would be prepared to participate in the ultimate purpose for which he was created. God created Joseph to share unconditional love with people in his life who least expected it and probably felt they least deserved it – his own brothers who had rejected and abandoned him, and even considered killing him.

If this was true for Joseph, let's trust that it is also true for you and for me. What we've experienced in our past, and what we're facing presently are necessary components of what we'll see unfold in our blessed future! God wants to turn our tests into our testimony. He wants to turn our messes into our message. He wants to turn our broken pieces into masterpieces!

Probably Not the Route We Would Have Chosen

I've found that many Christians have been taught (or assumed) that God's will is a straight, pain-free line that sounds something like this:

> **The better I am…** at *being good, making good choices, being with good people, having a good marriage, making a good living, raising good kids who make good choices and grow up and marry good people who also want to make good choices and have a good family, being good in my career, and having a good plan for retirement* **…the more I'm living in "God's will."**

Unfortunately, this was the path the Pharisees took, believing that if they learned, memorized, taught, perfectly demonstrated, and held others accountable to the 613 laws of the Jewish Torah, they would stand righteous before God. Jesus wasn't too big of a fan of that path. In fact, He intended the path of our lives to look quite the opposite.

I recently ran across a simple hand-drawn illustration on social media that really captured this for me. The upper frame – "Your Plan" – showed a character riding a bicycle from the beginning of a perfectly straight, unhindered line extending slightly upward toward a checkered flag at the end of the line at the far right. In contrast, the lower frame – "God's Plan for You" – took the rider on a much more complicated journey. There were hills and valleys, dense wilderness and wide open spaces, deep water and no water at all, thunderstorms and sunshine, cliffs to fall from and steps to climb up, all leading to the checkered flag on higher ground at the far right.

Jesus' Unlikely Choice

As He often did, Jesus taught an important spiritual lesson through a very practical example. It is entitled "The Parable of the Pharisee and the Tax Collector."

> "To some who were confident of their own righteousness and looked down on everyone else, Jesus told this parable: "Two men went up to the temple to pray, one a Pharisee and the other a tax collector. The Pharisee stood by himself and prayed: 'God, I thank you that I am not like other people—robbers, evildoers, adulterers—or even like this tax collector. I fast twice a week and give a tenth of all I get.'
>
> But the tax collector stood at a distance. He would not even look up to heaven, but beat his breast and said, 'God, have mercy on me, a sinner.'
>
> I tell you that this man (the tax collector), rather than the other (the Pharisee), went home justified before God. For all those who exalt themselves will be humbled, and those who humble themselves will be exalted" (Luke 18: 9-14 NIV).

Jesus made it very clear throughout His earthly ministry that aligning ourselves with Him would take us on an inward journey of transformation, not an outward quest for performance-based approval and self-righteousness.

"Then the Lord said to him, "You Pharisees are so careful to clean the outside of the cup and the dish, but inside you are filthy—full of greed and wickedness!" (Luke 11:39 NLT).

"Woe to you, scribes and Pharisees, hypocrites! For you are like whitewashed tombs, which outwardly appear beautiful, but within are full of dead people's bones and all uncleanness" (Matthew 23:27 NIV).

"You hypocrites! Isaiah was right when he prophesied about you, for he wrote, 'This people honor Me with their lips, but their heart is far away from Me. But in vain do they worship Me" (Matthew 15:7 NLT).

If we believe God's will is like a straight line extended from the moment we're born to the day we take our last breath, we will tirelessly strive to comply to a set of man-made rules, responsibilities, and risk-reducing choices, many times attributing this to "being a good Christian." This belief seems to imply that when we stand before God one day, He will be pleased or impressed by how "righteous" we have been while on this earth. As I have studied the scriptures over many years, I have found that God's word teaches quite the opposite. Let me share two of the most poignant passages regarding the futility of our self-righteousness before God:

"He saved us, not because of the righteous things we had done, but because of His mercy. He washed away our sins, giving us a new birth and new life through the Holy Spirit" (Titus 3:5 NLT).

"God saved you by His grace when you believed. And you can't take credit for this; it is a gift from God. Salvation is not a reward for the good things we have done, so none of us can boast about it" (Ephesians 2:8-9 NLT).

We will discover true freedom only when we allow ourselves to view God's will from the perspective that I sense He does. We will come to understand that God did not create our lives to follow a single, narrow lane that we are obligated to stay within. On the contrary, God's wants us to put Him first as we move through the thousands of moment-by-moment choices and decisions we make in our everyday lives.

In a 2018 sermon at Southeast Christian Church, pastor Kyle Idleman shared this wonderful, practical wisdom regarding God's will:

> As people, we tend to focus on the direction, as if we're at an intersection and we're not sure what to do. We could go left or right, or we could go straight. So, "God, what's your will? Just tell me what to do." The emphasis God puts on His will is not whether you turn left or right or you continue straight. As long as each of these paths are honoring to God, He wants us to choose. His will has more to do with who you are on the path than which path you take. As long as the path is honoring to God, what He is paying attention to is who you are on the path, not which way you go.

It's About Being, Not Doing

Most of us have asked God in a thousand ways, "What is your will for my life?" Bottom line: God cares more about who you are than He does about what you're doing or where you're going. But you may be asking yourself, What about all the good things I've done in my life? What about the hurtful things others have done to me? Do You not care about my future? Doesn't all of this matter? Does it not count for something? Don't you care God?

In the life of a Christ-follower, these things matter only to the degree that they're moving us closer to Jesus and positioning us to show His unconditional love and grace to others. From this perspective, there really aren't good and bad things in life. There are just things, every one of them an incredible opportunity to encounter the unconditional, undeserved, unending love of Jesus. And there really aren't good and bad people in life. There are just people, every one of us with the potential to sin, and the need to experience God's grace and mercy, so that we may be made new in Christ.

Jesus wants to walk with each of us into the painful memories and hurtful experiences that have caused brokenness within us. Every one of these is a doorway to enjoy God's presence more deeply and intimately. The more fully we uncover the ache within us – to ourselves, to God, and to another human being – the more profoundly we'll encounter His life-changing love and grace. He's the only one who can fully know us, fully love us, and fully accept us! This is where the healing of our brokenness occurs.

The Truth None of Us Likes to Hear

Our human nature seems to fight against the most essential ingredient for real, authentic life change to occur. This element many Christians (myself included) struggle to implement in our lives is found in some of Jesus's most important spoken words:

> "For whoever wants to save their life will lose it, but whoever loses their life for Me will find it" (Matthew 16:25 NIV).

In this passage, is Jesus telling us that in order to discover a life of meaning and purpose we have to give up life as we've come to know it? I really believe that is what He is saying. It seems counterintuitive, or even contradictory to our human minds. Many of us who are reading this can't imagine how it could ever work. We are supposed to willingly make ourselves smaller and make Him greater? And somehow that is going to make our lives more joyous and fulfilling? Absolutely!

He's telling us to deliberately put to death all that makes us who we are in this world – past, present, and future – both happy and hurtful. And He promises to redefine our identity into who He created each of us to be. He promises to give our lives more meaning, purpose, and significance, in place of our shame, stress, and fear. It still seems daunting, doesn't it? Can I trust Jesus? Does He really know what's best for me?

Many of us still have a white-knuckle grip on the three biggest obstacles to experiencing a life of wholeness in Christ: CONTROL, CONTROL, and CONTROL.

A Radical Paradox: Dying in Order to Live

God is not speaking in this passage of us losing our life literally, even though there have been times on my journey when the emptiness within me was so great that I wished my life would end.

Dying to self means dying to our flesh – our fallen human nature. I did an online keyword search for words in the Bible that are synonymous with this concept of this "dying to self" we're talking about:

- **Surrender.** 46 occurrences in the Bible.
- **Self-denial.** 54 occurrences in the Bible.
- **Flesh / sinful nature**. 6,166 occurrences in the Bible.

God has a lot to say about this topic! Here are several passages from the Bible that I often turn to as a reminder of where my confidence should lie:

> "My old self has been crucified with Christ. It is no longer I who live, but Christ lives in me. So, I live in this earthly body by trusting in the Son of God, who loved me and gave Himself for me" (Galatians 2:20 NLT).

> "Then he said to the crowd, 'If any of you wants to be my follower, you must give up your own way, take up your cross daily, and follow Me'" (Luke 9:23 NLT).

> "Those who belong to Christ Jesus have nailed the passions and desires of their sinful nature to His cross and crucified them there" (Galatians 5:24 NLT).

> "I tell you the truth, unless a kernel of wheat is planted in the soil and dies, it remains alone. But its death will produce many new kernels—a plentiful harvest of new lives" (John 12:24 NLT).

> "If you try to hang on to your life, you will lose it. But if you give up your life for My sake and for the sake of the Good News, you will save it" (Mark 8:35 NLT).

"If you refuse to take up your cross and follow Me, you are not worthy of being Mine" (Matthew 10:38 NLT).

"He personally carried our sins in His body on the cross so that we can be dead to sin and live for what is right. By His wounds you are healed" (1 Peter 2:24 NLT).

"Don't be selfish; don't try to impress others. Be humble, thinking of others as better than yourselves. Don't look out only for your own interests, but take an interest in others, too" (Philippians 2:3-4 NLT).

"And so, dear brothers and sisters, I plead with you to give your bodies to God because of all He has done for you. Let them be a living and holy sacrifice—the kind He will find acceptable. This is truly the way to worship Him" (Romans 12:1 NLT).

"He must become greater and greater, and I must become less and less" (John 3:30 NLT).

"Don't copy the behavior and customs of this world, but let God transform you into a new person by changing the way you think. Then you will learn to know God's will for you, which is good and pleasing and perfect" (Romans 12:2 NLT).

"So you also should consider yourselves to be dead to the power of sin and alive to God through Christ Jesus" (Romans 6:11 NLT).

To Some, Surrender Sounds a Lot Like Losing

The Bible suggests that there is one primary step needed for us to die to our flesh – **surrender**. Literally one small step that feels like a giant leap. To some of us who are reading this, the word surrender is somehow linked to losing. And for those, losing is unacceptable. In war, if one side surrenders to the other, waving the white flag means they lose. Defeated. Second place. Humiliated. Losers!

We need to get that image out of our heads when we consider the context of the "surrender" God is inviting us to. He certainly doesn't see you and me as losers. I'm sure, when studying other scriptural messages, this image of waving the white flag may have its place, but not when it comes to the healing journey you and I are on. That type of surrender – "I'm a loser" – runs the risk of deepening our shame and may actually reinforce the times in our past that we were dominated, blamed, controlled, manipulated, abused, overlooked, and so on. To that person, losing isn't cathartic; it's tragic. And we'll do anything in our power to avoid it.

I've chosen to use an example from my own life to illustrate a perspective of surrender that I believe is best suited for the transformational work we're doing. When Jesus would do this, His examples became known as "parables." My students and clients have been known to refer to my use of modern-day metaphors as "davisms."

Ann and I have moved a few times over the course of our marriage, but only once to a different state. When we relocated from Kentucky to Texas, we were required to go to the DMV (which in Texas they call the Texas Department of Public Safety) to get a Texas driver's license. Even though we were entirely eligible for a Texas license, and we had brought all of the appropriate papers with us (social security card, birth certificate, proof of residence, etc.), they would not give us our new Texas license until each of us **surrendered** our Kentucky driver's license.

Why did I need to surrender my Kentucky license? They probably just destroyed it anyway. Or sent it back to Kentucky for them to destroy. The reason we were required to surrender our license was not because Texas was trying to prove we had lost some sort of battle. No, it was because **we could not be residents of two states at the same time**. Get that? We had to choose whether we were residents of Texas or residents of Kentucky. It was our decision. But we couldn't choose both.

Where Is My Residency?

God wants every one of us to give up our residency in this world – fallen, unfulfilling, and in decline – and live our lives as residents of His kingdom.

Similar to how Ann and I had to do when we moved to Texas, each of us must surrender our proof of residency in this world if we want to experience the fullness of Christ in our lives.

So, what is the proof of residency in this world that we need to surrender? We are to give God our shame, pride, and fears, our godless beliefs, thoughts, emotions, and behaviors, and our efforts to be "good." Basically, we are to surrender anything that elevates self and stands in front of God on our priority list. God accepts nothing else that we have to offer. To be a resident of His kingdom, we must let go of all that has defined us on this earth. Let's look at what the Bible has to say about this.

"But we are citizens of heaven, where the Lord Jesus Christ lives. And we are eagerly waiting For him to return as our Savior" (Philippians 3:20 NLT).

"Don't copy the behavior and customs of this world, but let God transform you into a new person by changing the way you think. Then you will learn to know God's will for you, which is good and pleasing and perfect" (Romans 12:2 NLT).

"Do not love this world nor the things it offers you, for when you love the world, you do not have the love of the Father in you. For the world offers only a craving for physical pleasure, a craving for everything we see, and pride in our achievements and possessions. These are not from the Father but are from this world. And this world is fading away, along with everything that people crave. But anyone who does what pleases God will live forever" (1 John 2:15-17 NLT).

"But they were looking for a better place, a heavenly homeland. That is why God is not ashamed to be called their God, for he has prepared a city for them" (Hebrews 11:16 NLT).

> "We know that we are children of God and that the world around us is under the control of the evil one" (1 John 5:19 NLT).

> "The world would love you as one of its own if you belonged to it, but you are no longer part of the world. I chose you to come out of the world, so it hates (rejects) you" (John 15:19 NLT).

If you're reading this with a desire to surrender your residency – and all of the baggage that comes with it – yet have little idea how to go about doing it, please allow me to walk you through what the Bible teaches on this subject.

Only One Answer Can Be Correct

Over the years in both my personal Christian journey and full-time ministry, I have had opportunities to ask men and women these two questions: *"Who is Jesus?"* and *"On what basis does God allow a person into heaven?"* At Life Training, these questions are part of our practice's client intake form. So, ever client responds to these questions before we ever meet them or could bias their answers in any way. Although my conclusions are generalized (and certainly not statistically analyzed), the responses I've received tend to fall within these buckets:

- "There is no heaven. When people die, they simply cease to exist."
- "All good people go to heaven. If God is loving, He would not turn away anyone who is good and sincere."
- "Going to heaven is on the basis of merit and good deeds – a sliding scale of good and evil – and we just hope our good acts outweigh our bad ones."
- "What about those who have never heard of Jesus? Because they're good people, surely God wouldn't send them to hell."
- "All ways lead to the same place. Certainly, Jesus is one of those ways, but so are Shiva, Buddha, Allah, and others."

- "Although some "bad" people may need punishment, most people are generally "good" and deserve to go to heaven."
- "Getting to heaven is not on the basis of merit, but on the basis of God's grace through faith in Jesus Christ."

Each of us certainly has the choice to believe about God, Jesus, and heaven as we choose. My personal conviction is that salvation is by faith alone in Christ alone. No other answer is accurate or correct.

> "Jesus answered, 'I am the way and the truth and the life. No one comes to the Father except through Me'" (John 14:6 NIV).

My prayer for you is that by the time you've read this entire book, you would agree that there is no greater, more important truth than this! And no greater hope than Jesus. **He is the only way that we can move from the brokenness within us to the wholeness God has prepared for us.**
The journey begins!

Questions from Dr. Dave

For personal reflection or group discussion of Chapter 2

"There **is** no way to follow Jesus without Him interfering in your life. Following Jesus will cost you something. Following Jesus always costs you something." This statement that I quoted in this chapter seems to push against what has been the prevailing Christian thought in America for generations. In what ways does it align with or stand in opposition to your personal belief system? Are you willing to pursue Jesus for the remainder of your life, no matter what it might cost you?

Like the Pharisees in the first century, we often focus more on what we do than on who we really are. The metaphor of Kintsugi pottery underscores God's desire to turn our broken pieces into masterpieces. Conversely, many of us have lived as though we have no broken pieces, and if any did exist, they were denied, hidden, minimized, or overcome. Which of these two views most accurately describes your story?

Many Christians are readily able to reflect back to a time in their life when they "accepted" Jesus, were baptized, or maybe had a mountaintop experience with God. These are all wonderful parts of a life in Christ but are not the entirety of it. Being entirely honest, has your Christian life been an ongoing story of surrendering to God one day at a time? Or was the last time you surrendered to Him when you originally placed your faith in Jesus?

"The closer you get to God, the better you're going to understand yourself."

Pastor Rick Warren

CHAPTER 3

Our Identity Is Always Found in Someone (Or Something)

The term "codependence" is a word that people tend to hear fairly often yet may not fully understand its meaning. What is it? Where does it come from? Do I have it? We sometimes make IT seem like an incurable disease. Let me comfort your fears. Codependence is not a clinical condition or disorder or diagnosis. It is a learned pattern of thought and behavior that we subconsciously believe will protect us from the possibility of abandonment and rejection.

In essence, we have learned that our identity (who we are) is defined entirely by how others see us, what they teach us, what they say about us, and how they treat us. Another term for this is being "externally defined." This makes it virtually impossible for our identity, worth, and acceptance to become any greater than the sum total of the external messages we've internalized.

New Wine Requires New Wineskins

> "And no one puts new wine into old wineskins. For the wine would burst the wineskins, and the wine and the skins would both be lost. New wine calls for new wineskins" (Mark 2:22 NLT).

Who puts new wine into old wineskins? According to Jesus' words in the passage above, no one should. While I'm certainly not an expert in the field of wine and wineskins, I can pretty easily understand why we shouldn't put new wine into an old wineskin. Over time, the new wine expands but, unlike new wineskins, old wineskins don't. And as a result, the new wine bursts the old wineskins, and both are lost.

Today's twenty-first century generation is crying out for meaningful guidance in connecting the Christian faith model with their real-life struggles. Many authors purport that today's society is more spiritually conscious than their predecessors, yet have difficulty trusting or accepting the belief systems of their forefathers. Unlike their predecessors who trusted the faith of their parents, present-day men and women tend to submit themselves only to systems they deem as trustable, pertinent, and beneficial.

What Would That Look Like?

I've yet to find a comprehensive book on the market today that: 1) offers decisive solutions for letting go of the past and finding enduring hope for the future, 2) is relevant and practical for members of today's pluralistic society, and 3) remains true to a Christian, Biblical ideology. The thorough, comprehensive route provided by *Addition By Subtraction* very effectively addresses these three objectives.

I have immense professional respect for the diligent work of Melody Beattie, John Bradshaw, Stephanie Tucker, and countless others who have provided decades of groundbreaking work on the effects of toxic shame in our lives. Notwithstanding, I believe there is an urgent need to revitalize these concepts in order to maximize their effectiveness in today's world.

Buckle your seatbelt. That's where this adventure is headed!

A Common Thread

Notable author Melody Beattie presented her groundbreaking work on the topic of codependence nearly forty years ago in her bestselling book,

Codependent No More. The principles and perspectives she explained have helped countless millions of men and women from all walks of life, including myself, discover freedom from the shame of our past. What I learned from Melody in the early years of my journey of soul work laid a solid foundation for who and where I am today.

Stephanie A. Tucker, in her publication entitled *The Christian Codependence Recovery Workbook,* provides a succinct Christian viewpoint of recovery from codependence. The soul work and spiritual growth that her book led me through has played an instrumental part in my personal recovery journey. I've been blessed with the opportunity to teach her material on multiple occasions, and each time, I have observed amazing life-change in those who participated.

Melody Beattie's writings and teachings seem to tend toward a non-religious perspective, leaving the God question for each reader to clarify for themselves. The benefit of this, obviously, is that it allows great latitude for men and women of diverse faith traditions and belief systems to find the help they are searching for. Stephanie Tucker's perspectives seem to discuss soul health from a Biblical, Christ-centered viewpoint. Although I have enormous respect for both authors and both viewpoints, I personally align myself with the strongly Christ-centered belief. As a result, this is the sentiment that flows through this entire book.

This difference makes little to no difference in a fundamental understanding of brokenness, shame, and codependency. However, it makes all the difference in how we find hope for lasting, internal change. Beattie's model seems to focus on <u>self-help</u> as its objective, whereas the Christian model focuses on <u>self-denial</u> in order to become more like Jesus. This seemingly "subtle" difference makes all the difference!

Trustworthy Definitions

Here is Stephanie Tucker's basic explanation of codependence extracted from her workbook:

> Historically, the term codependency or codependence was used to refer to the significant other of an active alcoholic.

33

That's because it became apparent that just as the alcoholic suffered from distinct symptoms, the dependent family members also shared in a unique pattern of behavior. Namely, tools of compensation and ultra-controlling behaviors used in an attempt to resolve the alcoholic's problem.

The definition, as we understand it today (2010), applies to much broader situations, although codependence is most obvious in the addiction cycle. For our purposes, we are going to define codependence as: "a set of learned coping skills used to function in an environment that is imbalanced and dysfunctional. It is a counterfeit method of expressing love and engaging in healthy, spiritually based relationships. Codependence manifests itself in a variety of behaviors, but the driving factor of a codependent is an **internal brokenness**.

In truth, codependence can develop or exist wherever relationships (past or current) are love deficient. It also occurs when we look for something from the outside to fill a void we have on the inside. Since that inner void can be filled only by God, a codependent unknowingly attempts to put a person, situation, or thing in Jesus's place. Before getting overwhelmed by that definition, recognize that, by default, all human beings do this to varying degrees.

Additionally, Melody Beattie wrote in her book, *The New Codependence:*

In my earlier book, *Codependent No More* (1986), I defined a codependent person as 'one who has let another person's behavior affect him or her, and who is obsessed with controlling that person's behavior.' But I now know that codependency is about more than that (although controlling and obsessing are good places to start).

While alcoholism in the family can help create codependency, it isn't essential (as was originally believed). How do we know whether to call codependency a disease or a problem? Does it help to call ourselves sick when we already suffer from low self-worth? The behaviors associated with codependency make perfect sense if we look closely enough. It's understandable that we would confuse control with love when control is all we've known. It makes sense that we think controlling will keep us safe, because it did – for a while. All codependent behaviors make sense if traced to their origins.

Altered Through the Generations

In the words of Melody Beattie: "Codependency hasn't disappeared. It's wearing new faces and using different names."

Although I believe that the presence of generational shame in today's society had its origins in the World War II generation, I can only assume that a similar claim could have been made by earlier generations in response to the dysfunction the World War I generation left in their wake. As Christians, we very much understand the Biblical origin of shame. So, no particular generation is to blame for having originated the toxic shame that plagues our society today. However, as it relates to the generations that have members living in today's America, our understanding must have a beginning somewhere in time. Much research and study has concluded that post-World War II America is the most appropriate starting point.

Let's look at these generational changes through the lens of experts Melody Beattie and Psychologist Dr. Perpetua Neo.

The first generation of recovering codependents (Early Baby Boomers) had parents who endured the Great Depression, fought in World War I or II, or suffered horribly from the Holocaust. Information about codependency wasn't in the consciousness yet; we didn't have a name for the problem or a solution. These first-generation codependents had martyrdom and deprivation embedded into their DNA. Their parents had been through a lot.

Many second-generation codependents (Generation X), born in the 1970s and 80s, have parents who wanted to make sure their children had everything they (the parents) didn't get. When Gen Xers become parents themselves, they began taking it a step further, attempting to protect their children from every problem and emotion. This created codependents with the opposite of deprivation – a sense of over-entitlement, over-protection, and inflated self-esteem that often crossed the line into narcissism. They expected life to be easier than it really was, and they wanted everything done for them no matter how they behaved. Then they become depressed and confused when they didn't get what they believed they deserved.

Today's most prevalent version of a codependent (often Millennials) is a person who puts the needs of their partner in front of their own needs because they have built their identity upon that relationship. Present-day examples of codependency center around unhealthy relationships with toxic people, or those who are nontoxic but trigger our codependent behaviors. Codependency is no longer limited to just romantic or family relationships as they once were. It now spills over into our friendships and work relationships as well.

"First Generation" Codependence

The concept of codependence in America first came on the scene following World War II. Amidst the post-war backdrop of victory, celebration, and abundance, many American families were experiencing something quite different in the privacy of their homes.

An exorbitant number of men returned home from the warfront emotionally traumatized, angry, and broken. To expect them to immediately step back into the roles they had left a few years earlier was a recipe for disaster.

Three conflicting messages were bombarding these men all at the same time:

- The new culture of prosperity and accomplishment in America demanded they and their families be (or at least appear to be) perfect, happy, and successful.
- Their family needed them to immediately resume their important roles of husband, father, and provider.
- Their view of life was now seen through the clouded lens of post-traumatic stress and flashbacks to the unimaginable things they had seen, done, and experienced on the battlefront.

I can only imagine how overwhelming this might have been for those men to have such expectations heaped upon them. On one hand, they strived to do everything within their power to create a family that society would deem acceptable, yet they had to live every day with the constant inner turmoil of fear, shame, grief, and who knows how many other painful emotions.

Many turned to excessive use of alcohol and others isolated themselves emotionally, but virtually all of these men exhibited significant issues with anger and rage that could at times become volatile and harmful to those around them, especially their wives and children.

Codependence Thrives in The Presence of a Dependent

Enter what we now have come to know as "codependence." Following World War II, alcoholism among men became rampant in American society. In their need for something – anything – that might help them cope with the weightiness of life, alcohol offered an escape from their painful memories of war, and their feelings of isolation, rejection, and failure. Not only had they become "dependent" on alcohol to help them function somewhat normally in everyday life. They had also unknowingly become "dependent" on the need for every member of their family to play along with their anger-based life, fearing what might happen if the secret was ever exposed.

This became like a never-ending dance, with toxic shame being the only record that was played. The man's dependency demanded that every member of his family cooperate with him in every way, or they would experience painful consequences. Therein lies the origin of the concept we now understand as "co-dependence" – family members cooperating with the dependent, even at the expense of their own individual needs and well-being.

I remember when I was growing up in the 1960s, there were still many women who had never learned to drive, as their husband had always insisted on taking them wherever they needed to go. Many women had spent much of their adult lives being homemakers, wives, and mothers – providing for the needs of their home, husband, and children. As a result, they had never been employed outside the home. They (the wife) had become entirely dependent upon the dependent (the husband) to provide for their needs, therefore, co-operating with the dependent. Knowing this, it's not difficult to understand where much of the generational shame we face today had its beginnings.

Classic Patterns of Codependence

The "classic" codependency model has been well described by the organization Co-Dependents Anonymous, Inc., and is referred to as "Recovery Patterns of Codependence." This organization has done an outstanding job of not only providing the important characteristics of codependency but organizing them into typical clusters in which they are most often observed.

Denial Patterns

Codependents often tend to:

- Have difficulty identifying what they are feeling.
- Minimize, alter, or deny how they truly feel.
- Perceive themselves as completely unselfish and dedicated to the wellbeing of others.

- Lack empathy for the feelings and needs of others.
- Label others with their negative traits.
- Think they can take care of themselves without any help from others.
- Express negativity or aggression in indirect and passive ways.
- Do not recognize the unavailability of those people to whom they are attracted.

Low Self-Esteem Patterns

Codependents often tend to:

- Have difficulty making decisions.
- Judge what they think, say, or do harshly, as never good enough.
- Are embarrassed to receive recognition, praise, or gifts.
- Value others' approval of their thinking, feelings, and behavior over their own.
- Do not perceive themselves as lovable or worthwhile persons.
- Seek recognition and praise to overcome feeling less than.
- Have difficulty admitting a mistake.
- Need to appear to be right in the eyes of others and may even lie to look good.
- Are unable to identify or ask for what they need and want.
- Perceive themselves as superior to others.
- Look to others to provide their sense of safety.
- Have difficulty getting started, meeting deadlines, and completing projects.
- Have trouble setting healthy priorities and boundaries.

Compliance Patterns

Codependents often tend to:

- Are extremely loyal, remaining in harmful situations too long.
- Compromise their own values and integrity to avoid rejection or anger.

- Put aside their own interests in order to do what others want.
- Are hypervigilant regarding the feelings of others and take on those feelings.
- Are afraid to express their beliefs, opinions, and feelings when they differ from those of others.
- Accept sexual attention when they want love.
- Make decisions without regard to the consequences.
- Give up their truth to gain the approval of others or to avoid change.

Control Patterns

Codependents often tend to:

- Believe people are incapable of taking care of themselves.
- Attempt to convince others what to think, do, or feel.
- Freely offer advice and direction without being asked.
- Become resentful when others decline their help or reject their advice.
- Lavish gifts and favors on those they want to influence.
- Use sexual attention to gain approval and acceptance.
- Have to feel needed in order to have a relationship with others.
- Demand that their needs be met by others.
- Use charm and charisma to convince others of their capacity to be caring and compassionate.
- Use blame and shame to exploit others emotionally.
- Adopt an attitude of indifference, helplessness, authority, or rage to manipulate outcomes.
- Use recovery jargon in an attempt to control the behavior of others.
- Pretend to agree with others to get what they want.

Avoidance Patterns

Codependents often tend to:

- Act in ways that invite others to reject, shame, or express anger toward them.

- Judge harshly what others think, say, or do.
- Avoid emotional, physical, or sexual intimacy as a way to maintain distance.
- Allow addictions to people, places, and things to distract them from achieving intimacy in relationships.
- Use indirect or evasive communication to avoid conflict or confrontation.
- Diminish their capacity to have healthy relationships by declining to use the tools of recovery.
- Suppress their feelings or needs to avoid feeling vulnerable.
- Pull people toward them, but when others get close, push them away.
- Refuse to give up their self-will to avoid surrendering to a power greater than themselves.
- Believe displays of emotion are a sign of weakness.
- Withhold expressions of appreciation.

The presence or absence of these traits in a person's life does not infer any type of mental or behavioral disorder. I have presented this in great detail simply to vividly illuminate the real-life effects of shame in the lives of individuals who were immersed in a toxic environment during childhood.

Codependency is the fertile soil in which all compulsions, obsessions, addictions, and shame-based patterns are cultivated.

The New Twenty-First Century Codependent

Author Melody Beattie, in her book *The New Codependency*, provides another meaningful glimpse into how codependency has adapted to an ever-changing world:

> Although second, third, and forth generation codependents have many traits in common, and not all new codependents have been coddled (many are still horribly abused), the new codependents are a different breed from the classic ones. The new codependency has changed too.

41

Since codependent behaviors have mainstreamed into the culture, many people have learned to be codependent under the radar. They understand that certain behaviors aren't appropriate or therapeutically correct, so they hide what they are doing. It's easy to disguise obsessing now. People don't have to sit at home staring at the phone, waiting for him to call like codependents used to do. Instead of detaching, the new codependents leave the house, bringing their cell phones and obsessions with them. It's also easier now to mask the anxiety, grief, and depression that accompany codependency by taking medications that weren't around when codependency recovery began. While using medication is a personal choice, it's important to not take prescriptions to endure miserable situations or lose touch with who we are and what we need.

Codependency survival behaviors, and the need to change them, hasn't disappeared. Ideas recycle every twenty, thirty, or hundred years. Codependency recovery is coming around again, stronger than ever before. Young people are flooding meetings, groups, and counseling offices like never before. They're learning to take care of themselves, not just other people.

While codependent relationships may seem complicated, the root cause – as well as the reason behind its evolution – is actually simpler than one might think. Put simply, codependency is when a person's self-worth is dependent on something external to themselves that is not emotionally healthy or beneficial, yet they unwittingly stay trapped in that dependency because they don't think they are worthy of a better situation.

Although somewhat similar to the characteristics of classic codependency, modern day codependents primarily tend to exhibit some or all of the following common characteristics. In creating this list, I've taken the liberty to paraphrase the comments of psychologist Dr. Perpetua Neo and psychotherapist Dr. Holly Daniels in their article entitled, *What Codependent Behavior Looks Like These Days – And How to Change It.*

People-Pleasing

The inability to say "no" as a means to keep those around them happy, is a common sign of today's codependency. The few times they've stood up for themselves, they feel bad or guilty about it. They're afraid of conflict, so they avoid direct confrontation, doing everything to smooth things over, even if it's obvious there is an "elephant in the room."

Being A "Fixer"

While wanting to help a friend or loved one is not a bad thing, excessively needing to fix people is a different story. The codependent is always jumping in to give solutions, even when they're not asked. They believe it's their duty to clean up someone else's mess, such as compensating for their shortcomings, covering their financial obligations, or making excuses for them. They become so fixated on everyone else, they forget to take care of themselves. Then when they halfheartedly ask for solutions, they either sabotage them or claim, "I've tried that, and it didn't work. I'm beginning to think nothing can be done."

Minimizing Their Own Needs

While deep-set habits and behaviors are best dealt with through the help of a professional, some initial steps can include asking themselves, "What is it about my own needs that I might be running away from?" Dr. Neo states: "We procrastinate on things that matter, out of fear of doing them wrong. So, projects, issues, and goals that are the most personally meaningful might be the very ones we run away from. When something strikes a deep chord with us, it's possibly the last thing we want to sit down and honestly face. So, we distract ourselves with the needs of others."

Being Defined by Their Job or A Relationship

Often when a codependent's job or meaningful relationship is taken away, they tend to feel a substantial loss of self-worth. Codependents often deny this with statements such as: "I cannot help that it/they mean so much to me. I'm must just be too caring and dedicated." They use this as an excuse why they get exhausted from dealing with these very things, while at the same time justifying, in their own minds, why they cannot stay away from them.

This characteristic is driven by the desire to feel wanted and needed, in hopes of proving they're a good person, worthy of love and acceptance. This individual is not able to feel worthy of love by just being themselves. They believe they must be "externally defined," which inevitably leads to the development of a fear of abandonment (removal of love and acceptance).

Lack of Boundaries

Within the issue of people-pleasing lies boundless behaviors and relationships. These can be toxic if they go unchecked. The codependent fears that if they don't do these things, the person will leave them, which will mean they are less of a person. This causes even well-intentioned boundaries to erode. When a person is codependent and someone tramples on their boundaries, they tend to make excuses for them. This tells the other person their boundaries can be lowered, which systematically gives toxic people a "free pass" to hurt them.

Obsessing Over A Relationship

Another sign of codependency is obsessing about and wanting to control a meaningful relationship. Because the relationship is the primary way that someone who is codependent identifies their worthiness and lovable-ness, they spend an inordinate amount of time thinking about that relationship. They wish their partner would do this or that and may even resent their partner for not fulfilling their fantasy of the perfect relationship.

A New Name: Identity Dependence

In having dedicated a great deal of my work as a Christian counselor, teacher, and author to the study of generational shame and human identity,

I believe it is warranted to minimize the use of the term "codependence" in my professional practice. I feel this terminology has become inadequate and not easily recognizable in today's diverse world. It oftentimes is misused and tossed around lightly. It certainly has served us very well for over a half century and has become a part of the regular vernacular for many of us. Through much prayer and consideration, I suggest that the new, commonly accepted name for codependence become **Identity Dependence.**

If not already, you will soon come to appreciate that the pivotal element of codependency is **identity**. False identity develops through a myriad of shame-based messages in childhood. True identity emerges in a life surrendered to Jesus Christ. One concept – two sides!

This book is devoted entirely to providing a responsible pathway for us to personally make this transition from our broken "false" self to our God-given "true" self. We become dependent only upon Jesus. **We give no one else that power!**

Questions from Dr. Dave

For personal reflection or group discussion of Chapter 3

First-generation codependence was a byproduct of men returning to their homes and families after World War II in the 1940s. These men's emotional trauma, anger, alcoholism, and emotional isolation caused many of their wives and children to fearfully live their lives "walking on eggshells." Even if you're not a first-generation codependent, in what ways has this period in American history contributed to the culture of your family of origin? What shame-based dysfunctions do you personally deal with that may have been passed down to you through the generations?

In this chapter, I emphasize that all compulsions and addictions originate from unresolved shame from our childhood. Compulsivity is not a God-given, inborn trait. Rather, it is the result of us growing up without an accurate measure of what is "enough." What compulsivities, obsessions, addictions, or "not-enoughness" do you deal with today that may be drawing their energy from unfinished emotional business from your childhood?

In this chapter, I outlined common characteristics of a person who has become identity dependent. Which of these traits seem to be the most evident in your life today? What are some of the factors that may have contributed to you being defined by someone or something outside of yourself rather than Jesus' spirit in you? How has this been an obstacle to discovering a meaningful life of faith, hope, and love?

*"The footprint we leave in this world
will not be a measurement of what we do
but a reflection of who we are."*

Dr. Dave Ralston

CHAPTER 4

Our Shame-Based Identity

Two or three decades ago, I became very involved in a men's ministry called *Promise Keepers*. What I experienced during those years was life-altering for me. I attended regional and national PK events in huge sports stadiums jammed full of men committed to learning how to become men of God. For several years, I pored over countless books, studies, and teaching videos, to glean nuggets of wisdom that would help me be a more effective husband, father, and citizen. I met weekly with a small group of like-minded men who were committed to deep, honest vulnerability and accountability.

Although I sat under the anointed teaching of countless men of God, it was something I heard one particular national conference speaker say that has continued to resonate in my mind and heart since the day I first heard it:

"We teach what we know, but we reproduce who we are."

That is so powerful and profound! I teach this principle in my counseling practice nearly every day. I've tried to engrain it into my adult children ever since the day I first heard it. I strive to live it as a mantra in my own life. So, obviously I feel strongly that the readers of my first book need to understand it. This paradox serves as a quiet voice underlying every aspect of every word, page, and chapter of this book.

I feel certain the intent of the one who first spoke this was entirely neutral, not qualitative at all. No implied meaning. Nothing between the lines... Its relevance would depend upon the lens in which the hearer (or reader) processed the statement that would attach either a positive or a negative value to it.

There is an intrinsic part of these words, though, that sends a message even more relevant than the nature of <u>what</u> is "taught" or "reproduced." It is the implication – maybe even claim – that **the footprint we leave in this world will not be a measurement of what we do but a reflection of who we are.**

There is a not-so-common word assigned to this concept of reproducing who we are. The word is to **impart**. The *Merriam-Webster Collegiate Dictionary* defines "impart" in this way: "To give, convey, or grant from."

What makes imparting unique is that it is more about the learner than it is about the teacher. More about what is being learned than what is assumed to be being taught. Shame works that way. Human beings have a propensity to have shame imparted to (into) them when the source may not even know they are imparting it.

Over the past fifty years or so, our American culture has come to associate the concept of "shame" with something that is necessarily undesirable or hurtful. In all fairness, shame is an integral part of how we as human beings effectively function in this world, but it has been hijacked by the enemy and turned into an obstacle to our experiencing the unconditional love of our Creator.

Heads or Tails?

I often use the metaphor of a two-sided coin to illustrate the tension inherent in living a life in Christ. Shame is the first example of that. One concept – two sides.

Two Sides of Shame

The moment we received Christ as Savior, the Holy Spirit (the spirit of Jesus sent to His followers after He ascended into heaven) came to live in our hearts. Billy Graham said, "There is not a person anywhere who can be a

Christian without the Holy Spirit. There is not a person who can follow Christ without the help of the Holy Spirit."

As you can imagine, the presence of a Holy God taking up residence in the heart of a less-than-holy individual tends to create an inner tension. This tension is illustrated by the two sides of an imaginary coin: 1) the side surrendered to God's spirit within, and 2) the side driven by the needs of self.

The apostle Paul described this ongoing battle within himself in Romans 7:19-25 (MSG):

> "I need something more! For if I know the law but still can't keep it, and if the power of sin within me keeps sabotaging my best intentions, I obviously need help! I realize that I don't have what it takes. I can will it, but I can't do it. I decide to do good, but I don't really do it; I decide not to do bad, but then I do it anyway. My decisions, such as they are, don't result in actions. Something has gone wrong deep within me and gets the better of me every time. It happens so regularly that it's predictable. The moment I decide to do good, sin is there to trip me up. I truly delight in God's commands, but it's pretty obvious that not all of me joins in that delight. Parts of me covertly rebel, and just when I least expect it, they take charge. I've tried everything and nothing helps. I'm at the end of my rope. Is there no one who can do anything for me? Isn't that the real question? The answer, thank God, is that Jesus Christ can and does. He acted to set things right in this life of contradictions where I want to serve God with all my heart and mind but am pulled by the influence of sin to do something totally different."

You and I are really no different than Paul. Mere men and women living life with an inner battle – not a battle for good versus bad or right versus wrong or black versus white, but a struggle between **flesh** and **spirit.** Our nature versus Jesus's nature. Control versus surrender.

The A-Side of the Record

Long before the internet and MP3s were ever even thought of, "A-side" and "B-side" were terms frequently used to refer to the two sides of a phonograph record. The A-side usually featured a song that its artist, producer, or record company focused their promotions toward in hopes of it becoming a hit record. The B-side (or "flipside") was a secondary recording that typically received much less attention, and in many cases was hardly worth listening to.

The A-side of the two-sided coin is a life lived in grace – a daily relationship with Jesus, defined by love and grace and mercy and forgiveness and acceptance and connectedness and true freedom. This life can only be realized in the presence of healthy, productive shame.

God sometimes uses the unhealthiest, most undesirable experiences in our lives to produce some of His most amazing results. So, I tend to refer to this positive side of shame as "productive shame" rather than "healthy shame" as many in this field have described it. Only in Christ can unhealthy shame be positively productive in our lives despite having painful origins. Shame only becomes "toxic" when it robs us of our correct and accurate view of God, ourselves, and others.

> "And we know that God causes everything to work together for the good of those who love God and are called according to his purpose for them" (Romans 8:28 NLT).

John Bradshaw, in his book *Healing the Shame That Binds You*, helps us understand productive shame (he refers to as "healthy" shame) in this way:

> One of our basic needs is structure. We ensure this by developing a boundary system within which we safely operate. Structure gives our lives form. Boundaries and form offer us safety and allow a more efficient use of energy. Without boundaries we have no limits and easily get confused. We begin to lose our way. We sometimes don't know what is enough, how to stop, or when to say "no."

Healthy shame keeps us grounded. It is the emotional energy that tells us we are not God – that we have made and will make mistakes, and that we need help. Healthy shame is a normal human emotion that lets us know we are limited, which is part of our humanity. It signals us about our limits and motivates us to meet our basic needs.

By knowing our limits and finding ways to use our energy more effectively, healthy shame can give us a form of personal power. Healthy shame does not allow us to believe we "know it all," but spurs us to make significant life changes. In knowing that we have made mistakes and are not perfect or always right, we can continue to strive to grow and discover. Healthy shame gives us permission to be human!

Psychotherapist Joseph Burgo, in his book entitled *Shame: Free Yourself, Find Joy, and Build True Self-Esteem*, speaks of the important benefits of productive shame in this way:

Productive shame focuses on discrete traits or behaviors rather than the entire person. Instead of making global statements about someone as completely worthless and irredeemable, productive shame leaves room for the individual to feel good about themself as a whole, while also suggesting changes that might help themselves grow and develop.

Our forefathers used shaming and shunning to invoke change, to help tribal members reform their transgressive behavior and then reintegrate. Helpful shame always leaves room for improvement rather than making someone feel fundamentally worthless, with no hope for growth.

For my clients, and for human beings everywhere, shame often has an important lesson to teach and can be a guide to personal growth. Shame sometimes tells us we need to pay attention and work harder. It may let us know we've been insensitive or irresponsible. Rather than the divisive weapon it has become in many environments, shame continues to be an instructive tool on the personal level, helping us to grow and feel better about ourselves — provided we can listen to it.

The development of productive shame frames our understanding of our finiteness and limitedness as human beings. It provides safe boundaries that protect us from seeing ourselves as bigger than we really are. It is what differentiates the created (you and me) from the Creator (God) – omnipotent (all powerful), omniscient (all knowing), and omnipresent (all present). Here are a few real-life examples of productive shame that may help us understand this concept more clearly.

- Not feeling the compulsion to be perfect or right or in control.
- Asking for help when I'm unable to do something by myself.
- Admitting I'm wrong when discussing something important with another individual.
- Accepting that I can't make another person love me.
- Creating healthy boundaries in in my relationship with a member of the opposite sex.
- Keeping my thoughts to myself, when sharing them might show disrespect to another individual.
- Sincerely apologizing to a person I've hurt or dishonored in some way.
- Allowing a friend to feel the pain of grief without my feeling responsible to fix it.
- Trusting God to do the things that I'm either reasonably not able or responsible to do, or that are His to do.
- Establishing healthy boundaries for ourselves of what is "enough."
- Accepting the fact that I cannot (and should not) change another person.

Every one of these illustrates an acknowledgement of reasonable human limits. Our admission that God truly exists… and we're not

Him! Although the examples on this list all seem sensible and logical, an overwhelming segment of today's society find these fundamental life perspectives to be very difficult, if not impossible, to live out. Surely there is an explanation as to why.

God's Original Design

I'm going to make the assumption that most people who are reading this book have at least heard, if not studied, the story of Adam and Eve in the Garden of Eden, recorded in the first chapter of Genesis at the beginning of the Bible. They enjoyed a wonderful, intimate connection with God. That was until they made a choice.

God extended to Adam and Eve full access to all of the breathtaking goodness of the garden, with only one exception. They were to steer clear of the only object in the garden that would give them what only God could possess – "the knowledge of good and evil" (Genesis 2 and 3). This phrase is an example of the type of figure of speech known as merism, a literary device that pairs opposite terms together in order to create a general meaning, so that the phrase "good and evil" would simply imply "everything" – the entire spectrum.

The Enticement

Even when we are provided with much, we tend to want the things we're told we cannot have, and often lack gratitude for what we have been given.

This lone, off-limits tree represented the choice between submitting to God's law (denying self) or seeking to pursue independence and self-sufficiency (choosing self).

If Adam and Eve had merely been obedient, that would have ultimately resulted in greater wisdom, maturity, and freedom. But that is the "promise" the serpent tempted them with, as if God had no intentions to give them those good things. The serpent said: "You shall be as gods, knowing good and evil" (Genesis 3:5 NIV). Put differently, you shall judge for yourselves. You don't have to be like little children, having good and evil dictated to you.

Adam and Eve were lured by the offer of "entitlement" to an autonomous, empowered adulthood while bypassing their need to learn to submit to God. The serpent persuaded them by way of disobedience.

These same fulfillments could have been achieved through obedience every bit as well as they were with disobedience, and without the lasting consequence of sin. From the beginning, Adam and Eve were destined by Creator God to rule creation. But God's design was that this would be achieved in the same way the rule of Jesus was achieved – by humility and submission to God (see Philippians 2:8-9).

And there began the internal struggle you and I still face today – the choice whether to submit to God or to focus on ourselves. This dichotomy holds both the problem and the solution. The explanation of our inner battle. And the profound answer for us to be made new – transformed from brokenness to wholeness. You and I get to choose.

The Flipside of the Record: Toxic Shame

By God creating a limit to Adam and Eve's liberty in the garden, there was a type of "productive shame" imposed on them. Boundaries. Limits. To protect them. Not to control them. But to shield them from what? or who? The answer: **Themselves**!

Toxic shame was what they brought upon themselves by choosing to live outside the natural order of God's perfect creation. The Bible refers to this as sin. Not merely breaking the Ten Commandments, but willfully choosing to put self ahead of God in their hearts. My will ahead of His. A disease that every one of us – past, present, and future – is inborn with. And Jesus is the only cure!

Loss of Our Inborn, God-given Identity

Bradshaw describes toxic shame (referred to through the rest of this book as merely "shame") as more than an emotion that signals human limits, as we've learned earlier about productive shame. In stark contrast, toxic shame literally robs a person of their true identity and purpose.

Toxic shame creates beliefs that one's true self is defective and flawed, creating a false sense that one is substandard as a human being. If this false premise of defectiveness is believed, then a person begins to create a false self that is not defective or flawed. Once someone creates a false self, then he or she ceases to be an authentic human being.

People who have toxic shame believe that they are a failure. Self-contempt, isolation, and a strong sense that they are untrustworthy are also feelings which often accompany those who believe themselves failures. Sadly, when shame becomes a core belief (or a core identity), the individual will most probably shut down from human relationships.

The issue of guilt versus shame plays into this discussion. Guilt can also be healthy (productive) or toxic. Healthy guilt helps form our conscience. We would not want a world with no conscience where people would be shameless and do anything they wish.

Healthy guilt reveals to us when we have violated our own values. It usually persuades us to change or make amends. It also provides a fear of punishment, which is a healthy deterrent.

Unfortunately, if someone is shame-based, he or she (due to unhealthy guilt) believes punishment is not only warranted, but deserved, whether they've actually done anything wrong or not. And in cases of chronic shame, this individual may even feel they deserve punishment and are responsible for the wrong someone else has done. The person often believes that there is no possibility for repair.

People who are shamed-based live in hopelessness and are locked into a set of very unhealthy beliefs. They believe they cannot fix their lives and will always be failing. Their sense of being trapped in failure and shame can lead to desperate acts including perpetrating violence.

Although it may relieve guilt, this feeling of being trapped in failure is why **punishment that doesn't lead to a healthy outcome intensifies shame**. It is, therefore, essential to realize that we must be very careful not to place so much shame on our children that they become convinced that they are flawed, and that they can never change or recover.

Dark Is Merely the Absence of Light

In the physical world, there are many characteristics we often perceive as opposite, when in reality one characteristic is actually the "presence of" and the other is the "absence of."

- Hot is the presence of heat; cold is the absence of heat.
- Bright is the presence of light; dark is the absence of light.
- Heaven is the presence of God; hell is the absence of God.

In following this same line of reasoning, this statement must also be true:

- Wholeness is the presence of productive shame.
- Brokenness is the absence of productive shame.

Understanding toxic shame is not the primary objective of this book. Although it may bring enormous relief, merely ridding our lives of collateral damage caused by toxic shame does not automatically lead to a godly outcome. We must be even more intentional to fill the vacated spaces in our soul where toxic shame once dwelled, with the truths, nature, and character of Jesus Christ and His spirit. In Matthew's gospel, Jesus speaks very clearly of the necessity that we allow God to redefine these inner voids and vacuums before the enemy is able to steal them back:

> "When an evil spirit leaves a person, it goes into the desert, seeking rest but finding none. Then it says, 'I will return to the person I came from.' So, it returns and finds its former home empty, swept, and in order. Then the spirit finds seven other spirits more evil than itself, and they all enter the person and live there. And so that person is worse off than before" (Matthew 12:43-45 NLT).

Whether you are familiar with contemplating the spiritual world or not, the message of this passage is still relevant for every one of us. Our soul will never be empty. It will contain the beliefs and truths that we choose to build our lives upon – either Truths imparted by God's word and Spirit, or truths internalized through our childhood past and our adult lives.

The Worst Pandemic in History

Shame has been a reality of the human condition – both productively and toxically – for as long as mankind has inhabited this planet. No person has ever escaped the influence of shame, with the exception of Jesus himself. The souls of people from every generation, nationality, ethnicity, race, and gender have been shaped by the impact of shame on their mind, their will, and their emotions.

So, does that mean we have our ancestors to blame for our personal issues? Is the toxic shame in my life the result of my parents' having failed me in some way? No, not exactly. The Bible's response to these questions is found within the narrative of the Ten Commandments.

> "I, the Lord your God, am a jealous God who will not tolerate your affection for any other gods. I lay the sins of the parents upon their children; the entire family is affected—even children in the third and fourth generations of those who reject me. But I lavish unfailing

love for a thousand generations on those who love me and
obey my commands" (Deuteronomy 5:9-10 NLT).

Simplistically, sin is every human being's affinity for self rather than
submission to God. It might seem that this passage is telling us that all of
the sins of our parents and grandparents and great-grandparents land in
our lap. So, are we really responsible for their sins? Will we one day stand
before God and be held accountable for the things our ancestors did?"

No. You and I are not responsible or accountable for our ancestors' sins,
especially as it relates to our eternal salvation. But… **we are absolutely
responsible for what we do with the sin we've inherited from our
forefathers.**

Sin is an offense against God – birthed in the heart and revealed in
our thoughts, words, decisions, and actions.

> "Then, after desire has conceived, it gives birth to sin; and
> sin, when it is full-grown, gives birth to death" (James
> 1:15 NIV).

We have all missed the mark of sinless perfection. And the Bible says
there is a consequence for this:

> "For the wages (results of wrongdoing) of sin is death, but
> the gift of God is eternal life in Christ Jesus our Lord"
> (Romans 6:23 NIV).

There is only one solution for our sin problem – faith alone in Jesus
Christ alone!

Generational Shame: The Result of Inherited Sin

For every person who has placed their faith in Jesus Christ, the eternal,
spiritual consequence of their sin was paid in full at the cross. Nevertheless,
there remains the inescapable effect of human sin on this earth – brokenness
of the soul of every man, woman, and child. Some tragically shattered;
others only slightly damaged. But all are broken.

This is the legacy of generational shame: the trickle-down effects of disobedience to God. Adam and Eve immediately experienced shame when they sinned by disobeying God. The Bible describes them hiding behind some trees in the garden (see Genesis 3:8), wallowing in shame from the sin that was spawned in their deceived hearts.

This began a pattern every one of us knows all too well, albeit countless generations since the Garden: A perpetual loop where shame is both the "front door" into our sin <u>and</u> the "back door" byproduct of our sin. A vicious, self-sustaining cycle of sin and shame.

Questions from Dr. Dave

For personal reflection or group discussion of Chapter 4

In this chapter, I made the statement, "We teach what we know, but we reproduce who we are." Reflect on how your current issues with brokenness and shame stem from what you were taught versus the ways you were influenced during childhood. Are the emotional struggles of your life today tied to unhealthy things you were taught, or to the emotionally unhealthy, unsafe, or unavailable adults you interacted with in childhood?

If you were to die today, what would be the "footprint" you would leave in this world? Would it be a reflection of the things you have accomplished, achieved, or acquired? Or would it be a reflection of the man or woman you've become, and how that has affected others? If you don't like the answer, what are some areas in your life that may need to change?

Have you ever stopped to realize that you are not obligated to pass down the same shame-based messages and behaviors you were raised in? Ask God to reveal to you any areas where you are perpetuating generational shame into your children or grandchildren. Remember, God blesses a thousand generations of those who turn from the sins of our forefathers and turn toward the ways and truths of God.

PIECE 2

Shame: *Am I Acceptable?*

"If our emotional needs weren't well met when we were children, we're not alone and it wasn't our fault. We deserved to feel loved and supported by the people closest to us."

Dr. Dave Ralston

CHAPTER 5

Shame's Menacing Effects

Toxic shame is experientially acquired more than it is cognitively learned. It evolves from an unmet need, into a chronically unmet need, into a false belief, into an altered self-image. This will develop in uniquely different ways in the lives of individuals who have been exposed to the very same environment. For some, it may create internalized shame that is acted out through fear, depression, anxiety, drug abuse, self-harm, identity dependence, or isolation. For others, it may contribute to drivenness, control, perfectionism, overachieving, compliance, or fearlessness. Although the second group of characteristics appear much more "socially acceptable," both groups are responding to the same internalized shame messages and are therefore equally shame based.

What Does Shaming Look Like?

No one is born shamed. It is a learned emotion, beginning at a very early age. Although human beings are born with a capacity to experience shame, the ways in which we process and deal with shame is learned. This means that wherever there is shame there must also be a shamer. Children learn to be ashamed of themselves because someone of significance in their lives imposes shame upon them. And their response will be entirely unique dependent upon the needs of their inborn, God-given temperament.

Shame messages are more powerful when they come from people whom we are closest to, people we love and admire, and individuals God appointed as our primary caregivers. This is why parents' shaming has the deepest effects on children. Secondarily though, shame messages from older siblings, teachers, coaches, pastors, and peers can also create wounding of the child's self-image (identity). Although every one of us encounters shame messages throughout life, the ones we experience in childhood have the deepest effect on us and are virtually impossible to erase.

"Shame is different from other feelings such as embarrassment or nervousness because shame makes the individual feel that he or she is not acceptable or worthy as a human," says psychologist Dr. Carla Manly. Shaming implies that the child is wrong for perceiving, feeling, wanting, or needing something. This often occurs not only through others' spoken words, but also by facial responses, body language, physical consequences, removal of approval, relational absence, and a long list of others. The point is, shaming oftentimes occurs when the "shamer" may not even be aware, because shaming isn't merely what they do, it has become who they are.

Brene' Brown, bestselling author, professor, and lecturer, has spent her entire professional career performing research on the topic of shame and vulnerability. In a recent posting on her blog, Brene' spoke of shame in this way:

> The intensely painful feeling or experience of believing that we are flawed and therefore unworthy of love and belonging – something we've experienced, done, or failed to do makes us unworthy of connection. Shame is much more likely to be the source of destructive, hurtful behavior than the solution or cure. The fear of disconnection can actually make us dangerous. I believe that if we want meaningful, lasting change, we need to get clear on the differences between shame and guilt and call for an end to the use of shame as a tool for change. That also means moving away from labeling of people."

Remember, we duplicate who we are. And we base who we are on how we perceive ourselves. We may pride ourselves in who we perceive ourselves to be, even if that identity has been built upon a myriad of shame messages and false beliefs and is toxic in the lives of others. Nearly every week in my counseling practice I hear a client say, "I'm just made that way" or "That's just how I was raised." Is it really ok to rest on that, with little motivation to become anything different?

We must learn to see others' hurts not through our own lens, but through the lens of how we are impacting the wellbeing of their soul and spirit.

Subtle Shaming Messages

John Bradshaw, in his book *Bradshaw On: The Family*, offers an understanding of five of the most subtle, yet damaging, aspects of shaming that occur in American families. These are referred to as the "Five Freedoms." Affirmation of these freedoms moves a child toward full self-acceptance and the ability to begin integrating the complexities of life. Personal power and self-worth results from such freedoms. All the person's energy is available to interact with the world and establish healthy, meaningful relationships.

The absence of these freedoms in a child's life tragically results in a host of shame-based traits, including issues with trust, intimacy, confidence, responsibility, and countless more.

Shame is not necessarily a result of hurtful or demeaning things done to a child. Rather, it is the child's inward response to the chronic, ongoing absence of something that was essential and developmental to their emotional well-being.

The Five Innate Human Freedoms

Renowned author and therapist Virginia Satir speaks of the five freedoms that accrue when we are loved unconditionally. Shaming occurs when any or all of these are overlooked or under-validated within a family relationship system.

- **The freedom to perceive.** If a child's God-given need to perceive is not affirmed, he or she will believe that they cannot trust their own perceptions or opinions.

- **The freedom to think.** If a child's God-given need to think independently is not affirmed, he or she will believe that their views are not correct or worthwhile.
- **The freedom to feel.** If a child's God-given need to feel what they feel is not affirmed, he or she will believe that feelings and emotions are bad, inappropriate, or unnecessary,
- **The freedom to dream**. If a child's God-given need to dream is not affirmed, he or she will believe there is nothing worth hoping for today, tomorrow, or in their future.
- **The freedom to risk.** If a child's God-given need to risk is not affirmed, he or she will believe they must always play it safe, and never allow the possibility of doing something wrong, making a mistake, or failing.

Commonly when I am working with an adult in our counseling practice, they will argue that they could not have internalized toxic shame because they came from a healthy family with wonderful parents. They've never experienced a traumatic event in their life, especially during childhood. Undoubtedly, it is difficult to comprehend how deeply internalized shame might occur within an environment that by all standards seems healthy.

In the family I grew up in, there seemed to be an unspoken rule that we do not show emotion or feelings. The adults seemed to present themselves as always having their lives together, carrying themselves as if they always lived above the fray, and seeing emotions as an indication of not being under control. At least that's how I perceived it. It wasn't that they wanted to control anything or anyone, but more importantly always being under control – meticulously punctual, reliable, and responsible, almost to a fault. These are certainly all good traits of character, except if a person experiences shame when they can't uphold them or becomes a compulsive perfectionist in order to sustain them. I know this because I've lived it.

No member of my family ever had any intention to harm anyone in any way and were always people of good character in what they believed, said, and did. That's why when I admit that I still deal with shame from childhood even today, it brings with it a certain amount of guilt for inferring that the older members of my family weren't perfect. Shame can be imparted in the most subtle of ways.

Wounded by Perfection

Early in my counseling career I had the opportunity to work with a young woman in her late 20's. She sought counseling due to feelings of depression, low self-esteem, and the belief that she was inadequate as a woman, wife, and mother. She felt like giving up on all of it.

In discovering more about this young lady, her description of her family of origin sounded like something from a Hallmark movie. Dad was kind and caring. He had a great work ethic and glowing reputation with his employer, and he was very good at maintaining a healthy life-work balance. He was a deacon at the local church and participated in the spiritual development of each of his three children, now all adults with their own families.

Her mom had been a public elementary school teacher for many years and was that teacher that every parent wanted their kids to be in her class. She was a wonderful mom and grandma, an excellent cook and baker, kept a beautiful and welcoming home, and adored her husband.

My client was the youngest of three children. All were raised with a good balance of ambition and groundedness. The older sister was a schoolteacher with her mom, and arguably they were best friends. Her life, marriage, family, and home were a veritable duplication of her mom and dad's – ideal in nearly every way.

Her brother was very popular with everyone around him. He was a high-level athlete who was lauded since childhood by the small community they lived in. He received much of the praise and accolades of the family and was the kind of young man every family dreamed they could raise or that their daughter would marry.

Then there was my client – a committed wife, mother, schoolteacher, church volunteer, and friend. Very unassuming and faithful. But in her mind, she was just not enough. She saw herself as a disappointment when comparing herself to her parents and siblings. And she assumed others perceived her in the same way. No matter how hard she tried, she never seemed to get the kudos that her sister and brother did. And regardless of encouraging words her husband spoke into her, she still assumed she could never measure up to the woman, wife, and mother her family expected her to be. She was overwhelmed by the fear of disappointing them.

Did her parents impose these shame messages upon her? Certainly not. At least not overtly or knowingly. Nevertheless, this young woman was trapped in a prison of fear and shame. Just because there was no specific individual or shame message or trauma to attribute this to, it was nonetheless very real in her life. Yet to speak of it, she felt enormous guilt because of a false belief she had internalized that told her, "I need to be thankful for how wonderful a family I've been blessed with."

So, it was not uncommon for her to share her honest feelings with me, then in the very next breath undermine her emotions with justification of why she was wrong and ungrateful for having those feelings. She was in bondage to a spiral of guilt and shame that she saw little hope of ever escaping. And it had become like an emotional cancer inside of her.

Just Trying to Raise Good Kids

As adults, we may play a part in another's internalizing of shame messages, many times without being fully aware. This is most often a result of invalidation of the child's natural, innate expression of their emotional needs.

> Child: "I want to be a doctor when I grow up."
> Adult: "At the rate you're going, you'll be lucky to graduate high school."
>
> Child: "Can I help make dinner?"
> Adult: "Get out of the kitchen before you mess something up."
>
> Child: "I'm really sad my best friend moved away."
> Adult: "You have other friends. Don't let that bother you."
>
> Child: "Our house is just five blocks down from the school."
> Adult: "You're wrong. It's five and a half if you count the parking lot."

Child: "Do you like the picture I drew for you?"
Adult: "It's hideous. I can't even tell what it is."

Child: "I'm finished mowing the yard."
Adult: "What part of putting the mower away did you not understand?

Child: "Can I ask you a question about my homework?"
Adult: "Don't you ever interrupt me when I'm reading."

Child: "Will you be at my ballgame tonight?"
Adult: "You know I have to work. You want to eat, don't you?"

Child: "Can I ride my bike to the park?"
Adult: "I don't know. Can you?"

Many would say that these adults' responses were necessary to teach the child the difference between "right" and "wrong," "good" and "bad." Verbal punishment is common in almost every home and school. It relies on shame as the deterrent, in the same way that spanking relies on pain. For over a century, our society has endorsed shaming as one of the most common methods used to regulate children's behavior, with the underlying false belief that this is how to raise "good" kids.

What If Our Parents Were Wrong?

I love the way Robin Grille and Beth Macgregor, in their article entitled *"Good" Children – at What Price?* help us consider what they call the "secret costs of shame."

Our parents and caregivers' voices are the first we hear, and in childhood, theirs are the words that echo most strongly through our days and in our minds. Our parents show us the world and our place inside it. They witness our first steps and help us navigate the delicate mechanics of falling. They tell us who we are as best they know how to.

But what happens when what they tell us is wrong? What if you fall and, instead of offering you a hand, they chide you for losing your footing?

Many parents invalidate their children's feelings. Some children grow up believing their accomplishments are never enough, that their emotions are bad and harmful. Some people go through life believing their parents do not love or want them.

If this sounds like you, you're not alone. If you felt invalidated by your parents as you were growing up, we want you to know that your feelings matter, and you deserve to feel loved and supported.

Grille and Macgregor asked their large, diverse online community to describe the "signs" that they felt invalidated as children. Here are the top 25 signs those community members shared in common:

- We were told we were "too emotional."
- We sought validation from others.
- We never allow ourselves to be vulnerable as an adult.
- We weren't told we were loved.
- We apologized for everything, even if it wasn't our fault.
- We felt invisible.
- We were told our feelings were wrong.
- Our career dreams were made fun of.
- Our parents missed basic details.
- We were told we were selfish.
- We're now perfectionists.
- Our parents didn't want to hear about our problems.
- We self-sabotage as adults.
- We never heard a genuine apology.
- We now struggle to get in touch with our true feelings.
- We were told our struggles were "all in our head."
- We thought love had to be earned.

- We second-guess ourselves all the time as an adult.
- We sought affection from strangers.
- We feel the need to justify ourselves to others as an adult.
- We were made to feel unwanted.
- Our family members played favorites.
- We were constantly put down, teased, or criticized.
- Our parents didn't show up for us.
- We're uncomfortable with the kindness of others as adults.

If your emotional needs weren't well met when you were a child, you're not alone and it wasn't your fault. You deserve to feel supported by the people closest to you. If reading this has been hard for you, please commit to take care of yourself and remember that your feelings do matter. No matter how dark or painful your past, there truly is hope. His name is Jesus. My sincere prayer for you is that this book will lead you on a wonderful journey from the brokenness of your past to wholeness in Christ for your future!

Shaming Can Also Be Very Overt

I've devoted much of this chapter to helping you understand the more subtle – even "unintentional" – ways that shaming occurs. I would be remiss, though, to not commit space in this book to address the more obvious forms of shaming. I wrote this book for the person who has been overtly shamed through experiences of being abused or demeaned within their own family culture, and also for those of us who internalized shame while in family environments that outwardly appeared to be very healthy and, in some ways, even enviable.

Heartbreaking Real-Life Examples

Undoubtedly, many who are reading this book have experienced shame in ways that were far from subtle. In fact, everyone may have been aware of it. That, in itself, may be the worst part of the shaming – that other adults were present or aware, yet seemed to condone the shaming we received, and made no effort to protect us.

Allow me to share paraphrased versions of several stories of parental / family shaming that I've heard from my clients over the course of two decades as a Christian Counselor.

- "Any time my dad would get mad at me, he would make me sweep our entire gravel driveway until all the rocks were perfectly even."
- "My parents divorced when I was in high school. My mother told me that if I went to or even talked to my dad that she would move everything I owned out onto the street curb. After I came home from seeing my dad, I found all of my possessions in a pile next to the street. For the next forty-five years until her death, I never spoke to my mother again."
- "For about six or seven years, when I was between the age of five and about twelve, my parents would use me as a sex toy for them and their friends. There was a shed behind our house where they would do this. Sometimes it was just my parents – my dad sexually abusing me and my mom videotaping it. Other times there were several other men there who would take turns molesting and abusing me while my parents watched."
- "Any time I was sick and vomited, my step-dad would make me eat my own vomit. I grew to hate that man."
- "I grew up on a farm, pretty far away from other people. One day when I was a very young girl, my older brother came home drunk and beat my mom to within an inch of her life while I was there in the room."
- "Before I reached puberty, my mom's husband would come into my room when I was in bed, and he would pinch my testicles until they nearly bled. Then he would deny to my mom having done it."
- "My husband was so wounded and compulsive that the house had to always be spotless. He wouldn't let the kids step foot on the floor after it had been cleaned, so they had to jump from one rug to another in order to get through the house."
- "At the private high school I attend, to make an example of me for getting in trouble, the principal called all of the other kids

and their parents together in a big room, then spent a long time berating me in front of them for what I had done. And my parents were there the entire time."

- "My mom and dad divorced when I was in middle school. When I would visit my dad's house and stay overnight there, he and his girlfriend would have loud sex in my dad's room. And he had taken off the door so it couldn't be closed."

- "For some reason, when I was a young girl, my dad could not stand for a girl to have bangs. So, one day he came home, and I had done my hair with bangs. He didn't say anything, but just went and got the scissors and cut my bangs off all the way to the root."

- "My husband's grandfather had eight children: the first three were born of his wife, and the next five were born of his oldest daughter."

A Family Culture of Shame

There is a significant difference between not aware and not responsible. Many adults whom I talk to about them perpetuating generational shame assert that there is no way they could know they had shamed their child in these ways because they did "the best they could." Really? By simply duplicating their shame-based childhood pain into their own children – whether unknowingly or intentionally – they considered that the best they could do? The pain in their own lives should have been proof enough that something needed to be radically changed.

What the parents are implying is that they cannot be responsible to provide their child something their own childhood did not provide them. I won't argue that this makes reasonable, logical sense. How can a person give away something they don't possess? But I believe God sees it differently.

You and I always have a choice. Whether we were raised in church or in the bars; whether we had two parents, one parent, no parents, foster parents, adopted parents, or grandparents… as adults, we still have the choice to either impose our pain onto others, or find a way to do better – no matter what it takes!

If we fail to parent our children from the foundation of the love and grace of Jesus, and the truths of God's word, then we are guilty of perpetuating generational shame for three to four generations. Our grandparents represent the first generation, our parents would be the second generation, we are the third, and our children are the fourth. The passage in Deuteronomy clearly states that God will "lay the sins of the parents upon their children; the entire family is affected--even children in the third and fourth generations." And if you're reading this book, there is a pretty good chance that you're one of those four.

The Great Cover-Up

Common sense might say that if we just do the opposite of the shaming we witnessed in childhood it will produce a healthy life, marriage, children, and family. The flaw in this reasoning is that, without of a person's heart being regenerated through Christ, the opposite of shame-based is not self-worth, but rather pretentiousness and a façade created to cover up our internal toxic shame. Although it may not look as outwardly unhealthy as what was experienced in childhood, it still derives its motivations from the very same shame messages.

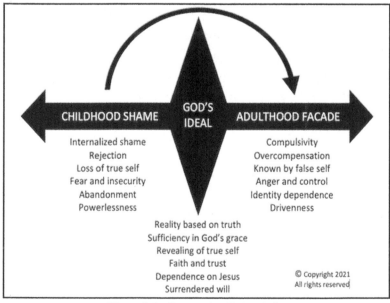

Equal & Opposite Principle

76

The Equal and Opposite Principle ©

Sir Isaac Newton's third law states:

> For every action in nature there is an equal and opposite reaction. In every interaction, there is a pair of forces acting on the two interacting objects. The magnitude of the forces on the first object equals the magnitude of the force on the second object, and the direction of the force on the first object is opposite to the direction of the force on the second object. Forces always come in pairs – equal and opposite action-reaction (cause-effect) pairs.

Through counseling thousands of clients across many years, I began to notice a very predictable trend: Deeply soul-wounded people unconsciously were compelled to create a world around themselves that was internally similar yet externally 180 degrees opposite to the painful experiences of their childhood.

This brought me back to the principle I learned in Physics 101 way back in the 1980s – equal and opposite. I feel certain that Newton had no intensions of his discovery of the Third Law of Motion applying to the non-physical world. I feel strongly that it does!

In the diagram above, consider the horizontal line as the "shame" line. The center point reflects the virtues an individual develops as they grow closer and closer to Jesus – theoretically the place of no toxic shame. No doubt this ideal is unachievable while we're on this earth. Nonetheless, God calls His children to actively pursue these qualities in growing measure through the process of sanctification and being transformed into the very nature of Jesus.

- Reality based on truth
- Sufficiency in God's grace
- Revealing of true self
- Faith and trust
- Dependence on Jesus
- Surrendered will

The Childhood Shame side of the diagram helps us visually consider the effects progressively more or less shame have on us. In equal yet opposite proportion, we can visualize on the Adulthood Façade side of the diagram the manifestations in adulthood of greater or lesser shame in our childhood. Obviously, none of us were raised in the perfect family, as it certainly doesn't exist. But we can see clearly how the more closely our family of origin is to the healthy ideal God intended, the more authentic and whole the individual becomes in adulthood. This diagram provides a few representative examples so you may need to insert the equal and opposite realities that make this illustration applicable to your individual story.

- Internalized shame
- Rejection
- Loss of true self
- Fear and insecurity
- Abandonment
- Powerlessness

As we trace the arched line from left to right, we can see traits of the pretentious outward "façade" on the right that correlate with each specific soul wound on the left.

- **Internalized shame** from childhood unknowing leads us to **compulsivity**, addictiveness, and black/white thinking as adults. We lack the healthy shame needed to function within our finiteness as human beings.
- **Rejection** during childhood causes us to **overcompensate** in an effort to prove to others (and sometimes ourselves) that we're enough, based upon an arbitrary measurement relative to an arbitrary standard of perfection.
- **Loss of our true self**, a subconscious response to our childhood – believing we're flawed or unacceptable – leads to being known only by our "acceptable" **false self** as an adult.
- We protect our **fears and insecurities** resultant from life in our childhood family by expressing **anger and control** over anything

78

or anyone in our adult life that might threaten our need to always feel safe and secure.

- In response to any form of **abandonment** we faced in childhood, we become **identity dependent** and people-pleasing in our meaningful adult relationships.
- **Powerlessness**, the belief that we were weak, invisible, or not heard as a child, provides the motivational energy for relentless **drivenness** in our adult endeavors.

Shame Does Not Have to Be Passed Down

Just because we learn something doesn't mean we are obligated to live it or to teach it. Just because our parents did not create an environment during our childhood where our soul needs could be consistently met, does not obligate us to duplicate the same patterns into our home, marriage, family, and children.

For the pattern to change, for the shaming to stop, for the generational "curse" to end, we must make some radical adjustments to our lives.

- Turn from toxic people, places, and things.
- Uncover the lies and false beliefs of our past.
- Rediscover our true identity in Jesus Christ.
- Nurture lasting hope in others.

Later, in Chapter 12, we'll explore the twelve Bible-based principles that are essential in shifting your family tree from generations of sin, shame, and brokenness to a lasting legacy of faith, love, and grace.

Questions from Dr. Dave

For personal reflection or group discussion of Chapter 5

God created every human being with inborn, non-physical needs. If these are cultivated during childhood, we experience certain freedoms in our adult life and relationships – the freedom to perceive, think, feel, dream, and risk? If these needs were unmet, undermet, or met in unhealthy ways, we experience fear rather than freedom. Which of the five freedoms is most present in your life today? Which is most absent? Are you ready to allow God to do make you whole in these ways?

Many of us just can't bring ourselves to admit that our parents might have been wrong in some of the ways they parented us or the things they taught us. We feel an overwhelming loyalty, and the responsibility to "honor our parents" as the Ten Commandments teaches. Have you allowed yourself to take your parents off the throne of your life? If not, is leaving them in that high position costing you anything?

The Equal and Opposite Principle© vividly illustrates how the opposite of shame-based is just as shame-based. Are there any facades you've constructed in your adult life that you're now able to see are built largely on unresolved shame and brokenness from your past? What might it cost if you were to tear down those facades and begin to live a fully authentic life? What might it cost if you don't?

"All compulsivity is a consequence of unresolved toxic shame within us."

John Bradshaw

CHAPTER 6

Adding to Our Own Shame

I wish I had come up with this quote: "The definition of insanity is doing the very same thing over and over and expecting a different result." Why do we do that? What is it within us humans that takes us back to the same painful choices again and again?

In the year 700 BC, Solomon, Son of David, King of Israel wrote what the Bible refers to as the Proverbs. This collection of Solomon's writings simply compiles numerous short instructions for living an effective life on earth. Listen to this interesting proverb: "As a dog returns to its vomit, so a fool repeats his foolishness" (Proverbs 26:11 NLT). Yuck!

There is an enormous amount of strong metaphorical language in this thirteen-word sentence. As is common in Solomon's proverbs, he utilizes simile to make a comparison between a natural event and a moral principle. Similes are identified by their use of "like" or "as." In this way, Solomon makes very clear the "foolishness" of us living in a repetitive cycle of sin and shame. Even if we don't have a spouse or children to be the recipients of our shame, we can still do substantial soul damage merely by perpetuating it (continuing it indefinitely) in our own lives.

We're Not the Only Ones

The apostle Paul, one of the most prolific leaders of the early Christian church, battled the very same inner nature you and I do. In Paul's letter recorded in Chapter 17 of his letter to Christians in Rome, he is super honest in revealing his struggle within:

> "I do not understand what I do. For what I want to do I do not do, but what I hate I do. And if I do what I do not want to do, I agree that the law is good. As it is, it is no longer I myself who do it, but it is sin living in me. For I know that good itself does not dwell in me, that is, in my sinful nature. For I have the desire to do what is good, but I cannot carry it out. For I do not do the good I want to do, but the evil I do not want to do—this I keep on doing. Now if I do what I do not want to do, it is no longer I who do it, but it is sin living in me that does it" (Romans 17:15-20 NIV).

Notice a fundamental shift in what Paul is saying about himself within this passage. At the beginning, Paul speaks of his outward struggle – unable to do "right." But later in the text, he confesses, "It is sin living in me" that continues the cycle of sin and shame in his life.

You and I must get to the same place Paul did – taking full responsibility for the sin and shame within ourselves. No excuses. No blaming. No justifying. It's ours now, regardless how it got there.

No matter how shaming or toxic or rejecting or abandoning our childhood may have been, it is still our responsibility as adults to deal with the sin within us, and to do whatever it takes to not duplicate it into the lives of others, especially our own children. Rest assured, God provides us the only way out: His son, Jesus Christ.

The Shame Cycle

The more deeply shame-based an individual is, the harder it becomes to break the cycle of shame. In many instances, this cycle has become a "normal" part of life. But for others, this seemingly endless battle devolves into what seems more like a shame "spiral," where toxic shame leads to even more shame, and the individual's sense of identity, self-worth, and inner power concurrently spiral further and further down, to the point of self-deprecation, or even self-destruction.

Through the remainder of this chapter, I'll be introducing you to each element of my perspective of the shame cycle in hopes you'll better understand how we can literally get trapped in our own sin and shame. In thinking about what the most effective way might be to illustrate this, I've chosen to share an honest glimpse into my own personal story that I battled from adolescence into young adulthood.

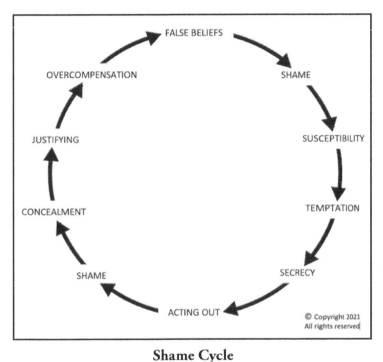

Shame Cycle

False Beliefs

Our conscious mind generates our conscious choices. Our subconscious mind generates our subconscious choices.

Much of what comprises our conscious mind is information we have accumulated, in one way or another, over the course of our lifetime. This is a myriad of information that allows us to make decisions throughout each day; from large (such as purchasing a house) to small (such as deciding which shirt to wear). The more reliable the information, the more accurate the decision.

However, unlike the conscious mind, our subconscious is not primarily made up of information and facts, but of life experiences and emotions – both productive and toxic in nature. Also, our subconscious houses the emotions that those experiences spawned. Practically speaking, the reason these are subconscious (beneath our conscious awareness) may be related to a range of factors:

- Lack importance or relevance in our current needs and priorities.
- Not aligned with what our conscious mind understands.
- Lead to undesirable outcomes.
- Too painful for us to consciously process.
- Rekindle memories of pain and loss.
- Occurred a long time ago.

Max-Planck-Gesellschaft, in their 2008 *ScienceDaily* article, entitled *Decision-making May Be Surprisingly Unconscious Activity*, concluded that,

> Contrary to what most of us would like to believe, decision-making is a process handled to a large extent by unconscious mental activity. The brain actually unconsciously prepares our decisions. Even several seconds before we consciously make a decision, its outcome can be predicted from unconscious activity in the brain.

There is a proclivity for our false beliefs to be linked to what we came to believe early in our lives were the answers to these six unspoken questions:

- **Identity** – "Who am I?"
- **Significance** – "Am I acceptable?"
- **Worth** – "Am I enough?"
- **Intimacy** – "Am I known?"
- **Belonging** – "Am I safe?"
- **Maturity** – "Am I complete?"

False beliefs largely smolder somewhere in our subconscious mind. These beliefs were created by how we interpreted shaming experiences during childhood, and they are solidified through "validating experiences" throughout adulthood. A validating experience is an encounter in our adult life that validates or reaffirms the already deeply held false beliefs we internalized during childhood. For example: If we don't perceive ourselves as being overweight and have no insecurities related to our body image, then our feelings won't be hurt if someone teases us about our eating habits or lack of exercise. But, if we are extremely insecure about our body image, having repeatedly been told by our parents that we're chubby or lazy or unacceptable as a child, that shame message will be triggered by any type of comment related to our appearance, work ethic, or accomplishments, regardless the intention of the one communicating it.

On my own personal journey, there was a period of several years where I was scared to death that someone whom I loved might remove their love from me. I did all that I could to please them and keep them happy. I took responsibility for things that really weren't even mine to own. I kept my mouth shut when I would have rather said how what I was thinking. All of this in hopes of securing the certainty of their love and approval. This internalized fear was heightened any time I felt that I may have failed or disappointed that person.

This performance-approval pattern began when my parents divorced and my dad moved away – a time over fifty years ago when one of the two adults whom I most loved, trusted, and needed seemed to "remove their love" from me. Because I was young and not sure why they would do such a thing, I drew my own conclusion. I convinced myself that I must have made a mistake, done something wrong, been disobedient, or disappointed them in some way. And that was why they broke up, and why my dad left without even telling me. This was my childhood reality, and in some strange way, these false beliefs allowed my immature mind to make sense of things, even though they were painful. The truth didn't really matter. Feelings did.

This really became a problem when I carried it with me into adulthood – marriage, family, friendships, and work. I knew that my wife loved me dearly, and that she wanted to be with me. Yet when in a situation where I had to stand my ground or share a conflicting viewpoint with her or tell her something that I had done wrong, I would feel enormous anxiety on the inside. Shame had convinced me that if I was totally honest and transparent with her, she would remove her love from me and possibly even leave.

My conscious mind was saying, "I know she loves me and wants to be with me." But the underlying shame in my heart was whispering into my subconscious mind something different: "If I disagree with her or disappoint her, she will get angry and go away. I can't imagine living without her, or even worse, what other people might think of me if my marriage ends like my parents' marriage did." More often than not, which of these two messages do you think had the greater power?

Many times, the internalizing of a false belief is not necessarily based upon actual reality, but more on the child's <u>perception of reality</u>. If the child craves a caregiver's approval, and that adult seems disappointed when the child doesn't get it just right, then the child will grow to become an adult who believes they are powerless to honestly share their opinion or needs or feelings without running the risk of losing the love, approval, and presence of that person. In a twisted way, they believe it is better to have no opinion, to minimize their own needs, or to stuff down their true feelings than it is to risk losing someone because they were honest with them. Is that thought based on factual information held in their conscious mind? Absolutely not. It's far more real than that!

Shame

False beliefs tend to activate the shame messages internalized from our past. From that irrational yet familiar place, we begin to relive the "old tapes" that have played over and over in our minds more times than we care to admit:

- I'm fat
- I'm ugly
- I'm unlovable
- I'm worthless
- I'm stupid

- I'm unacceptable
- I'm a failure
- I'm not enough
- I'm unforgivable
- I'm supposed to be perfect
- I don't matter
- I'm bad

From my early adolescence through my young adult years, I had a tape that played relentlessly in my mind. Its message said that the only way I could be loved was to earn it through performance, perfection, and approval. I (the sin within me, as Paul would say) had convinced myself that I would never be enough. Enough of what? I really had no idea. All I knew was that if I really was enough, my dad who I loved so much would not have abandoned me for "more important" priorities in his life.

This shame-based false belief provided the fuel to sustain a cycle of sin and shame in my life for nearly twenty years – from age twelve to into my early thirties. Make no mistake, it cost me dearly along the way.

The enemy is well aware of these chinks in our armor. So, they are exactly where he targets his arrows. He makes promises to provide relief for the shame-based pain we're experiencing, all the while focusing his sights on our weakest, most susceptible places. He is a master of deception and lies and uses them as the impetus behind the only three arrows in his quiver: to steal, to kill, and to destroy.

Susceptibility

Depending upon context, the word "susceptible" can be understood in numerous ways: yielding readily to; lacking protection or defense; responsive to external stimuli; open to being acted upon; readily persuaded or convinced; easily bent or redirected; and multiple others. What all of these definitions have in common is the lack of a personal boundary (productive shame) to protect us from temptation or risk. This leaves us wide open to believe we are strong enough to resist temptation, despite our past track record that would prove otherwise.

The author Homer, in his 800 BC mythological story *The Iliad and the Odyssey*, tells of a warrior by the name Achilles. Achilles was a powerful hero in Homer's Iliad, and undoubtedly the greatest warrior on the battlefield at Troy.

When Achilles was just an infant, his mother immersed him in the river Styx, which separated the land of the living from the land of the dead, to confer on him immortality, and to make him invincible in battle. But when doing this, she committed a grave error. Through her oversight (neglect), she held Achilles by his left heel when immersing him in the river and forgot to immerse his heel as well.

And so, in spite of his great power, strength, and unsurpassed skill and prowess in battle, Achilles moved through life with one weak, susceptible spot, his left heel, which would ultimately become his demise. In the final battle of the Trojan War, Achilles was shot in his left heel with a poisoned arrow, which finally killed him.

I've been in this place of susceptibility more than once in my life. Strong and resolved on the outside, yet insecure on the inside. Fully mindful of the love and acceptance of God and others, yet unguarded and exposed to the enemy's plans and tactics. Shame, many times, would overpower my objectivity and awareness. My Achilles' heel would leave me greatly unprotected.

Most of the time, people-pleasing, being highly responsible, and putting the needs of others ahead of my own allowed me to maintain the approval needed to hold my shame at bay. In spite of my gallant efforts, there were still times when there would be what felt like disapproval (or the absence of approval) – whether real or imagined – and I would almost instantaneously open my mind to the enticements of the enemy. It felt like rejection, whether it really was or not.

We all have our weak or susceptible areas – our Achilles' heel. Some are a result of our own sinfulness. Others, like Achilles, are a byproduct of someone else's neglect or omission. Either way, they are ours now. Although every human being has areas of weakness, American culture has convinced us that any weaknesses is unacceptable. We must hide our weaknesses from others, or else they may not accept us or approve of us or love us. It's like we're so desperate for other fallen human beings to validate us that we'll sacrifice virtually anything, even ourselves.

Matthew 16:26 (NLT) says, "And what do you benefit if you gain the whole world but lose your own soul? Is anything worth more than your soul?" We often go to great lengths to outwardly appear acceptable and well put together in hopes of hiding our authentic humanness. We create a façade that tells others we're strong and under control – that is, until the enemy releases an arrow that targets and exploits our Achilles' heel. At that point, we're totally defenseless, and our weakness has been exposed.

Temptation

The Bible assures Christians in 1 Corinthians 10:13 (NIV): "No temptation has overtaken you except what is common to mankind. And God is faithful; He will not let you be tempted beyond what you can bear. But when you are tempted, He will also provide a way out so that you can endure it."

We must look deeper into the meaning of this verse in order to interpret it accurately and understand it in context of our situations. Online author Lyn Dove does a wonderful job of helping us interpret this passage, not only correctly, but in a way that clarifies how our battle with temptation is often handicapped by the toxic shame in our lives:

> The misinterpretation of that verse makes people question God and decry the unfairness of life. Why does God allow me to be tempted? He promised we would never face more than we can bear! This perspective completely misses the meaning and message of that Bible verse because we have completely misinterpreted it!

> The reader must consider this scripture in proper context to glean its full meaning. Paul, in 1 Corinthians 10 (NIV), is warning the church, using Israel's past history to prove his point: That they will face all manner of temptations, but as long as they anchor themselves to God, He will give them the spiritual strength to handle whatever they may face. God will not allow any temptation to come their way that they are unable to resist. The entire passage is about

temptation and the fact that people fall into temptation when they are being disobedient. Verse 12 warns: "So, if you think you are standing firm, be careful that you don't fall!

Sin is insidious. When people are not following God, when they insist on going their own way and not obeying God, sin, disguised as temptation, will lure them in. Verse 14 says the solution to being tempted is to "flee," but if we ignore that advice and instead succumb to temptation, God will, in His mercy, help us by providing a way out. He will ask us to repent (turn from the sin), to be restored to a right relationship with Him first. Leaning on Him, we can endure the consequences that follow as a result of our disobedience. He won't remove the consequences, but He will give us the strength we need to handle them.

The promise is not that God won't let bad things happen, but when they do happen, **we can trust that God is bigger than any problem, trial, or temptation we may go through in life**.

Even when I knew that anchoring myself in God would give me the spiritual strength to withstand whatever temptation life may throw at me, I was often complacent about doing what was necessary for that to happen. I wish I could tell you why. Maybe there was something exhilarating about being vulnerable to temptation, because it allowed me to continue in the earthly pleasure it had provided since I was twelve years old.

I was first exposed to pornography at the vulnerable age of twelve. Long before the internet, it was in the form of magazines. Lots of them. I never even needed to purchase or own a single one. Several young guys in my life had drawers full of them. Mine for the taking.

At twelve, I was just curious. Those were things I had never seen before. No acting out. Just a growing curiosity.

But it was only a few months before hormones began to do something totally unfamiliar within my body, and unfortunately, to my eyes as well.

What once was curiosity was now beginning to turn into desire. Like a drug, pornography and masturbation began to make the pain of my dad's abandonment and the absence of approval melt away — at least for a few minutes. There's a huge brain science behind this whole thing, which I know little about. All I know for sure is, that when I was hurting inside, this seemed like the best answer.

What began as novelty turned into frequent acting out — call it sin, regardless my young age. At some point (I can't even tell you when it was), my occasional habit crossed the line into becoming an addiction — a pattern I was unable to stop. I'm not really sure what I was addicted to. Pornography? Naked women? The rush it gave me? The emotional and physical release I experienced? The vicarious feeling of being wanted, pursued, or accepted? Or could it have been something much deeper?

I took this self-destructive secret with me from junior high to high school to college to marriage to young adulthood. Saying and doing all the right things on the outside. Hurting, lonely, and ashamed on the inside. My brokenness had gone from a byproduct of choices my parents had made, to now, a cycle of shame I repeatedly imposed upon myself. The sin had gone from initially being theirs to now being fully mine.

Secrecy

Shame has a deceptive way of convincing us that we need to hide ourselves from the outside world — at all cost — much like the way Adam and Eve hid themselves from God. We go to great lengths to protect our secrets. At its worst, shame will lead us to sacrifice good things in our lives just to preserve and protect the secrets inside. Many a person has sacrificed their marriage, family, career, reputation, and so much more at the altar of shame and secrecy.

By the time we get to the secrecy element of the shame cycle, we've pretty much locked in on following through with acting out, whether big or small. Our inhibitions have been drastically lowered by the shame messages we've played over and over in our heads, so we have set ourselves up to be vulnerable to nearly any temptation that promises to numb our pain. If God is in the conversation at this point, it's typically us begging

Him to give us the strength to say "no" to ourselves. Then when we cave in to temptation, we're mad at God for not hearing our prayer.

It's not our sin that we're hiding at this point. We're actually trying to hide ourselves and our internalized shame because we don't want anyone to witness our vulnerability or try to talk us out of succumbing to our indulgence. Our shame has prevailed over our will, and we've reached the "point of no return."

I became a master of hiding my secret. Not just my occasional secret rendezvous with pornography. I mean the secret reality that my interactions with people I cared about would evoke a wave of insecurity inside me. An insecurity that if I said or did the wrong thing, or if I didn't say or do the right thing, the person might disapprove of me. Wow, that sounds ridiculous as I hear myself say it.

Acting Out

The Bible tells us that each of us is made by God as a composite of three distinct components: "Now may the God of peace make you holy in every way and may your whole spirit and soul and body be kept blameless until our Lord Jesus Christ comes again" (1 Thessalonians 5:23 NLT).

In a world without sin, we would truly be blameless in these ways. The word blameless means "innocent of wrongdoing." We would have no wrongdoing in our spirit or soul or body. But unfortunately, that's not the world we exist in. This characterizes one of the most important reasons Jesus died on the cross – to pay the penalty for the wrong you and I have done (justification), and to satisfy God's wrath toward us as sinful man (propitiation).

Scripture uniformly traces voluntary, intentional sin to its root cause in sinful human nature. Sinful acts are the fruit of a "depraved" nature (see Proverbs 4:23; Mark 7:20-23), which is simply a nature bent toward impurity or immorality.

So, what does this have to do with acting out? As human beings, our Creator gave us a free will. Sin created in us a depraved nature. When our free will mixes with our depraved nature it creates a recipe for disaster! Human history has proven that when humans allow shame to spiral to a progressively lower and lower state, depravity may manifest in ways we would have never imagined.

My pet method of acting out was to secretly view pornography. Private, secret, not hurting anybody, right? This was in the days before the internet was "invented." So, believe it or not, there were actually times I would go to a video store (my local Blockbuster) and rent not only a video, but also the VHS player to play it with! Speaking of desperate. I can't even begin to tell you the lengths I went to so that I wouldn't be found out.

I recently viewed a TV documentary that chronicled the story of infamous serial killer Ted Bundy. A quote from an interview with this man clearly illustrates the slippery slope of succumbing to the shame within us, no matter how seemingly small it seems at first: "With the clock ticking toward his scheduled execution, Ted Bundy tearfully blamed a growing addiction to pornography for fueling one of the most gruesome killing sprees in recent history… ''Pornography…was the fuel for his fantasies to do all of the things he did."

If we don't allow the darkness of our hearts to be exposed to the regenerative light of Jesus Christ, the inclination of our human depravity might lead us into choices we thought we could never make.

Needless to say, acting out can take the form of any or all of the three inborn components of our nature: spirit, soul, body. Consider these few examples:

SPIRIT	**SOUL**	**BODY**
Idolatry	Anger	Sexual immorality
Pride	Hatred	Impurity
Greed	Discord	Over-indulgence
Envy	Rage	Laziness
Vanity	Selfishness	Drunkenness
Witchcraft	Lust	Self-harm

Some of you reading this book may be thinking to yourself, "Even my worst choices aren't anywhere near as bad as these examples." Praise God. I'm certainly glad they're not. But this information still may be for you. None of us should accept being captive to a repeated cycle of shame and acting out, even if it's as benign as compulsively reading romance novels or eating too many Oreos. The issue is more than just the nature or extent of the behavior being acted out. It's the unchecked influence of our internalized shame that is driving us to do the compulsive behavior in the first place. Even seemingly innocuous choices can keep the shame cycle spinning if they lead to greater feelings of guilt and shame, and the desire to conceal our behavior from others.

Your secret may be the compulsion to sneak a package of Oreos out of the cupboard late at night (which I've been known to do), hoping to relieve your feelings of rejection and unworthiness through your compulsion to consume your favorite comfort food in excess. This may lead to feelings of guilt, which convince us to keep our behavior a secret. Or maybe going on a shopping spree for things we don't really even need, in hopes that this will placate the pain of loneliness we feel in the midst of a struggling marriage, all the while keeping the items and the receipt for what we purchased secret from our partner.

A powerful quote by Pastor Ravi Zaccharias very poignantly illustrates the topic of us acting our shame: **"Sin will take you farther than you want to go, keep you longer than you want to stay, and cost you more than you want to pay."**

Shame

Shame that is a product of our acting out (I'll refer to this as "post-shame") is somewhat different than shame that was the precursor to our acting out (I'll refer to this as "pre-shame"), although both weeds share the same roots.

As we looked at in detail already, pre-shame leads to discomfort that we feel we need to make go away. Typically, the deeper the pain, the more extreme our acting out behaviors become. Certainly, there is a wide gap between gorging on Oreos verses being a serial killer. But believe it or not, the toxic shame that underlies both examples might not be all that different. The serial killer probably allowed the shame in his or her heart to go unchecked, and to spiral progressively further down over the course of many years.

Every single time, after succumbing to my secret sin, I would be overwhelmed with a heavy cloak of shame. Sometimes I would cry out to God, asking Him to have mercy on my wretched ways. Other times I would just sob as messages of shame, guilt, and worthlessness ran through me. Suffice it to say, there was never a time after viewing pornography that I was glad I had.

Post-shame typically presents itself in some sort of self-deprecating thoughts and feelings. I've read hundreds of books throughout my life, and another one of my all-time favorites is *The Search for Significance* by Robert McGee. This book is actually one of the top ten most read Christian books of all time!

McGee writes from the premise that every human being is on a constant search for significance (e.g., worth, meaning, purpose, identity). In his career as a Christian counselor that spanned several decades, McGee discovered that people tend to separate into four distinct tendencies in our relentless search for significance, even when we know consciously that these will not bring the ultimate fulfillment we are searching for.

> **The Performance Trap**: "I must meet certain standards to feel good about myself."

> **Approval Addict**: "I must be approved by certain others to feel good about myself."

> **The Blame Game:** "Those who fail (including myself) are unworthy of love and deserve to be punished.

> **Shame**: "I am what I am. I cannot change. I am hopeless."

Once we've acted out our drug of choice, the enemy is right on our heels trying to convince us of how worthless we are for failing again, despite the fact that he is the one who urged us to do it. In my use of the phrase "drug of choice," I'm employing a broad use of terms which could include meth as a drug or alcohol as a drug or marijuana as a drug, but also pornography or gambling or adultery or binge watching or overeating or sneaking Oreos as drugs as well.

Through my own work as a counselor, I've come to agree with Robert McGee that the clients who seek counseling due to the pain of unresolved toxic shame seem to disperse into these same four groupings. He went even further in his book to break down the most common consequences of these four false beliefs. If these four groupings seem to fit your story, you may want to read his amazing book sometime on your own. It was life-changing for me.

Wrong Place to Search	False Belief	Typical Consequences
The Performance Trap	I must meet certain standards to feel good about myself	The fear of failure; perfectionism; drive to succeed; manipulation of others to achieve success; withdrawal from healthy risks
Approval Addict	I must be approved of by certain others to feel good about myself	The fear of rejection; attempts to please others at any cost; overly sensitive to criticism; withdrawal from others to avoid disapproval.
The Blame Game	Those who fail (including myself) are unworthy of love and deserve to be punished	The fear of punishment; punishing others; blaming others for personal failure; withdrawal from God and others; drive to avoid failure
Shame	I am what I am. I cannot change. I am hopeless.	Feelings of shame, hopelessness, and inferiority; passivity; loss of creativity; isolation; withdrawal from others

Concealment

I'm guessing that the words "concealment" and "secrecy" might be listed as synonyms if you were to search them online. For the purpose of describing the shame cycle though, I see them as not quite the same. Secrecy, which we discussed in great detail a few pages back, has to do with hiding ourselves: "I don't want people to see me – even if they're right next to me – because they might interfere with or make me feel guilty for my self-indulgent behavior." I can almost hear the righteous among us saying, "I can't imagine a mature person ever doing something like that; being that secretive." But for those of us who have ever ridden the cycle of shame, it seems entirely fathomable.

It's almost embarrassing to admit the lengths I would go to in order to conceal what I had done…again. I vividly recall compulsively cleaning the inside of my vehicle to make sure a video rental receipt was not mistakenly left on the floorboard or in a cup holder. Another time, I asked to meet with the manager of the movie rental store, and practically begged him to take off our account any hint of my having rented an adult video. If I disclose any more stories of my outlandish efforts to conceal my sin, you'll begin to think I'm making them up just for the shock factor. Enough said.

Concealment, by my definition, is not about hiding me. It's about hiding what I have done.

I reflect on the storyline of the fictional book, *The Tell-Tale Heart*, when I think of the concept of concealment. I can still remember reading this story way back when I was in seventh grade, and for some reason it has always intrigued me. It tells of a man who killed another man, apparently for having a strange looking eye. After having buried the dead man's body under the floorboards of his own home, his feelings of guilt caused him to perceive that he could still hear the man's beating heart. Although well concealed, the effect of the man's actions still held power over him.

The man in the story is making every effort to resume mainstream life as if nothing has happened, but his heart is in turmoil from the guilt and shame of the very behavior he personally chose, yet ironically detests.

Justifying

The word "justify" basically means to be aligned with the desirable result. When typing a document, we justify the text to the prescribed margins. In a court of law, to justify means to show a sufficient lawful reason for an act that was done. The Bible teaches to justify means to be proven righteous based upon God's standards. I think you get the idea.

In order to return to the demands of everyday life, our mind must find some means of diminishing the relentless chatter of guilt and shame in our mind. Later in the book I go into great detail about God's plan for us to squelch the insistent lies of the enemy in our heads. When in the throes of the shame cycle though, it seems God's voice is only a faint whisper, if present at all.

Quoting C.S. Spurgeon, nineteenth century English preacher and author: "If the heart is foul, the eye will be dim." What I believe he is inferring is that the more toxic our heart, the less interested we become in hearing and seeing the heart of God.

I'm pretty certain that every one of us has attempted to justify our wrong actions in some way, whether associated with our brokenness or not.

- "I can spend my money however I want. I earned it."
- "I can stop drinking any time I decide to."
- "She should be thankful that all I do is look at porn. At least I'm not sleeping with another woman."
- "I have to have comfort food or I can't relax and unwind."
- "Marijuana is legal pretty much everywhere, so it's no big deal that I smoke a few joints just to get through the day?"
- "The reason I kept it secret was to protect the people I love."
- "I only had sex with him because my husband isn't attracted to me anymore."
- "I guarantee she won't be complaining when I hit it big at the casino."
- "I'm not hurting myself. It's no big deal. I can cover them up and nobody will know."

My justification was a lie I told myself a million times: "My (first) wife isn't interested in having sex with me anymore, so I can look at porn to get my needs met. That way I won't put our marriage in jeopardy." One of the first realities that smacked me in the face many years later when I was in school to become a Christian counselor was that my porn habit wasn't the solution to us not having sex. It was the cause! This revelation totally broke my heart when I finally got to the place where I could admit that.

Regardless of what unhealthy habit or secret indulgence or sin we may choose, they all have one thing in common: They all lead to greater and greater shame, guilt, and brokenness.

Overcompensating

Overcompensating is the only way we know how to effectively re-enter life – by creating a façade of what we believe to be acceptable, in hopes of safeguarding our inner brokenness. In constructing the façade, however, the shame messages within us cause us to go overboard, thinking we can will ourselves to be whole – or at least appear to be. Chronic overcompensation predictably morphs into compulsivity and the need for control. As shame-based people, we have a tendency to exert control over any outcome we fear. If this paradigm is threatened or jeopardized or compromised, the worst aspects of our character may unwittingly become exposed.

Bradshaw claims that "**shame is transmitted within family systems and is the root cause of all addictive and compulsive behaviors.**" It's not merely the behavior or habit or tendency that is problematic. The root issue is that we can't not do it, despite our firm resolve to the contrary. Any concern about what our compulsivity might cost us is far outweighed by our fear that our secret shame may be laid bare.

The online resource Wikipedia defines compulsive behavior as: "Performing an action persistently, repetitively, and excessively without it necessarily leading to the 'promised' outcome or pleasure."

So, if our compulsiveness hasn't already manifested itself in the midst of our preferred form of acting out our shame, it will most certainly rear its head as a desperate, compulsive attempt to overcompensate externally for our shame and brokenness on the inside. We become experts at creating and maintaining an "acceptable" façade to protect our pain.

- A woman experienced shaming by her parents after becoming pregnant while still in high school. Now as a mother, she compulsively controls every action and decision her teenage daughter makes.
- A man who, as a child, was teased day after day by his family for being chubby, now compulsively runs several miles every single day and refuses to ever miss a day. He believes that if he doesn't run every day, he'll become fat and unacceptable.
- A person who was raised in a home where life felt out of control, is now compulsively perfectionistic in an effort to create a controlled, perfect, and predictable environment around themselves.
- A woman experienced deep emotional woundedness from her father while she was a child and adolescent. As a result she has unknowingly become "over-sexualized," subconsciously hoping her need for male affirmation and affection will be satisfied through provocativeness and sex.

The nature of our acting-out behavior and the nature of our compulsivity often have little resemblance to one another. Our compulsiveness is merely our way of distracting ourselves from the reality of the pain inside us, while projecting an image around ourselves that portrays the image that we want others to see. Although we may not consciously realize it, all of this compulsive effort serves as our well-constructed strategy to protect our shame, brokenness, and humanness from ever being seen by others.

The longer I continued in my pattern of pornography and lust, the more compulsively "perfect" I presented myself to others. I needed them to see how "good" I was so they would never suspect anything dark and secret going on in my private life. Somehow people had become convinced they needed to apologize to me if they said a cuss word in my presence. Co-workers wouldn't invite me to social get-togethers because they knew I "didn't drink." Any time there was a gathering of family or friends, I was always the person they asked to pray before the meal, because I was the "most religious." Others perceived me as a godly man, husband, father, and citizen. All the while, I was protecting my secret at all cost. **The opposite of toxic shame is not wholeness. It is pretentiousness.**

But I thank God every day that wasn't the end of my story. In fact, it's where my real story actually began. And God is still writing it today!

Through that long season of inward brokenness and outward pretentiousness, God in His mercy saw fit, over twenty years ago, to allow me to crash and burn, losing almost everything that meant anything to me – fired from my job, publicly humiliated, lived on unemployment, filed bankruptcy, and eventually divorced my wife of twenty-one years.

Then, from the ground up, God began growing within me a new life filled with grace, hope, authenticity, and purpose. He took all of my broken pieces and made them into a masterpiece!

Wash, Rinse, Repeat

At this point in the shame cycle, each of us faces a significant fork in the road with two opposing choices. Fully surrender our lives – our sin, shame, and brokenness – to Jesus Christ. Or repeat the cycle all over again, only now with even more false beliefs and internalized shame to embolden it.

Questions from Dr. Dave

For personal reflection or group discussion of Chapter 6

Have you ever gotten yourself trapped in a cycle of shame that felt like being stuck on a hamster wheel you just couldn't get off of? What were the false beliefs that kept this endless pursuit going? Have you become free of those false beliefs today? If not, what have you learned in this book that has offered you hope to find freedom from the bondage of your shame-based compulsions?

There are six core questions every one of us unknowingly gets answered through our childhood: Who am I? Am I enough? Am I acceptable? Am I known? Am I safe? Am I complete? Which of these did you receive affirming answers to as a child? Which were answered in ways that contributed to the toxic shame you deal with today? Are you willing for God to re-frame all six of these questions with life-affirming answers?

We seek significance in four typical ways that inevitably leave us still feeling as though we're "not enough." Which of these most accurately reflects the story of your lifelong search? The Performance Trap? The Approval Addict? The Blame Game? Shame? Do you sincerely believe that God can and will change this pattern within you? Are you ready for Him to?

"Without complete honesty and vulnerability, unresolved shame can become a barrier to God turning our broken pieces into masterpieces."

Dr. Dave Ralston

CHAPTER 7

Toxic Shaming: An American Icon

I've had the wonderful opportunity to meet numerous high-profile people throughout my life – professional athletes, celebrities, dignitaries, and government leaders – Ronald Reagan, Jalen Rose, Michael W. Smith, Dick Vitale, Bo Schembechler, Steve Urkle, Larry Bird, Hulk Hogan, Bill Clinton, Chris Webber, Tom Landry, John Baker, Mitch Albom, Magic Johnson, Gerald Ford, Kyle Idleman, and countless others. Yet none of these encounters was as memorable as when I personally spent an afternoon with Muhammad Ali in his grand hotel room in Atlanta, Georgia.

Ali is what many in America would refer to as a cultural icon. Webster's defines the word "icon" as: "An object or person that is identified by members of a culture as representative of that culture." For decades his face and message appeared routinely in all forms of mainstream American life. Muhammad Ali had become a significant part of the cultural landscape.

Toxic Shame – An Icon?

As far back as the Mayflower Pilgrims landing on Plymouth Rock in 1620, America has had the cultural norm of utilizing shaming as a means of discipline, particularly in the discipline of children, woven into its DNA. A methodology we in the twenty-first century have come to perceive as detrimental is what our predecessors considered to be right, godly, and necessary.

Check out this excerpt from an article by the Journal of Family Studies:

> As early American Puritans broke from the English church, the subjugation of children was formalized, dissuading (discouraging) them against challenging or rebelling against authority in the slightest. Puritan children were taught that by disobeying their parents they were forcing God to condemn them to eternal death, and that strong discipline through physical punishment could bring salvation to children. If disobedient, children were whipped in public and forced to make public confessions in front of a meeting of adults. Matters such as rights of children were never considered.

These harsh forms of discipline apparently defined the American family, church, and community for centuries, rising to the status of a cultural icon worth aspiring to. It became the outwardly visible representation of their dedication to purity, morality, and righteousness, which many believed were foundational to the life in godliness that our nation was built upon.

According to The Bible

Respectfully, our forefathers believed these cultural standards were fully corroborated by the Bible, using these and similar Old Testament scriptures as their foundation:

> "A rod and a reprimand impart wisdom, but a child left undisciplined disgraces its mother" (Proverbs 29:15 NIV).

> "Do not withhold discipline from a child; if you punish them with the rod, they will not die" (Proverbs 23:13 NIV).

> "Punish them with the rod and save them from death" (Proverbs 23:14 NIV).

> "Folly is bound up in the heart of a child, but the rod of discipline will drive it far away" (Proverbs 22:15 NIV).

"Physical punishment cleanses away evil; such discipline purifies the heart" (Proverbs 20:30 NLT).

I have no intention to create a theological discussion over the deeper meaning of any of these proverbs, or to judge other generations' belief systems. I concur that every word of the Holy Bible is without error, each part written entirely through the inspiration of the Holy Spirit.

We must be honest with ourselves though. Any flaw or contradiction we might perceive in God's word is not a mis-step on God's part, but a mis-interpretation on ours.

When each of us reads the words of the Bible, we all have a tendency to "interpret" what we read through the lens of our own personal needs, beliefs, and life experiences. I'm confident that God did not provide us His word that we might interpret it in a way that would fit it into <u>our</u> will and purposes, either individually or corporately. Rather, I believe we were given this precious gift to guide us, as a cohesive church, in understanding <u>God's</u> will and purposes.

In order to even begin to understand God's heart in the scriptures, it's critical we read it through the only lens that is capable of capturing God's heart fully and accurately: Jesus Christ. Jesus is not merely the central character in the Bible. or a man who freely gave his life on a criminal's cross as a substitute for the punishment you and I should have received. **He IS the unfolding story of the Bible** -- cover to cover, Genesis to Revelation. It's all about Him – His love, His joy, His peace, His patience, His kindness, His goodness, His faithfulness, His gentleness, and His self-control. These characteristics can only become a part of us as His followers through His grace and our faithful submission. Any lens other than Jesus will lead us to conclusions that do not accurately reflect that nature and character of God we see personified in Jesus.

But What About These Proverbs?

When we, as Christians, are unable to reconcile passages like these proverbs with the very nature and character of Jesus, we must come to the conclusion that we are in error in how we're interpreting them. Nothing in scripture will every contradict Jesus. Not His nature. Not His character. Not His words. Not His actions.

With this being said, I have no right to criticize or second guess those who came before us, and their efforts to build their families, homes, schools, churches, and communities upon the foundation of God's word. I presume that each previous generation merely duplicated into their own families the very principles and practices their parents and grandparents employed in their families. They did what they thought was right.

As Christian adults today, though, our Christian responsibility is not to debate whether we are to raise our kids or run our schools or lead our communities the way our forefathers did, but to infuse the very love and grace and character of Jesus Christ into every element of life we are a part of – in spite of historical precedent or family history.

Fast Forward to the Twentieth Century

Prior to the twentieth century, adults demanded strict adherence to a very stringent code of behavior and conduct – privately and publicly – for both themselves and their children. Despite many of their techniques appearing harsh and primitive by today's standards, history appears to show that the effects of these methods were not as emotionally detrimental as we might think. Fundamentally they were an expression of society's deeply held Christian beliefs, and the intent of people's hearts was to develop noble character in their children. They sincerely believed that shaming was a God-given instrument for creating a culture that aligned with the teachings of the Holy Bible as they understood them.

Although discipline through "shaming" has existed for centuries in America, what was once religion-based discipline subtly mutated into emotion-based discipline on the heels of our society's painful journey through a global pandemic, the Great Depression, and two World Wars of the early twentieth century.

After the United States and their allies won the war in Europe in May 1945, morale reached all-time highs across our nation. Unemployment, which had reached twenty-five percent during the Great Depression, had dropped to a mere 1.2 percent at war's end. With the war finally over,

American consumers were eager to spend their money, on everything from big-ticket items like homes, cars, and furniture to appliances, clothing, shoes and everything else in between. New car sales quadrupled between 1945 and 1955. Driven by growing consumer demand and optimism, the US reached new heights of prosperity in the years after World War II.

Amidst this new-found affluence, though, an insidious disease was beginning to covertly infect the nation's collective consciousness: **Toxic Shame.** Envision a freeway that, by all appearances, seems perfectly safe, solid, and smooth to drive on. While drivers and their families enjoy travelling this way day after day, a steady undercurrent is slowly eroding the freeway's base, until one day, the road collapses.

Men came home from war radically changed from when they went. Marriages suddenly functioned differently than ever before. Children were now being raised with an entirely new set of rules and standards. Everything was changing as a half century of seemingly endless emotional trauma reached its crescendo.

Numerous authors identify that, as a means of managing the stresses of life after World War II, there was a shifting of parenting models, from a Biblical system of "training up" a child, to an emotional system defined by the transferring of toxic shame as a means of "controlling" a child. Despite this having affected the very fabric of the collective American soul, no one is to blame – yet we're all responsible to be a part of the solution.

PTSD Was Born

Author Steven Mulvey wrote in his BBC news article, "World War I and Vietnam are the wars most often associated with post-traumatic stress – but it was also a huge problem for the combatants in World War II, and one that is still affecting their children and grandchildren today."

Carol Schultz Vento, in an interview documented by Stephen Mulvey entitled *The Long Echo of WW2 Trauma*, speaks of her memories of her father after his return home from World War II:

> When my dad (Dutch Schultz) returned from war in 1945, he returned home to the US entirely different. The

happy-go-lucky joker his girlfriend had been waiting for since 1943 had turned somber and melancholy. After they married in December 1945, she had her first experience of his nightmares. As they travelled west by train to visit his parents, he shouted in his sleep and tried to climb out of the window. She also noticed that he had begun to swig regularly from a flask. "My father was a functioning alcoholic," says Schultz's daughter. "It was self-medicating, really.

The dominant narrative at this time was relentlessly upbeat, she says. The heroes of World War II were now building a prosperous post-war society. People who remarked upon the large numbers of marriages in the immediate post-war period tended not to mention the record number of divorces. The fact that veterans' hospitals were full of men with serious mental health problems went undiscussed. The movies of the 1950s and '60s did not depict the reality of war. "People did not want to know what it was like," her father told her.

Writer and author Tim Madigan, in a 2015 Washington Post article entitled, *Their War Ended 70 Years Ago – Their Trauma Didn't*, wrote these words regarding the emotional effects of World War II:

> They told me of night terrors, heavy drinking, survivor's guilt, depression, exaggerated startle responses, profound and lingering sadness. The symptoms were familiar to the world by then, but **post-traumatic stress disorder** (PTSD), the diagnosis that came into being in the late 1970s.

> Though it was referred to by other names (shell shock, combat fatigue, neuropsychiatric disorders) the emotional toll of World War II was hard to miss in the immediate postwar years. But with the passage of time and the

prevailing male ethos — the strong, silent type — World War II was soon overshadowed by the Cold War and eventually Vietnam. By the 1990s, amid the mythology of the Greatest Generation, the psychological costs of the last "good war" had been forgotten. **Yet those costs, as hard as the nation tried to ignore them, did not go away.**

In 1947, nearly half of the beds in every VA hospital in the nation were still occupied by soldiers with no visible wounds. While there were no reliable statistics on the topic, the epidemic of alcohol abuse was widely known.

Emotional Trauma and the American Family

A landmark article by the US Department of Veterans Affairs National Center for PTSD explains how the emotional trauma World War II imposed on American men profoundly changed how they functioned as men, husbands, fathers, and citizens.

PTSD can make somebody hard to be with. Living with someone who is easily startled, has nightmares, and often avoids social situations can take a toll on the most caring family. Early research on PTSD has shown the harmful impact of PTSD on families.

This research showed that US war Veterans have more marital problems and family violence. Their partners have more distress. Their children have more behavior problems than do those of Veterans without PTSD. Veterans with the most severe symptoms had families with the worst functioning.

How does PTSD have such a negative effect? It may be because those suffering with PTSD have a hard time feeling emotions. They may feel detached from others. This can cause problems in personal relationships and may even lead to behavior problems in their children. The numbing and avoidance that occurs with PTSD is linked with lower satisfaction in parenting.

It Makes Sense

Consider with me what the outcome in mid-twentieth century America might be when the effects of PTSD intersect with an already staunchly religious, legalistic environment. Suffice it to say, an entirely new conversation was born in many homes and families: "How do we survive?"

What was going on that family members needed to survive? It was the fear, anger, and control that now governed the average American family.

John Bradshaw explains the common theme that emerged in these homes as the emotion rose to an intense level, especially between the husband and wife. "Typically, the result is that the partners settle their issues with an "emotional divorce," yet cannot make this known to the outside world in the midst of a culture of high expectations. So, the family would make everything look good on the outside – a façade of happiness – yet beneath the surface there was a shame-filled struggle with fear, anxiety, pain, and loneliness within each family member."

It is from this backdrop that the shame-based family "rules" I presented in an earlier chapter family were born:

DON'T FEEL – DON'T TALK – DON'T TRUST

Families learned the "don't feel" rule, largely because authentic feelings would expose deep shame and emotional pain. WWII veterans knew that to open themselves up to their feelings would open a floodgate that probably would take them to a place of no return. So, they categorically held all of their feelings in, and expected everyone in their home to do the same. Secondarily, feelings were taboo, as they would cause a person to appear weak, lacking faith, or discontent in a world that expected everyone to be overtly religious, proud, prosperous, and happy.

The "don't talk" rule morphed into the "don't air our dirty laundry" rule of the '60s and '70s (and maybe still today in some families). The belief was that if anyone in the family were to "talk" (to speak of anything that might challenge or expose the fragile make-believe world within the family), others outside the family might perceive us as not being perfect and would surely judge us for our issues. A multigenerational gag order was placed upon the US family, and only now are courageous individuals beginning to challenge its validity.

The rule of "don't trust" was much more subtle than the others. In this context, trust had little to do with the fear of someone being dishonest or corrupt. What family members could not trust was the emotional state of the man leading their home. One day he may come home jovial and happy, bringing gifts for the kids and kisses for the wife. The very next day, the same man may enter the house angry and raging, yelling at the wife that something wasn't just the way he thought she should be, and taking out his anger on the kids. This lack of consistency and predictability instilled enormous amounts of fear into every family member. This is the very scenario where the concept of "codependency" began to emerge as an effective (yet unhealthy) means of surviving within a toxic, shame-based home.

To some degree these continue to govern many families in our country today. More often than I can count, I meet with husbands and wives in my office who are struggling because of these exact issues. Typically, the husband works hard to provide financially for the family, yet displays little or no emotions or feelings, has little to say of any substance, and cannot be trusted to be emotionally safe within the family. Folks, we need to do better than that.

Erosion of Godly Foundations

In light of the foreboding cultural climate of the early twentieth century that we've explored, we can't help but consider factors that may have contributed to the nature of the world we live in today. Natural characteristics such as creativity and vision were subdued by forced compliance. Respect turned into fear. Work ethic became drivenness. Discipline became punishment. Excellence became perfectionism. Contribution became control. Attentiveness became compulsivity. Conversation became conflict. Beliefs became dogmarism. Faith became religion. The inner fiber that had defined America since its inception was being weakened right before our eyes, and we were not able to recognize it.

The late 1940s and 1950s saw a marked upswing in church attendance across the country; yet, in retrospect, experienced a steep decline in the "faith" of the average American family. Biblical Christianity, which had once been the cornerstone of our American heritage, had now begun to devolve into merely a stage where adults would bring their families to display how devout, happy, and successful they were. History shows this to be the start of American culture beginning to tolerate the removal of God from many aspects of American life. The Christian community moved from being culturally prominent to now being functionally passive and superficial.

It's not difficult to begin to see the connection between "brokenness" in the souls of men in 1940s post-war America and the cultural and personal responses of every generation since. What is the nature of the shame that has been passed down? How was it communicated through each generation? What traits should we cling to, and what needs to be left in the past? We'll dig deeply into these, and many similar questions, as the remainder of this book unfolds.

Honor with Honesty

How can we appropriately honor those who have preceded us and served our nation so sacrificially, yet at the same time be objective about the generational impact their emotional brokenness has had on the wellbeing of our souls today?

The Bible records God's response to the prophet Micah centuries ago, as he posed a very similar question to God: "The Lord has told you what is good, and this is what He requires of you: To act justly, to love mercy, and to walk humbly with your God" (Micah 6:8 NIV).

This passage speaks to the paradox between deserved <u>justice</u> (being honest about how we've collectively been hurt) and undeserved <u>mercy</u> (compassion and empathy for those who fought to defend our freedom nearly a century ago). This span can only be bridged, as we read in Micah, by our walking in <u>humility</u> with God, understanding in our hearts that every one of us is deserving of God's wrath, yet graciously saved by His unending mercy.

Respect for My Elders

Before I explore the nature of the toxic shame that has become propagated – often unknowingly – through the generations of the past hundred years, I must first give honor to those who have come before me. My wonderful parents, grandparents, and great-grandparents, in their own unique ways, instilled faith, family, character, and purpose into my life. I'm especially proud to say that my father served as a US Marine during the Korean War. What a wonderful legacy of pride and patriotism he gave our family!

I believe that if my ancestors were still living today, they would be proud of the man, husband, and father I have become, and I would have the chance to tell them how grateful I am for each of them.

An inherent part of living on this planet, however, is our coming to the realization that society isn't always emotionally healthy, life isn't always fair, and people aren't always kind. The more pronounced these realities become, the more wounded and broken our souls will be. Despite my love for my family, my childhood wasn't without issue, and my family-of-origin was not without its own generational stuff. And it had an effect on me.

In writing this book, I was careful to not imply that my purpose was to criticize or demean my family (or yours) in any way. I love and respect every one of my relatives very much. Concurrently though, I owe it to myself and my own family to explore the lingering effects of shame and brokenness experienced during my childhood. Without that level of honesty, unresolved shame can become a generational barrier to God turning our broken pieces into masterpiece. Honor your family. Respect yourself.

To the Third and Fourth Generation

Walk with me as I explore the nature of each of the seven generations that co-exist in America today, and how each may have uniquely contributed to the dysfunctional aspects of our today's culture: The Greatest Generation > The Silent Generation > Baby Boomers (Early and Late) > Generation X > Millennials > Generation Z > Alpha Generation.

Every one of us — no matter our age, family history, or life choices — is faced with the decision whether to pass down the worst of what we've received from our ancestors, or to create a new generational legacy built upon the nature, character, and reality of Jesus Christ. We have the opportunity to be the generation that pivots our family tree from self-focused to Christ-focused.

The **Greatest Generation** is generally defined as people born from 1901 to 1927, and their remaining members are the oldest generation still living today. I can't even imagine what our society might look like had it not been for this generation's selflessness and courage. You and I enjoy the freedoms every day that these brave individuals fought so dearly to preserve.

Objectively though, this was this generation that introduced toxic shaming into American culture. In spite of their great heroism, we cannot overlook the realities of what they introduced into life in America in the 1940s and 50s, and how that altered the trajectory of every following generation. The unspeakable inhumanity, tragedy, and death they witnessed fundamentally changed the emotional core of American society. From this generation came the "DON'T FEEL" rule.

Members of the **Silent Generation** were born between 1928 and 1945. These were the younger brothers and sisters of the WWII generation. These are the individuals who fought during the Korean War. The children who grew up during this time worked very hard and kept quiet. It was commonly understood that "children should be seen and not heard." Leaders in Washington, DC passed legislation making it unacceptable for Americans to speak freely about their opinions and beliefs that might appear counter to the nation's post-war narrative. Therefore, the people were effectively "silenced." And thus the "DON'T TALK" rule was introduced.

The **Baby Boomers** categorization of Americans is made up of men and women who were born between 1946 and 1964 and is subdivided into two broadly defined subgroupings: **Early Baby Boomers** (born 1946 – 1955) are those who came of age during the Vietnam War era. They were the direct recipients of their fathers' harsh, shame-based parenting methods, and their lives became a reflection of what had been done to them – "DON'T TRUST." **Late Baby Boomers** (aka "Generation Jones") were born between 1956 and 1964 (this is my generational group). We did not grow up with World War II veterans as fathers, and there was no required military service or political cause that defined us. We never lived in a world without television. We were raised in homes where "keeping up with the Joneses" was a cultural norm. This generational group introduced the presence of "entitlement" into American culture.

The generation to follow is known as **Generation X**, born between 1965 – 1980. Growing up in a time of shifting societal values, Gen Xers are often called the "latchkey generation," due to reduced adult supervision compared to previous generations. They were the first generation to grow up in homes where their mothers weren't there every day when they got off the school bus. As children born of the adult children of emotionally traumatized World War II fathers, this generation felt the sting of the emotional absence of both their father and mother.

Millennials, originally known as Generation Y, were born between 1981 to 1996. They are the children of the "Jones" generation. The entitlement of their parents contributed to this generation being overindulged as children. As a result, the concept of the "child-centered home" was born. Now parents built their lives and families around the preferences and whims of their children, doing whatever necessary to keep the kids happy. The Millennial generation is generally marked by elevated usage of and familiarity with the Internet, mobile devices, and social media, which also made them the first to have uninhibited access to pornography, violence, and immorality at their fingertips.

Members of **Generation Z** – born between 1997 and 2012 – tend to be well-behaved, self-controlled, and are risk averse. Having been raised by latchkey Generation X parents, they tend to live more slowly than their predecessors when they were their age, causing them to sometimes be perceived as lazy. They have lower rates of teenage pregnancies, and they consume drugs and alcohol less often, largely due to having seen the destructive results in their parents and older siblings. Having been raised either by divorced parents or a single parent, they are concerned about academic performance and job prospects, in hopes of being able to "take care of themselves" without the help of a family. This generation has the highest frequency of mental health problems, experts assume due to the lack of family stability and cultural morality during their developmental years.

The youngest generation living in today's world are members of the grouping referred to as **Generation Alpha**. Researchers gave them this name because they are the first generation born entirely in the twenty-first century – with birth years from 2013 to today. In various articles about this generation's future, authors anticipate Alphas being the best educated generation ever, the most technologically immersed, and the wealthiest. Yet they will be the generation more likely than any in the past century to spend some or all of their childhood in living arrangements without either of their biological parents.

Every Generation Is a Gift to Society

The effects of toxic shame on individuals, families, and American culture cannot be fit into a nice, neat little box. These are not one-size-fits-all. Each generation, family, and individual are distinctive in the way they process shame as it was imparted to them, and to what extent they convey it into the lives of those they influence. Nonetheless, I hope this generational overview has provided a snapshot of the ripple effects of toxic family shame that was birthed more than seventy-five years ago.

We Can Do This Respectfully

We need to be careful to not accuse or make assumptions about individuals, as if they shamed us or others intentionally or maliciously. Rather, our objective is to identify and acknowledge the toxic effects of shame in our own individual lives, and to take courageous steps to allow God to bring healing and wholeness to our hearts.

Questions from Dr. Dave

For personal reflection or group discussion of Chapter 7

Every generation in human history has had to reckon with the sins of their forefathers. Over the past century of American culture, the introduction of toxic generational shame has been unprecedented. What aspects of your family's culture may have generational roots stemming back to post-World War II ancestors? In what ways has this had an adverse effect on your emotional and spiritual health?

Each successive generation since the World War II Generation has had to negotiate these three unspoken dysfunctional family rules: DON'T FEEL (from the Greatest generation) – DON'T TALK (from the Silent generation) – DON'T TRUST (from the Baby Boomer generation). Are you able to connect any of these to difficulties you have faced in your life and relationships? In what ways has this book shed light on the roots of these false beliefs? Have you been able to find hope that you had not before?

Every one of us is a member of a people group born and raised during some point in United States history. Although just brief generalizations, how does the description I provided for your generation help you make more sense of what you've experienced in your life? Are you able to see your parents in a different light, knowing what they might have experienced in their own childhoods?

"The unique nature of who we are is reflected most accurately through the characteristics of our inborn temperament."

Dr. Dave Ralston

PIECE 3

Soul & Spirit: *Am I Enough?*

CHAPTER 8

Same Experiences.
Different Effects.

At this point in our journey, you're most likely beginning to make significant connections between the experiences of your childhood and the intra- or inter-personal turbulence plaguing your adult life. To clearly and uniquely consider the solutions we'll be discussing in detail later in this book, there is one last foundational block that must be laid.

You see, this book is not simply a philosophical discussion of how brokenness and shame may have derailed your hopes and dreams. From the beginning, my passion has been to offer a roadmap for your one-of-a-kind journey toward soul health and personal wholeness.

In the preceding chapters, I've provided extensive content to help us understand the origins, causes, and effects of toxic shame in our lives. Without a doubt, this has been powerful in and of itself.

Nonetheless, that Information alone does not bring about the level of change each of us has longed for: a deep heart change. Transformation at that level requires more than merely controlling our thoughts or modifying our behaviors. We must identify how our childhood experiences have uniquely bruised, wounded, or broken our hearts in ways that others who had seemingly identical exposures weren't affected, or were affected in markedly different ways.

Was Sigmond Freud Correct?

In the nineteenth century, an Austrian neurologist by the name Sigmond Freud put forth a very un-Biblical perspective of human identity. He (and others preceding him) referred to this concept as "tabula rasa," which translated into English means "blank slate." His hypothesis was that every human being ever born came out of their mother's womb identically non-defined – literally a blank slate.

Freud claimed that individual personality traits were formed entirely by family dynamics. His theories implied that, from birth, humans lacked free will, that inborn influences on human personality were very miniscule, and that a person's specific identity was largely determined by their upbringing. Further, he theorized that all human knowledge came from experience or perception, and not from any inborn characteristics or tendencies.

It was in response to this illogical, irrational teaching of Freud that the debate of "nurture versus nature" ensued. The nurture perspective claimed that a person's environment was entirely responsible for who they would become. The nature perspective claimed that a person's unique inborn design established their identity. And, surprisingly, this discussion went on for decades.

Although Freud was certainly not the first to explore this notion, many believe that the implementation of this thinking within western culture from the late nineteenth and early twentieth centuries was largely a result of his research and writing. In fact, many of us reading this book may have been taught the uncorroborated theories of Sigmond Freud in mainstream public education. I know I was.

Regardless, Freud's theories were not only very secular and humanistic, but markedly incorrect, unfounded, and un-Biblical.

The Christian Perspective

Although Freud and his teachings were highly circulated, what he claimed completely flies in the face of what the Bible teaches about human identity.

The natural extension of Freud's "blank slate" theory would be that our identity is merely the sum total of our past experiences, both good and not so good. Scripture clearly reveals that an omnipotent God uniquely, and individually formed each of us in our mother's womb. Who we are is not defined by our past, but by our loving Creator.

This dichotomy often arises in my sessions with counseling clients. They insist that their relationships or occupation or family history "made them" who they are. They make statements like, "I'm just like my mom," "Smith men are just that way," or "My boyfriend makes me feel so stupid."

Would you consider that the more correct view might be entirely the opposite of what you've always thought? In each of these examples, their environment did not make them who they were, but rather, they chose how to interact with, perceive, or respond to their environment based upon their perspective they already had of themselves. I promise, it will make much more sense as we continue through this chapter. But please don't miss it.

If I'm entirely honest, much like you, I had never really considered either point of view. It had not ever seemed to matter. That is, until it did.

The Gold Standard of Christian Counseling Education

Over a decade ago, when I made the decision to retire from my lengthy professional career and to pursue education and training to become a pastor and Christian counselor, there was an overwhelming number of educational options to choose from. Suffice it to say, once I had done my due diligence in researching them all, one track clearly stood out from all others.

My seventy-two-credit hour course of study – accredited by the National Christian Counselors Association – culminated in my becoming nationally licensed as a Clinical Christian Counselor and conferred a PhD degree (magna cum laude) from Colorado Theological Seminary.

The entire curriculum had one fundamental theme woven through every course, clinical experience, and assignment: man's God-given, inborn nature, and its profound influence on our beliefs, thoughts, emotions, and actions throughout life. The flagship course was entitled *Creation Therapy,* written and taught by Dr. Richard and Dr. Phyllis Arno, founders of the National Christian Counselors Association.

National Christian Counselors Association

In 1981, the Arnos established the National Christian Counselors Association (NCCA) as a non-profit corporation in order to conduct extensive research in the development of a therapeutic assessment procedure based upon scripture. Through more than seven years of systematic research with over five thousand individuals, Drs. Arno developed a system that, still today, is considered the "gold standard" of client assessments. This instrument is known as the **Arno Profile System**.

Arno Profile System

The Arno Profile System (APS) is utilized by thousands of Christian leaders, ministers, and professional Christian counselors throughout America and around the world. It is the preferred instrument for assessing the unique, inborn identity of the individuals we serve. Over the past forty years since its inception, the APS has consistently been validated to a 95 percent accuracy rate in identifying an individual's inborn, God-given temperament.

The APS does not measure a person's personality, character, or behavior. To the contrary, it thoroughly describes a person's inborn temperament – the unique nature the Creator "knit together in our mother's womb" (Psalm 139:13 NIV). We are not merely a blank slate waiting to be defined, as secular science would claim. No, we are intentionally, miraculously, and beautifully crafted, distinct from all others.

Personality is a "mask" we put on, specific to each environment we're in and the people we'll be interacting with. Our personality may be starkly different at a birthday party than it would be at a funeral. **Character** is the person we've "learned" to be over the course of our lives, known best by those closest to us. **Temperament**, however, is the "inborn" nature we were given by God, and may very possibly not be fully known, even by ourselves.

Consider an old, white wooden table. Its "personality" is white. Its "character" is marred and blemished from years of use. But its "temperament" is the natural wood underneath the many colors that have been layered over it through the course of its life.

In contrast to Freud's suppositions, the person God created each of us to be (our true identity) and the person we have become through life in a fallen world (our learned, false identity) can be considerably different. This is creatively illustrated in a quote that many attribute to Albert Einstein: "If you judge a fish by its ability to climb a tree, it will live its entire life believing it is stupid!"

The APS profile intricately and accurately identifies the inborn nature of the "fish" we were created to be. Traditional profiles, designed to measure an individual's personality, simply reveal the outward behavioral and relational characteristics of our ability or propensity to "climb the tree."

The Human Soul

The Bible goes to great lengths to make it known that each one of us has been deliberately created by God. Countless scriptures affirm the truth of creation. And in the creation narrative, God not only created man and woman, He placed a specific design within each and every one of us.

The apostle Paul, in one of his letters, refers to this amazing design that separates man from all other living creatures: "May your whole spirit, soul, and body be preserved blameless at the coming of our Lord Jesus" (I Thessalonians 5:23 NIV). This affirms that we consist of body, soul, and spirit. Our material bodies are evident, but our souls and spirits are less distinguishable.

The meaning of the word Paul used for "soul" embodies our mind, will, and emotions. These three are evident in our personal preferences, choices, and desires, as well as our interactions with other human beings. **The nature of who we are is reflected most accurately through the unique characteristics of our inborn temperament.**

The Greek word for "spirit" is *pneuma*. It refers to the part of man that connects and communicates with God – much like the wind, very real yet not humanly visible. It is given to us by God and is the source of life (see

John 6:63). Our spirit differs from our soul, in that only through our spirit can we experience the very presence and nature of God.

While everyone's soul is fully active, not everyone's spirit is, because when Adam fell to sin, the spirit died and was separated from God. Only in Christ is the spirit reconnected and reconciled: "At one time you were separated from God. But now, by his death, Christ has made you God's friends again" (Colossians 1:21-22 NIV).

Layers of Temperament

The APS temperament profile is greatly effective in describing the inborn nature of a person's soul – **mind, will**, and **emotions**. The effects our lives have had on these three elements – both developmental and detrimental – are the essence of what we have been unpacking in the preceding chapters.

In creating the APS, Drs. Arno designated the three elements of human temperament in this way: **Inclusion** (our mind, and how it interfaces with the environment we're in), **Control** (our will, and how it carries out and responds to decisions, tasks, and authority), and **Affection** (our emotions, and how they express and respond to human feelings).

Metaphorically, these three temperament elements exist in what I conceptualize as "layers."

> **Inclusion** (mind) is how our five senses interpret to what extent the people, places, and things in our surroundings might sufficiently meet the needs of our temperament.

> **Control** (will) acts upon, decides, or responds to the information our mind has gathered, both consciously and subconsciously, present and past.

> **Affection** (emotions) causes us to emotionally process and respond to the input from our mind and will, both desirable and undesirable, present and past.

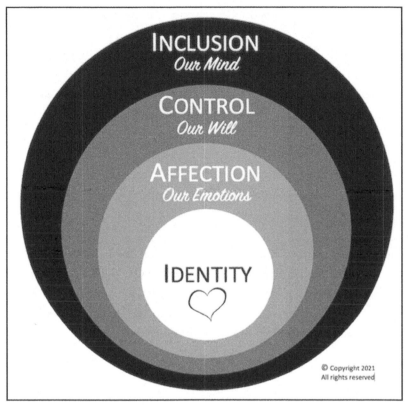

Temperament Layers

Drs. Richard and Phyllis Arno, in their book *Created In God's Image*, do a magnificent job of explaining the interconnection between these three temperament elements:

> The interpersonal relationship will be established and maintained according to the temperament needs that the individual is endeavoring to meet. This illustrates how temperament needs determine how we behave.
>
> Inclusion, Control, and Affection are comprised of needs within the temperament that must be met and are determining factors in other personality traits as well.

The area of Inclusion determines intellectual energies, whether we relate better to tasks or people, and how impulsive our behavior may be. The area of Control determines how well we make decisions, carry out our responsibilities, and how dependent or independent we are. The area of Control also determines how strong our will is. The area of Affection will determine how many of our emotions we share or how emotionally guarded or open we are. This area also helps determine the depth of our feelings, and how intimate we are with deep relationships in our life.

Our mind, our will, and our emotions are each fashioned by God with inborn **needs**, **strengths**, and **weaknesses**. This is common to all mankind. What makes us unique, though, is the combination of these inborn needs we were given, and how adequately our childhood, as well as our life as a whole, has attended to these needs.

Temperament Needs

We do not always recognize or acknowledge that our heart cries out for fellowship with God. Drs. Arno refer to this desire as "heart hunger," which often drives us into the things of the world in hopes of satisfying the longing within us. Our hunger for God will drive us, in our ignorance, to attempt to meet our temperament needs in ungodly ways. **Until we surrender our heart to Jesus Christ and become a child of God, our spirit will never be satisfied.**

In our own striving to be reconciled to God, we are unknowingly attempting to meet the needs of our temperament. If we could meet every one of our temperament needs in ways that would be fully pleasing to God, we would be perfect, complete, and have no need for God. In reality, our inherited nature keeps us from doing this; sometimes we walk in the flesh (that which is contrary to the spirit). We must face the fact that our identity (wholeness) can never be found within ourselves or the world in which we exist, but only in and through Jesus Christ.

Quoting Kyle Idleman, **"We'll not fully place our faith and hope in Jesus until our earthly idols have all failed us."**

Temperament Strengths and Weaknesses

Each element of our God-given, inborn temperament is comprised of **strengths** and **weaknesses**. Our inborn temperament strengths, when properly used, bring glory to God, the grace of Jesus to others, and fulfillment within. In order for our strengths to be realized, there needs to be a balance in all three areas of our temperament – Inclusion, Control, and Affection. Our temperament strengths are effectively and beautifully revealed in our lives when the specific needs of our inborn temperament are consistently met in healthy, godly ways.

However, because we experienced life and relationships in ways that were unhealthy, ungodly, or shaming, our mind, will, and emotions became drastically imbalanced, and the fundamental needs of our temperament went unmet. **Unmet needs always expose the weaknesses of our temperament.**

Certainly, issues such as depression, anxiety, addiction, crime, disobedience, disrespect, adultery, fear, worry, and so on, are obvious expression of temperament weaknesses. That largely goes without saying. But the enemy's deception often conceals our weaknesses in ways we very possibly might not recognize.

Often, behaviors that we typically might consider relationally and socially "acceptable" are essentially an equal-and-opposite reflection of our temperament weaknesses. Perfectionism, stringency, control, hypervigilance, and even serving the needs of others can be subtler expressions of temperament weaknesses, making it difficult to consider they might really be weaknesses. Temperament weakness cannot be assumed based upon outward behavior, but rather, by the inner motivation that provides motivational energy to behavior. Regardless whether outwardly "good" or "bad", if our attitudes, decisions, and actions derive their motivation from the shame within us, then they are weaknesses.

You Can't Judge A Fish by Its Ability to Climb A Tree

Let's consider that simply because we seem to effectively accomplish "good" things in our lives, it's very possible that these may be very self-focused, inhibiting the possibility for others to see Jesus through us. That's what makes them weaknesses. I often make the analogy to a young business that rapidly experienced enormous growth which visibly outpaced the organization's administrative ability to "keep up" – outwardly it appeared successful and thriving; yet its infrastructure was weak, underdeveloped and insufficient. Even though the results looked impressive, their weak foundation would inevitably falter.

> "Therefore, everyone who hears these words of mine and puts them into practice is like a wise man who built his house on the rock. The rain came down, the streams rose, and the winds blew and beat against that house; yet it did not fall, because it had its foundation on the rock. But everyone who hears these words of mine and does not put them into practice is like a foolish man who built his house on sand. The rain came down, the streams rose, and the winds blew and beat against that house, and it fell with a great crash" (Matthew 7:24-27 NIV).

Putting the Pieces Together

No doubt, the amount of information I've given you in this chapter may begin to seem overwhelming. I felt the very same way when the temperament concept was first presented to me.

Let me help you visualize the interconnection between all of the elements we've learned about, and the role each plays in the continuation of generational shame.

The child experiences an environment of rejection and abandonment

The child's unique inclusion, control, and
affection needs are largely unmet

Toxic shame begins to unknowingly become internalized by the child

To protect itself, the child's mind begins to
subconsciously suppress the true self

By adolescence, the child's temperament
needs have chronically gone unmet

In searching for their identity, the adolescent
allows a false self to emerge

The false identity is reflected in the adolescent's
attitudes, words, and behaviors

This familiar false identity carries into adulthood,
contributing to a lack of fulfillment

Unwittingly, the adult duplicates these patterns into their children

Let's Make It Personal

Understanding temperament can be very complex. I consider myself a trustworthy expert on this subject now, but when I was initially trying to wrap my mind around it, the information and concepts became almost overwhelming. Don't allow that to happen to you, ok? We're not studying for a PhD here. Our objective is simply to consider how our God-given, inborn temperament combination played a major part in not only how we experienced childhood shame, but also how we've responded and adapted to it in our adult life. Further, we'll learn the basics of how two individuals with two different temperament combinations can have two radically different responses to the very same environment.

Dating all the way back to the writings of Hippocrates in 400 BC, it seems that man has had this unquenchable desire to understand the inner design of human beings. Over the decades and centuries, countless theories, teachings, books, and assessments have emerged on this subject, each attempting to more clearly objectify human tendencies within the framework of four basic "types."

The four-type model was never challenged until nearly a half-century ago when Drs. Arno carried out extensive research for the purpose of creating an assessment instrument that could be effectively used in the Christian counseling environment. In so doing, they supplanted the traditional assessment models with two landmark discoveries:

- All previous assessment theories had apparently developed their assumptions based upon traditional, secular understandings of human nature and behavior existing within a fallen world. In stark contrast, Drs. Arno constructed their assessment tool based upon the manifold nature of Jesus Christ, illuminating teachings and principles of the Bible. These two premises are vastly different.
- From this Bible-based perspective, it became apparent to Drs. Arno that a critical piece of the identity matrix was missing: the humble, meek, submissive, self-sacrificing nature of Jesus himself. He described this in the Beatitudes, recorded in Matthew 5:3-12. Where secular science could not consider

the nature of an individual with these temperament traits as being whole, let alone desirable, our Christ-centered worldview affirms this description as a reflection of the very One who lovingly gave His life on the cross for us, that we might fully know Him.

The Arno's two groundbreaking findings led to the introduction of the fifth temperament – the Supine* – into the ancient four-type model that many assumed would never be redefined.

The _Five_ Temperaments

The result of the Arnos' tireless work birthed an entirely new paradigm from which to consider the God-given, inborn nature of human beings. Where there had long been four types, there were now five. For those of us who may have encountered a four-type assessment somewhere in our past, it's important to use caution in allowing those perspectives to overlay the profoundness of the innovative five-type APS model.

The names that Drs. Arno assigned to each of the five temperaments within the Arno Profile System are as follows: Melancholy, Choleric, Sanguine, Supine*, and Phlegmatic. As we've come to understand earlier in this chapter, each of these five temperament types is identified by an extensive set of inborn needs, strengths, and weaknesses. In my experience with literally thousands of clients and students who have completed the APS questionnaire, each of the five temperaments has one primary need (specific to that temperament type) that governs all of the other needs within that type. If this principal need goes unmet, or is met in unhealthy or ungodly ways, the person with this temperament type will predictably experience stress, anxiousness, and insecurity. Universally, individuals of all temperament types and combinations make choices – often unknowingly – that allow us to dodge the pain and insecurity of unmet needs.

Melancholy
Need: Appear competent
Avoid: Rejection

Choleric
Need: Control
Avoid: Failure

Sanguine
Need: Approval
Avoid: Absence of approval

Supine
Need: Acceptance or inclusion
Avoid: Abandonment or exclusion

Phlegmatic
Need: Protect energy
Avoid: Over-obligation of energy

Five-Temperament Matrix

Through the next several pages I have attempted to provide a very detailed look into the needs, strengths, weaknesses, and common shame-based responses of each temperament type. The more toxic the shame within us, the more profound, unhealthy, or even sinful our expression of this shame will become.

MELANCHOLY (M)	Inclusion	Control	Affection
Common Needs of An Individual with The Melancholy Temperament	Needs to appear competent and in control; needs to be respected; needs quiet time alone to regenerate; needs limited interaction with people; needs to not be controlled or manipulated; needs freedom from required socialization; needs freedom to think creatively; needs to function in an orderly,	Needs to appear competent and in control; needs to be respected; needs quiet time alone to regenerate; needs freedom to be creative; needs to not be controlled or manipulated; needs truth, order, reliability, and dependability from others, or they will feel they have been lied to; needs	Needs to appear competent and in control; needs to be respected, needs to be accepted and approved of for who they are; needs to not be controlled or manipulated; needs truth, order, reliability, and dependability from others, or they will feel they have been lied to; needs to be free from romantic

	stable environment; needs to fulfill their desire for knowledge; needs financial and economic security.	freedom to create and work independently; needs to work with tasks and systems; needs to be respected by other people, especially for their abilities.	demands; needs a relationship built on authenticity more than on emotion.
Common Strengths and Tendencies of An Individual with The Melancholy Temperament	Is extremely creative and artistic; highly productive; genius-prone; constantly seeking information; seeks excellence; persistent; self-sacrificing; friendly and personable; aware of how much they are loved by the people closest to them; moderately outgoing; see both the steps and pitfalls of a situation; visionary; loner; relationally cautious; homebody; strong-minded; methodical; perfectionistic; relentless thinker; vivid, detailed mind	Is capable of wonderful things; makes very good decisions; highly responsible within areas of competence; highly productive; seeks excellence; adheres to rules; exerts very little control over the lives of others; relentlessly motivated; sees both the steps and pitfalls of a situation; visionary; strong-willed; task oriented; works at slow, steady pace; very good leadership capabilities, especially when on their terms; highly independent; tolerate very little interference in their life; interferes very little with other people's lives	Is very faithful and loyal friend or partner; self-sacrificing for deep relationships; deep, tender feelings, but rarely reveals them; can easily empathize with others; able to make very deep commitments; shows very little emotional affection; needs very little affection shown to them; approaches very few people for deep relationships; deep personal relationships they do establish are very few; low self-esteem; feels unworthy of love; distrustful and suspicious; easily hurt
Common Weaknesses of An Individual with The Melancholy Temperament	Focuses on their imperfections; searches environment for messages to confirm their low self-esteem; sets unrealistic standards for themselves; fears rejection; has self-doubts; has mind that won't shut off; fears being wrong; pre-rejects others; projects façade of being competent and in control; seldom tells	Focuses on their imperfections; searches environment for messages to confirm their low self-esteem; pre-rejects others; projects façade of being competent and in control; seldom tells others their intentions; dwells on past criticism and rejection; sensitive to criticism or correction; can't admit when wrong or incorrect,	Focuses on their imperfections; searches environment for messages to confirm they are unlovable; vengeful if hurt or betrayed by a deep personal relationship; emotionally unavailable; unable to be emotionally vulnerable; demands to receive more love than they give; lonely; self-destructive;

	others their intentions; dwells on past hurts and failures; is easily insulted and hurt; can't admit when wrong or incorrect, making a mistake, being discovered to be inadequate, or making a fool of themselves; keeps emotional score card; throws past rejection back at others; justifies their anger; is hyper-sensitive; holds grudges; takes vengeance; unhealthy fantasies; angry; alcoholism; depression; stress; fear; drug addiction; sexual addiction; insomnia; suicide.	making a mistake, being discovered to be inadequate, or being seen as incompetent; procrastinates; rebellion; difficulty submitting to authority; projects façade of competence to hide real or imagined inadequacies; only submits to authority perceived as more competent; fears being wrong; rigid; inflexible; fears failure; fears the unknown; rebellious; angry; stress;	dissect the past; critical of others; angry; cruel; emotional; low self-image; hyper-sensitive to rejection; devastated by the loss of one of their few deep relationships; grieving seems to have no end; sexually oriented but not romantically inclined
Common Shame-Based Responses of An Individual With The Melancholy Temperament	Dark thinking; depression; drug use, abuse, and addiction; truancy; self-harm	Perfectionism; rebelliousness; altercations with others; quitting; retaliation; vengeance	Criticism of others; becomes idealistic and controlling

CHOLERIC (C)	Inclusion	Control	Affection
Common Needs of An Individual with The Choleric Temperament	Needs control; needs social interaction for the purpose of motivating others toward their goals; needs to be followed by others; needs to make decisions based on facts; needs achievement and accomplishment; needs constant recognition for their achievements and accomplishments; needs a great amount of control over	Needs control; need achievement and accomplishment; needs constant recognition for their achievements and accomplishments; needs to have tasks performed correctly, efficiently, and to their expectation; needs to be followed by others; needs a great amount of control over people's lives and behaviors; needs to associate with people who need	Needs control; needs to receive love and affection on their terms; needs to be followed, trusted, and respected; needs to be with people who are supportive of and believe in them; needs time away from people who aren't supportive

	their environment; needs mastery over pertinent information and content; needs accuracy, efficiency, and perfection; needs time away from people and socialization	them or are weaker than them; needs time away from people and interaction	
Common Strengths and Tendencies of An Individual with The Choleric Temperament	Is confident; outgoing; tough-minded; perfectionistic; good mind for envisioning new projects; extrovert of highly selective nature; highly personable and charming, open, and friendly, but doesn't really like people; able to inspire great numbers of people; socially very optimistic and well-liked; draws others into their charm; appears relational but is actually task oriented; high intellectual abilities; fast paced; undertakes projects quickly and efficiently; very good at envisioning new projects and goals	Is very organized and disciplined; leads by influence; tough-willed; excellent leadership abilities; efficient, well-disciplined, and military-like in carrying out responsibilities; capable of making quality decisions based on facts rather than feelings; makes quick, intuitive decisions; capable of taking on great responsibilities that might overwhelm others; has will-power to carry things through to completion; prefers to lead people who support their plans and goals; attracts weaker or needy people	Is bright; open; optimistic; outgoing; expresses a great deal of love and affection; approaches only select people for deep relationships; affectionate; appears to want deep relationships, but in reality, does not; turns away when approached by others for affection; must be shown love and affection according to their terms; very few emotions and feelings; cautious in expressing the emotions they do have
Common Weaknesses of An Individual with The Choleric Temperament	People user; walks over people; uses social connections as a means of reaching their goals; can appear arrogant; cruel, abusive temper; uses intellect as a weapon; ignore pitfalls in their plans and goals; questions other people's means and methods; always know the "best" way; angry if accomplishments aren't recognized	Capable of undertaking any behavior necessary in order to control outcomes; end justifies the means; tolerates almost no interference from others; seldom trusts others with projects; believes no one can do it as well as them; often experiences burnout; angry if accomplishments	Pushes away deep relationships if not on their terms; indirect behavior; rejects people; rejects the love and affection of people; angry and cruel to those who resist their manipulation for love and affection; extremely self-centered; disregards the emotional needs and wants of others;

		aren't recognized; accepts no input or control from others; leads by domination; puts down and discourages others; loses respect for and holds in contempt those they perceive as weak; treats weak people cruelly; avoids people they cannot control	considers compassion, tenderness, and warmth as weak and undesirable;
Common Shame-Based Responses of An Individual With The Choleric Temperament	Dominates surroundings; proves others to be wrong or inferior;	Causes physical harm or destruction; dominates tasks and people; creates hierarchy with them at the top; crushes anyone who goes against them	Selfish and hurtful; emotionally, verbally, physically, or sexually abusive

SANGUINE (G)	Inclusion	Control	Affection
Common Needs of An Individual with The Sanguine Temperament	Needs approval; needs to be with people; needs to have money to go places and do things with other people; needs to be the center of someone's attention; needs the freedom to talk loudly, behave distinctively, or dress in a way that draws attention; needs to not be alone; if alone, needs to have internet, phone, or TV on in order to feel they are with people; needs to perform tasks quickly so they can return to being with people again	Needs approval; needs others to understand their swing from the independent nature (similar to the Choleric temperament – in charge and dominant) to the dependent nature (similar to the Supine temperament – weak and a indulgent); needs opportunities to volunteer for difficult tasks, and will complete them as long as their need for recognition and approval are being fed; will be endlessly driven back and forth between the independent and dependent needs like a pendulum	Needs approval; needs to be told in some way every day that they are loved, needed, and appreciated; needs love, romance, acceptance, approval, and to be touched in ways that don't necessarily lead to sex; needs to hold hands; walk arm in arm, or just be affectionately touched; needs to do things of a romantic nature with their spouse or loved one; needs sex to be an expression of love and emotional oneness; needs to appropriately touch and be touched by family members and

			friends as a means of communicating love and acceptance; needs deep emotional connection
Common Strengths and Tendencies of An Individual with The Choleric Temperament	Social; fast-paced; approaches many people for surface relationships; responsive to their senses; brings life and energy to a room; cheery and humorous; inspiring and infectious; personable; desirable temperament to be around; optimistic; sees life as an exciting experience; drawn to colorful items; most impulsive of all temperaments; excels in communication-oriented things; outgoing; enthusiastic; warm; compassionate; constantly searching for something more exciting; makes a great best friend; apologizes very quickly, especially if acceptance is at risk; friendly; outgoing; relationship oriented; warm; able to see the bright side of life and the good in others; rarely found alone; freely interacts with people	Somewhat uncommon temperament; does not understand themselves, and are not understood by their family, co-workers, and friends; unquenchable need for recognition and approval; solicitous, caring person who will do things for other people, almost to the point of servitude; takes on the responsibility for making many decisions in order to receive recognition; charming; gracious; the longer they stay on one side of their temperament, the more they tend to be driven back to the other side	Most lovable temperament; expresses love and affection in an endless supply; accepts as much love and affection as others can show them; cares very little about possessions or things; entire existence is for relating to and establishing deep relationships with people; needs to touch and be touched, referred to as "skin hunger", but not in a sexual sense; least sexually inhibited; quick to reveal their inner selves in hopes their deep personal relationship will be just as revealing, to open up and share inner feelings, thoughts, and emotions; relate well to others' feelings
Common Weaknesses of An Individual with The Sanguine Temperament	Overly talkative; likes to be the center of conversation; impulsive; undisciplined; rude; needs to appear successful; sometimes will exaggerate their success; ignores	After taking on too many responsibilities and decisions, will be driven to be narcissistic, self-indulgent, lacking persistence, and weak-willed; nose-dives when criticized or	Easily devastated if not constantly reassured that they are loved and appreciated; very demanding of other people for love and affection; plagued with feelings of jealousy when love and

	responsibilities in order to be with people; feels punished when not accepted, whether for good or bad reasons; may undertake bad attitudes or behaviors to gain attention, as attention feels like a reward; can be rude and uncaring; may walk away if becomes disinterested; sometimes not faithful or loyal to others; since they live only in the present, they don't learn from their mistakes; prone to exaggerate in hopes of gaining approval or avoiding disapproval; may lie without realizing; acts and talks before they think; spends money while ignoring budget or future; apologies are often short lived, and may be used to manipulate others to meet their needs or to restore approval; lack organization	if recognition and approval are withheld by people they consider important to them; drops everything, shirks their responsibilities, stops caring, or just quits when criticized or not recognized; begins to feel the ugliness of guilt, worthlessness, and selfishness (oddly, these eventually turn them back to the responsible and dependable side of their temperament)	attention that they feel belongs exclusively to them is given to others; relationally undisciplined; poor boundaries in terms of showing affection and touching others; unable to deny themselves anything they feel might meet their deep need; weak-willed, especially in the face of something or someone who might meet their deep need for acceptance, approval, and touch; motivated by attention, not by morality; at risk of being drawn to pornography, adultery, or sexual immorality
Common Shame-Based Responses of An Individual With The Sanguine Temperament	Superficial; lack of focus; hyperactive mind; pretentious; exaggerates and lies;	Hot temper; sulking and pouting; self-indulgence; uncontrolled anger	Lust; pornography; adultery; dishonesty; deception; bad decisions

SUPINE (S)	Inclusion	Control	Affection
Common Needs of An Individual with The Supine Temperament	Needs to be accepted; need to be included; needs others to be genuine; needs others to recognize their needs and remove	Needs to be accepted; needs to serve others; needs to be included (consulted) in the decision-making process, especially	Needs to be accepted; needs others to understand their indirect behavior conflict: they express very little need for

	all the barriers to personally inviting them, with an insistence that "we need you;" needs others to interact with them with acute sensitivity, so they know they are accepted and included; needs social acceptance; needs for others to "read their minds" and provide them with the genuine invitation they long for	if the decision involves them; needs clearly defined rules, expectations, direction, and boundaries; needs for others to be kind and considerate; needs to be led, loved, and cared for in ways that make them feel "safe and secure;"	love and affection, appearing not to want deep personal relationships, yet they need a great deal of love, affection, and approval, and very much desire deep personal relationships; needs others to initiate affection, such as touching and hugging; needs to feel appreciated
Common Strengths and Tendencies of An Individual with The Supine Temperament	Inborn gentle spirit; servant; submissive to the needs of others; sees others as valuable and themselves as of less worth; feels they were created to serve others; expresses themself as an introvert, but respond as an extrovert; quiet and usually in the background; understands tasks as well as they understand people; performs tasks for the development of friendships; extremely accommodating of others, even at their own expense; if feels genuinely accepted, will become outgoing much like a person with the Sanguine temperament	Weak-willed; rule follower and rule enforcer, but not rule creator; puts the responsibility for their lives in the hands of others; easily motivated; dependable; serves those they follow, their caretakers, with absolute loyalty	Responds to love, affection, and approval after the other person initiates it and risk of rejection has been removed; responds to love and open up emotionally when they feel emotionally "safe;" if treated properly, are capable of absolute and total commitment to deep personal relationships
Common Weaknesses of An Individual with The Supine Temperament	View themselves as worthless, assuming they are neither wanted nor needed; indirect behavior that expects others to read their mind;	Cannot independently make decisions nor take on responsibilities; become anxious if forced to do so; becomes angry if credit due them is given to someone	Inability to initiate love and affection; as a result of their indirect behavior, people around them are unaware of their intense needs; others

high fear of rejection; can appear distant and disinterested; only responds when approached by others; often frustrated in their loneliness; natural born victim; will become angry if not genuinely invited and included, but regards it as being "hurt;" will withdraw into self as a means of protection from further rejection and hurt; harbors anger viewed as "hurt feelings"	else; feels inadequate and worthless; fearful of making a wrong decision that might lead to being left alone or having to take care of themselves; becomes very angry if not asked their opinion on a decision that involves them; harbors anger due to not being included in the decision-making process; difficulty saying "no" to others; do many things they do not want to do for people, then feel anxious, angry, and used; constantly searches for someone to take care of them; lacks self-confidence and strength to make decisions and take charge of their own lives; may vent their anger both verbally and physically (more pronounced in men); dominates through their words and actions as means of manipulating others into taking care of them; tends to not fight back, then turns on those who have dominated them; defensive against loss of position; weak willpower; tendency to feel powerless and at the mercy of others	seldom initiate love, affection, and approval because the Supine has sent strong signals indicating they neither want nor need love, affection, and, approval; experiences frustration and unfulfillment due to deep affection needs often going unmet; requires constant and current reassurance that they are loved, needed, and appreciated; expects others to recognize their deep emotional needs by "reading their mind'; becomes angry, yet define it as "hurt" feelings, when others fail to meet their needs
Common Shame-Based Responses of An Individual With The Supine Temperament		
Aloof; self-righteous; back bighting; vengeful; anger-based control	Powerless; helpless; victim; weak-willed; compromise own morality; anger-based control	Desperate; clingy; manipulative; internalize unresolved anger; anger-based control

PHLEGMATIC (P)	Inclusion	Control	Affection
Common Needs of An Individual with The Phlegmatic Temperament	Needs to conserve energy; needs to be in environments that require a minimal amount of interaction with people; needs a minimal number of commitments in their day; needs to be free from excessive social demands; needs employment that is methodical rather than physically demanding; needs a peaceful and tranquil environment	Needs to conserve energy; needs to undertake tasks that require a minimal amount of interaction with people; needs only moderate control over the lives and behaviors of others, and accepts only a moderate amount of control over their own life and behavior; needs to share responsibilities and decisions with others; needs to make decisions without being pressured and to have all the facts; needs to rest or take breaks regularly	Needs to conserve energy; needs others to provide the energy or sacrifice to build a deep relationship or to keep it going; needs only moderate demands placed on them with regards to romance and affection
Common Strengths and Tendencies of An Individual with The Phlegmatic Temperament	Extremely slow-paced and stubborn; able to identify injustices; inspires others to action; socially flexible and well-rounded despite having little need to interact; able to relate to both tasks and people; calm; easy-going; extremely efficient; perfectionistic; functions well in hostile social setting; dry sense of humor that may irritate others	Extremely well-rounded; very stable and practical; always seeks the "path of least resistance;" natural negotiator and diplomat; seeks "peace at all costs" without becoming involved in the conflict; the only temperament who can handle the Choleric temperament – does so by using humor to keep the Choleric from pushing them into doing something they don't wish to do; great capacity for work that requires precision and accuracy; doesn't struggle with anger, rejection, and other destructive emotions that are often seen in other temperaments; uses dry sense of	Extremely well-balanced; most stable of all temperaments; calm; easy-going; non-demanding; does not smother others, nor do they appear coldly distant; able to show a moderate amount of love and affection; has very realistic demands when it comes to how much love and affection they need from those close to them; has no fear of rejection; able to handle unaffectionate and hostile people; does not engage in conflict, as it requires too much emotional energy; no emotional outbursts, exaggerated feelings, anger, bitterness, or unforgiveness that are

	humor to keep others from placing unwanted demands on them; uses verbal abilities as a defense mechanism (often in form of witty humor or sarcasm)		often seen with other temperaments
Common Weaknesses of An Individual with The Phlegmatic Temperament	Observer of life rather than a participant; will identify injustices, yet not initiate action against the injustice; in inspiring others to action, they are seldom willing to get involved themselves; allow their lives to become stagnant because it takes too much effort to use their talents; goes through life quietly doing as little as possible; often has little energy left for family at the end of the day; observes the actions of other temperaments and identifies all the things being done wrong or that need to be changed; uses their dry sense of humor to protect themselves from over-obligation.	Self-righteousness, which makes them nearly impossible to change, regardless of the circumstances; stubbornly resists change; the more they're pushed, the more stubborn they will become (in their mind, to change takes energy, to stay the same does not); uninvolved in life, even their own; difficult to motivate; appears indecisive; tends to procrastinate in making decisions, partly due to being a slow mover, and partly to avoid wasting their energy on a decision that may later became unnecessary	Observer of deep relationships; doesn't get overly involved or expend much energy; unemotional; avoids conflict at all cost, so may not involve themselves in working out problems; appears cool, complacent, and disinterested in regard to love and affection; when others are angry, may ignore the anger, coolly observe the participants, or use their dry sense of humor to anger the other temperaments; may experience loneliness due to not giving emotionally of themselves, and therefore not receiving either
Common Shame-Based Responses of An Individual With The Phlegmatic Temperament	Apathy; uninvolvement; laziness; minimizing; extreme stubbornness	Passive; observer; back-seat driver; laziness; extreme stubbornness	Minimizing; lack of initiative; doesn't pursue; avoids conflict

Now that we've had the opportunity to dig through this matrix of information specific to each of the five temperament types, we can begin to insert ourselves into the picture. Please note that just reading these lists of characteristics and trying to find yourself within them does not provide the most accurate, reliable information available. However, we can certainly gain a general understanding of how our inborn temperament may have contributed to our shame-based responses to the experiences of our childhood.

My Real-life Example

To help each of us more effectively understand our temperament in ways that reveal unmet needs, weaknesses, and shame-based responses, I've inserted myself into a simple worksheet that will help us put all of these concepts together.

Completion of the Arno Profile System temperament questionnaire, administered by an NCCA Certified Temperament Counselor, is certainly the most accurate means of receiving a detailed analysis of your unique inborn temperament. With a 95 percent accuracy rating through nearly half a century of testing, it is certainly worth your time and expense to contact Life Training Christian Counseling to complete this online assessment.

NAME:

David Ralston

TEMPERAMENT COMBINATION:

Sanguine in the Inclusion area
Melancholy in the Control area
Sanguine in the Affection area

UNMET TEMPERAMENT NEEDS IN CHILDHOOD:

Sanguine in the Inclusion area: Need for approval; need to have money to go places and do things with other people; need to be the center of someone's attention; need to not be alone

Melancholy in the Control area: Need to appear competent and in control; need quiet time alone to regenerate; need to not be controlled or manipulated; need truth, order, reliability, and dependability from others, or they will feel they have been lied to; need to be respected by other people, especially for their abilities

Sanguine in the Affection Area: Need for approval; need to be told in some way every day that they are loved, needed, and appreciated; need to touch and be touched by friends and family members as a means of communicating love and acceptance; need deep emotional connection

SHAME-BASED RESPONSES TO UNMET NEEDS

Sanguine in the Inclusion area: history of being superficial; lack of focus; hyperactive mind; pretentious; exaggerate or even lie

Melancholy in the Control area: history of perfectionism; rebelliousness; altercations with others; retaliation

Sanguine in the Affection area: history of lust; pornography; infidelity; dishonesty; deception; bad decisions

Questions from Dr. Dave

For personal reflection or group discussion of Chapter 8

In this chapter, I provided a flow chart that illustrated the progression from being raised in a shame-based environment to duplicating many of the very same shame-based messages into our children. In what ways has this opened your eyes to something you maybe had not considered before? Hopefully it has given you an urgency to allow God to change the trajectory of your family tree for "a thousand generations."

In what ways has this chapter's detailed explanation of the five inborn temperaments helped you see yourself differently? Has this allowed you to have a better understanding of how specifically your childhood culture may have affected you, and why your siblings may have been affected in entirely different ways? God is ready to meet the unique, inborn needs of your temperament. Has what you've learned about your temperament given you hope that your life truly can change?

There is a tendency for us to compare ourselves to others. Individuals with the expressive Sanguine or Choleric temperament often compare others to themselves, while those with the responsive Melancholy or Supine temperament are more likely to compare themselves to others. How has considering your temperament combination been validating of who you are? How has it helped you to better accept others as they are?

"Jesus turns our ashes into beauty; our broken pieces into masterpieces!"

Dr. Dave Ralston

CHAPTER 9

Soul Work

"For the Word of God s alive and powerful. It is sharper than the sharpest two-edged sword, **cutting between soul and spirit**, between joint and marrow. It exposes our innermost thoughts and desires" (Hebrews 4:12 NLT).

In an earlier chapter, I reflected on a season in my early adult life when it felt as though my soul and spirit were literally running on two parallel tracks. As I allowed myself to become painfully honest with myself about myself, both the interdependence yet distinctiveness of these two elements – soul and spirit – became much clearer.

The decades since that time have acquainted me with countless men and women who had lived with very much the same disconnect that I had. They felt certain they had placed their faith in Jesus Christ yet found that the joy, peace, and hope of the Christian life eluded them. They considered themselves to be good Christian people yet could not comprehend why their belief system was insufficient when calamity or tragedy pierced their lives and relationships.

I don't want that to be the case with us reading this book. My sincere prayer is that all of the combined expertise and wisdom in what I've shared might provide a pathway that will radically transform our lives.

Trust the Journey

Oftentimes books that dig this deeply into our past, our family, and our shortcomings can feel a little scary and maybe even over our heads. I hope that's not the case here. I've attempted to break down every complicated, less-familiar word and subject in ways that make them understandable and applicable for the journey. But it still may seem daunting. I get it.

This chapter is filled with principles, verses, and teachings directly from the Bible. For some who are reading this, that is refreshing. Often, authors who teach soul healing principles offer a Christian approach to overcome the pain of our past yet lack in Bible-based substance. For maybe an even larger group of us, though, the "churchy" words and concepts in this book may cause you to feel less-than-qualified to benefit from these teachings, simply because you don't fully understand and comprehend them all.

Please trust me as I walk alongside you on this journey! I am simply a traveler, just like you. Whether you've been able to pick up every detail along the way, or if you feel like you're just hanging on for dear life, there's no "wrong" way to pursue your personal journey with Jesus. The only way to "fail" is to quit. And we're not going to quit! Hang in there with me.

Picture if we were all walking together through the woods. Some of us would notice all the different types of trees. Others would examine what's on the ground under their feet. Others would focus their senses on the sounds and smells of the woods. Some would repeatedly look behind them to not lose sight of where they came from. Others would analyze the most efficient way to get out of the woods. Regardless, <u>none of us would be doing the journey incorrectly</u>. We would all be experiencing and enjoying the journey together, while seeing it uniquely and exactly the way God wanted us to see it.

We're told in Romans 3:3 (NLT), "True, some of them were unfaithful; but just because they were unfaithful, does that mean God will be unfaithful?" God has a plan and a purpose for each of us (see Jeremiah 29:11). A keystone to our experiencing God's faithfulness is our growing awareness of who He is, who we are, and how He connects the two. In other words, how is learning all of this about God and ourselves going to make the pain and shame within us go away.? This chapter addresses that very question.

So, please don't miss it. Trust the journey. And more importantly, trust Jesus, our guide and our confidence on the journey.

"Cutting" Between Soul and Spirit

The passage from Hebrews, that I used to open this chapter, alludes to the fact that our soul and spirit are intimately connected, yet also distinctly separate. The Bible makes it clear that the soul and spirit are the primary non-physical aspects of our humanity, while the body is the physical container that holds them while we exist on this earth.

Although I have an earned doctoral degree, I know it's best that I admit when I'm not an expert on a subject. And this is one of those times. Do I have a thorough, Biblical understanding of the spirit-soul connection? Yes. Am I an expert on this subject? Absolutely not.

I feel certain that a Biblical scholar could write a lengthy, exegetical thesis about the incomprehensible soul-spirit connection. And certainly, there are countless aspects of the Christian life in which that would be beneficial, and even necessary.

I'm confident that, for our purposes, what I've included within these pages will serve us well on our journey.

What Is the Spirit?

Our spirit is God's life in us. It is our channel of communication with God through the Holy Spirit. It is what makes true worship of and communion with God possible. The spirit gives a "God-consciousness" to every believer. It translates the things of the Spirit of God for us as His children (see 1 Corinthians 2:14). It is the means through which spiritual gifts are given and expressed by the Holy Spirit within us (see 1 Corinthians 2:10-15). It is often referred to in the Bible as a "still small voice."

I've been very intentional to avoid what might open the door to controversy regarding differing doctrinal views. This book isn't about that. It's about helping individuals find hope in Christ to move beyond the shame and brokenness of their lives. Respectfully, I believe that man's spirit is **renewed** at the point of salvation, not necessarily **replaced**, as some believe. Regardless which theological camp we land in, the principal point is that, in Christ, God gives us a new spirit. And from that, He desires to reproduce the life of Jesus within us.

Numerous Christian writers concur that our spirit is comprised of three elements: conscience, fellowship, and intuition.

- **Conscience** – For us to discern right from wrong, to distinguish good from bad (see Romans 8:16; 9:1).
- **Fellowship** – For us to contact God and to commune with Him (see John 4:24; Romans 1:9).
- **Intuition** – For us to have a sense within our spirit of what our soul cannot perceive, regardless of reason or circumstance (see 1 Corinthians 2:11).

What is the Soul?

Our soul is the essence of who we are – the intangible nature of our tangible human being. It is comprised of our inborn, God-given temperament. In the Hebrew language, the word *nephesh* would be translated "soul" or "breath of life." These symbolize the non-visible lifeforce within us that animates our physical body.

As is the spirit, the soul is also comprised of three parts: mind, will, and emotions.

- **Mind** – For us to think, consider (see Psalm 13:2), know (see Psalm 139:14), and remember (see Lamentations 3:20). In the mind we have thoughts, ideas, concepts, reasonings, understanding, knowledge, and so on.
- **Will** – For us to have purposes and choices (see Job 7:15; 6:7), and to make decisions (see 1 Chronicles 22:19).
- **Emotions** – For us to experience emotional feelings, such as love (see 1 Samuel 18:1; 2 Samuel 1:7) or hate (see 2 Samuel 5:8), to like or dislike, to be joyful (see Isaiah 61:10; Psalm 86:4) or grieved (see 1 Samuel 30:6; Judges 10:16).

When we are saved (born again), our spirit is instantaneously renewed, but our soul is not. "Anyone who belongs to Christ has become a new person. The old life is gone; a new life has begun!" (2 Corinthians 5:17

NLT). While salvation does not make our soul new, a new hope and desire to serve and love God infuses into our mind, will, and emotions.

If we had received a new soul at the time of salvation, we would likely have lost all of our emotions, knowledge, and memory in that moment. In Christ we received a renewed spirit. Romans 12:2 (NIV) tells us our soul is to be "transformed by the renewing of our mind." As we continue on this journey, this renewing progressively develops our faith and trust in God. It is through the internalizing of God's word that we are sanctified and transformed into the image of Jesus.

Separate but Inseparable

Jesus makes it clear in the "Greatest Commandment" how spirit and soul, both distinctive in themselves, are intimately linked together within us as His followers:

> "'And you shall love the Lord your God with all your heart and with all your soul and with all your mind and with all your strength.' The second is this: 'You shall love your neighbor as yourself'" (Mark 12:30-31 NLT).

This passage illustrates how God's love is manifested in and through both our spirit ("love the Lord your God") and our soul ("love your neighbor as yourself"). But how are the two connected?

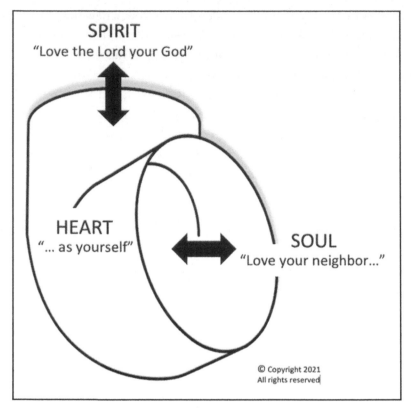

The Heart Is the Conduit

The Heart Is the Conduit

The soul and the spirit are inexplicably tied together by what the Bible calls the "heart." It's obvious that God was not referring to our physical, flesh-and-blood heart when He included this term within the pages of His word.

Throughout the Bible, writers seem to reference the heart in ways that pertain to matters of belief, behavior, conscience, moral character, courage, will, understanding, passions, intention, desire, and so on. Although we tend to assume these characteristics are all positive, they are actually value neutral. The "condition of our heart" is examined by honestly considering our answers to these probing questions:

- Who do I give the power to define my beliefs?
- In what ways are these beliefs affecting my relationship with God?
- In what ways are these beliefs affecting my relationships with others?

The Bible compares to stone the heart that is not surrendered to Jesus and describes it as "hardened" to the loving nature of God. The only One who can give us a new heart is the One who created us in the first place! We do not possess that power or capability.

> "And I will give you a new heart, and I will put a new spirit
> in you. I will take out your stony, stubborn heart and give
> you a tender, responsive heart" (Ezekiel 36:26 NLT).

Our human nature is the problem within us, not the solution! It would be ludicrous to think a wooden stick could be used to sharpen another wooden stick, wouldn't it? Likewise, our nature cannot sharpen our own nature. It requires something (actually Someone) much stronger and sharper to make us new.

While our spirit is renewed when the Holy Spirit enters into our being at the moment of salvation, our souls still carry spiritual dirt from our past – abandonment, rejection, abuse, and shame. Our souls still have stains that need to be removed and washed clean.

The Tale of the Two Seas

In his article entitled the *Tale of Two Seas,* author and communicator John Vaughan provides a powerful metaphor to help us contemplate the condition of our hearts.

> If you pull out the maps in the back of a Bible or online,
> and look at the Jordan River over Israel, you will see that
> it sources two different bodies of water: the smaller Sea of
> Galilee to the north and the larger Dead Sea to the south.
>
> If you've done any reading of the Bible, you recognize that
> much activity occurs in and around the **Sea of Galilee**

in the life of Jesus described in the New Testament. Throughout history, towns and cities have been situated on this sea, and it has served as a center of trade. Fish and plant life are abundant in the area. In stories recorded in the gospels, Jesus and the disciples travel by boat all around the Sea of Galilee, meeting people, fishing its waters, and participating in the local culture.

Contrast that with the body of water known as the **Dead Sea**. The Dead Sea is just that: dead. It's a lake in which nothing swims or grows. It is extremely salty and is a harsh environment in which animals, plants, and other aquatic organisms cannot flourish. In Hebrew writings, the Dead Sea is simply called the "sea of death."

Both of these bodies of water are sourced by the same fresh waters of the **Jordan River**. But they are opposites in their environment and impact on the life and people around them. What's the difference? The Jordan River sources the Sea of Galilee, and the Sea of Galilee's waters are then in turn used to source most of the population centers in Israel. Every drop of water that comes into the Sea of Galilee from the Jordan River flows back out to the people and land around. The Sea of Galilee serves as the source of much of the drinking water of the country. The Dead Sea, by contrast, is a dead end. The Jordan's waters pour into the Dead Sea only to come to their termination point, and as the Jordan's life-giving stream comes to a stop at the Dead Sea, it loses its vitality and sustaining qualities.

While the same waters feed both the Sea of Galilee and the Dead Sea, it's only when the waters are used and active and moving that they retain their productive, life-giving value. The Sea of Galilee gives back out what it is receiving from the Jordan River, while the Dead Sea is just a dead end, and every drop it gets, it keeps.

Both of these bodies of water have sufficient inflow to sustain life and share an abundance with others. One allows what flows in to freely flow out. The other exists only for itself and has become stagnant, toxic, and meaningless.

Each of us must make a choice which sea we will be: The life-giving Sea of Galilee, or the life-consuming Dead Sea. We are not the living water of the Jordan River. The love of Jesus is. We are merely a conduit (much like a siphon), holding loosely to the blessings of God and allowing them to flow from us just as freely as they have flowed to us.

Everything Begins in The Heart

All of our beliefs, thoughts, emotions, and behaviors originate from our hearts. In his book, *The Search for Significance*, Robert McGee describes this internal hierarchy "hardwired" within each of us. I've taken the liberty to add elements to it, while being careful not to compromise the author's original intentions.

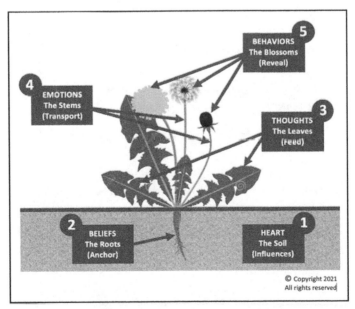

All Behaviors Begin in The Heart

There are five elements that are instrumental in the formation of every plant, whether beautiful and productive like a rose bush or apple tree or aggravating and undesirable like a dandelion. Metaphorically, the same components are present in our lives. The enemy goes to great lengths to cultivate weeds of sin, shame, and self in our lives. Our new life as a Christ-follower fosters the inborn, God-given nature (temperament) within each of us, and leads us toward the very purposes for which He placed us on this earth.

1. **HEART – The Soil.** In the same way the condition of the soil ultimately affects the plant's fruitfulness, the condition of our hearts leads us either to a life motivated by performance, approval, punishment, and shame, or an exciting journey defined by love, joy, peace, patience, kindness, gentleness, goodness, faithfulness, and self-control as God intends for us.

2. **BELIEFS – The Roots.** In the same way the plant's roots anchor the nature, growth, vitality, function, and yield of the plant, our deeply held beliefs influence the presence or absence of the healthy identity, maturity, passion, purpose, and impact that God intends for our lives.

3. **THOUGHTS – The Leaves.** In the same way the leaves of every plant feed the plant's needs for nourishment through the miraculous process of photosynthesis, our thoughts are the part of our humanness that exchanges conscious and subconscious information with our environment, establishing our place of significance, competence, and belonging amidst our surroundings.

4. **EMOTIONS – The Stems.** In the same way the stems of every plant transport nutrients to create the blossom of the plant, our emotions impartially transport feelings and emotions that initiate our externalized actions and reactions.

5. **BEHAVIORS – The Blossoms.** In the same way the blossom of a plant is merely a dependent result of the other components carrying out their functions, our behaviors and choices merely reveal the influence our life experiences have had on our beliefs, thoughts, and emotions.

Something I have learned through counseling thousands of men and women is the necessity of addressing our false, unhealthy, and toxic beliefs first and foremost. It is ludicrous for us to think we can meaningfully change or improve our actions, decisions, feelings, or thoughts without first examining and redefining the beliefs and environmental factors that influence them.

The TURN Approach

Section 5 in this book – TURN – is devoted entirely to a well-proven, Christ-centered approach to **Soul Work** – replacing our false beliefs with God's truth, moving us from brokenness to wholeness in our lives.

Our heart establishes the foundations of our conscience – the intersecting of God's perfect truth (spirit) with our human experience (soul). Proverbs 4:23 (NLT) says, "Guard your heart above all else, for it determines the course of your life."

There is nothing more important than our inner life – the condition of our heart (soil). While our spirit is renewed when the Holy Spirit enters into us at the point of salvation, our souls still carry spiritual grime from our past – abandonment, rejection, abuse, fear, and so on. This is why we often continue to struggle with sin and shame even after accepting Christ into our lives. It is a clear indication that our souls still have stains that need to be dealt with decisively.

Our Inner Battle

The human soul is constantly struggling to choose between the prompting of the Holy Spirit and the inciting of our fleshly desires for the world. Through the renewing of our mind, we become equipped to distinguish the "false beliefs" of this world from the "absolute truths" of God.

> "I do not understand what I do. For what I want to do I do not do, but what I hate I do" (Romans 7:15 NIV).

As we learn to submit our mind to God, our soul progressively becomes patterned to submit itself as well. Through faithfulness over time, we will become more in tune with the ways of God, and much less aligned with the lies of the world. The scales will begin to tip.

What's at Stake?

To understand the battle within our hearts, we must first acknowledge that we are in a war of sorts. Battles are merely smaller components of a bigger picture. By definition, battles involve combat between two persons or factions, and they consist of any type of extended contest or struggle. As Christians, we are in a spiritual struggle of some sort on a daily basis. Our spiritual battles are real, even though we cannot physically see the attacker.

It is important to educate ourselves on the nature of spiritual battles, even if we can't fully comprehend the reason for the fight, and often overlook its impact on our daily lives. War is very controversial in today's physical world, so it is common for our beliefs and convictions about war to spill over into the spiritual realm, where there is a battle going on regardless of our opinion on the subject. **We are either victors or victims in our spiritual battles!** Jesus has come and conquered. The war is already won in the heavens. But we must choose for ourselves how we will respond to that reality.

Jesus told us in Matthew 28:18 (NIV) that, "All authority in heaven and on earth has been given to Me." This verse is not only about our being saved from the penalty of sin. It is also very much about us experiencing everyday victory over our struggles, which adds up to victorious living in Christ here on this earth.

The Battle Is Partly Spiritual…

Many of us do not want to put much thought into a world we cannot see, when the world we do see is hard enough to deal with in itself. If we choose to ignore or not believe in the spiritual realm – let alone the spiritual nature of our inner battles – we will find ourselves not only confused and frustrated but will be extinguishing the peace that God has promised each of us, as well. Enlightening ourselves about the spiritual realm is half the fight. God has provided us everything else we need in order to come out on top.

> "For we are not fighting against flesh-and-blood enemies,
> but against evil rulers and authorities of the unseen world,
> against mighty powers in this dark world, and against evil
> spirits in the heavenly places" (Ephesians 6:12 NLT).

As Christians, we believe Jesus accomplished these things in the spiritual realm when He lived in the physical realm on earth. We believe this with the eyes of our heart, instead of with the eyes of our physical bodies. By believing in Jesus, we believe that He died to conquer the works of the devil so that we might be set free. There would have been no need for Jesus to come to die for us if life was limited to just the physical world.

... Partly Worldly

Earlier we read in Romans 12:2 (NIV) that we are to "no longer conform to the pattern of this world." This phrase is referring to how the people collectively choose to live on the earth. As Christians, we are to not conform to the norms and standards of how others live, but to live in ways that honor God and reflect the nature and character of Jesus. Not better than others. Not worse. Just different.

In John 17, Jesus speaks of how we are to live in the world yet not be influenced by the ways of the world. It quickly becomes clear that if we are in the world but not of the world, we are going to encounter conflicts and misunderstandings.

The world holds animosity towards those who follow Jesus today, just as it did in the first century. We are not called to be a reflection of the world, or worldly, but we are sent into that world to reflect the grace of Jesus Christ to those we know and love, as well as those we might consider our enemies.

… And Partly Within Ourselves

For some of us, the toughest battles we fight are fought within ourselves. Nearly every day I have a counseling client say to me, "I'm my own worst enemy." You may very well feel the same way.

Because of the shame we encountered throughout our childhoods, we can easily see how the enemy uses the circumstances and situations of life to destroy us. We can accept the truth of how the world lures and tempts us, because we've fallen prey to it many, many times. To some degree, we can understand that the battle in the spiritual realm is ongoing and real, even though we cannot see it. But, to wrap our arms around what is going on within our own hearts and minds can be the most difficult, exhausting battle of them all.

We must learn to fight against the very nature within us. Don't be fooled. Just because we may have walked a church aisle a long time ago or can recite scripture after scripture in the King James version, we are not exempt from the battle within. True change requires a radical shift of our heart.

> "But now you must also rid yourselves of all such things as these: anger, rage, malice, slander, and filthy language from your lips. Do not lie to each other, since you have taken off your old self with its practices and have put on the new self, which is being renewed in knowledge in the image of its Creator… Therefore, as God's chosen people, holy and dearly loved, clothe yourselves with compassion, kindness, humility, gentleness and patience. Bear with each other and forgive one another if any of you has a grievance against someone. Forgive as the Lord forgave you" (Colossians 3:8-13 NIV).

Soul Work Aligns Our Heart with God's

God has given us His Spirit who can and will empower us to overcome the battles within. But we must be willing to allow Him the authority to be in control of our emotions and behaviors, especially those surrounding the toxic shame and false beliefs we have internalized from childhood. This is the very nature of **soul work**.

Soul work is our intentional desire and commitment to do whatever it takes to align our soul – mind, will, and emotions – with the spirit of God who lives within us. The Bible refers to this as "sanctification," the process of being transformed progressively into the nature and character of Jesus Christ. It is our soul that must be transformed.

We must remember, "<u>All</u> have sinned and fall short" (Romans 3:23 NIV). Regardless of the darkness and dirtiness of our past, the blood of Christ has saved us from destruction. Though our internal battles may continue to rear their heads at times, the victory is assured because we have placed our faith in Jesus Christ!

Our opportunity to personally experience inner freedom is tied to our willingness to allow the grace of Jesus Christ to transform our hearts in ways that compel us to extend the same undeserved gift to those who have hurt us.

I love this quote by Robert McGee in his book *The Search for Significance*: **"Our ability to extend grace and forgiveness to others will be in direct proportion to our ability to understand our need for the same."**

I Want to Experience This in My Life!

Jesus died for the sins of every person who ever lived and who will ever walk the earth. The Bible tells us, "Jesus is the atoning sacrifice for our sins, and not only for ours but also for the sins of the whole world" (1 John 2:2 NIV). The term "atoning sacrifice" means that the death of Jesus on the cross covered the debt to God that humans owed for contributing to all the evil and death in the world. The blood of Jesus supernaturally washes away all of the damage and side effects of sin, purifying and sanctifying believers.

While Jesus offers forgiveness and salvation to everyone, unfortunately we don't all accept His gifts. Jesus, God's Son, saved the world from sin, the power of the devil, and eternity in a real place called hell. He did this through His own perfect life, His death, and His resurrection from the dead.

"For God so loved the world that He gave his one and only
Son, that whoever believes in Him shall not perish but

have eternal life. For God did not send His Son into the world to condemn the world, but to save the world through Him. Whoever believes in Him is not condemned, but whoever does not believe stands condemned already because he has not believed in the name of God's one and only Son" (John 3:16-18 NIV).

Many people choose to not believe in Jesus as their personal Savior. But there is no other way to heaven than through faith alone in Christ alone. Jesus said, "I am the way and the truth and the life. No one comes to the Father except through me" (John 14:6 NIV). The fact that this statement has become controversial – and even divisive – in today's world does not negate the absoluteness of its truth!

Jesus died for the sins of every person who ever lived – yours and mine, as well as those who may have committed harm against us. That's how much He loves each of us. If you believe in Him as your Savior, by faith, full forgiveness and salvation is yours.

You don't receive those gifts by anything you do or don't do – past, present, or future. Strict compliance to a list of do's and don'ts is not what Christian salvation is about. Romans 3:20 (NIV) reads, "No one will be declared righteous in God's sight by the works of the law." Titus 3:5 (NIV) says, "He saved us, not because of the righteous things we had done, but because of His mercy."

It's a free gift of undeserved and unconditional love given only by God's grace. The Bible says, "For it is by grace you have been saved, through faith – and this not from yourselves, it is the gift of God — not by works, so that no one can boast" (Ephesians 2:8-9 NIV).

Some May Just Have Never Been Invited

If you have never considered asking and allowing Jesus into your heart, could that be that no one has ever offered that to you? I personally and tenderly invite you to ponder that decision right now. Don't let anything keep you from it! Don't let shame or fear or pride or doubt or religion keep you from having a forever relationship with the only Person in all of creation who loves you unconditionally, accepts you fully, and will never shame, reject, or abandon you – Jesus Christ.

Here's a pretty comprehensive list of Christian truths you might sincerely pray about as you weigh the benefits and costs of committing to an <u>authentic</u> relationship with Jesus:

- Jesus is the only one in history who is both fully God and fully man.
- Every human being is born with an innate sin nature.
- Faith in Jesus is the only way to be in right relationship with God.
- We must believe in Jesus as our only hope of being saved.
- Jesus is the only way to an eternity with God in heaven.
- True belief requires putting our faith and trust in Jesus alone.
- Not every person will place their faith in Jesus.
- Not every person will spend eternity with God in heaven.
- Faith is rooted in knowing Jesus, not merely knowing about Him.
- True faith changes how we believe, think, feel, and act.
- Legalism, religion, and perfectionism are obstacles to knowing Jesus.
- Faith is in what He has done for us not what we can do for Him.
- Repenting of sin and self-centeredness are our priority.
- We are becoming more Christ-centered and less self-centered.
- Loving Jesus, and loving others in the same way, is our life mission.
- Humility replaces pride, performance, and control.
- Hope in Christ replaces shame, brokenness, and hopelessness.

As distinguished Christian author C.S. Lewis said in his book *The Case for Christianity:* "Now, today – this moment – is our chance to choose the right side. God is holding back to give us that chance. It will not last forever. We must take it or leave it."

Will you make this choice right now?

Where to Go from Here

"And they have defeated him (the enemy) by the blood of the Lamb and by the word of their testimony" (Revelation 12:11 NLT).

Many reading this book may have not spent much time in church, let alone reading the Bible. So, a sentence like this one surely makes absolutely no sense at all to you. And I respect that. It wasn't until I was twenty-two years old that I opened a Bible for myself, and actually began to take life and death and God seriously for the very first time in my life.

Verses like this one are not meant to be a form of code language. But sometimes it's beneficial to have someone help us understand it. This passage is simply telling us that the only way we are able to have victory over the spiritual enemy and to experience a transformed life and future is by the shed blood of Jesus and the renewing of our minds by the word of God.

> "'Come now, let's settle this,' says the Lord. 'Though your sins are like scarlet, **I will make them as white as snow**. Though they are red like crimson, I will make them as white as wool'" (Isaiah 1:18 NLT).

> "Do not conform to the pattern of this world but be transformed by the **renewing of your mind**. Then you will be able to test and approve what God's will is – His good, pleasing and perfect will" (Romans 12:2 NIV).

In English, Please

Shed blood? Word of God? I don't get it. Sounds like a lot of Christian jargon, doesn't it? Or at least some of us might be feeling that way.

There is no way for me to explain this part of our teaching without plunging a little deeper than we've gone up to this point. But it is far too critical for us to miss. It is what gives substance to our faith. Not only is this the very essence of being renewed and cleansed from the dirtiness and shame of our past, it is also the basis of our hope for the future, on earth and beyond!

When we place our faith and trust in Jesus, we are placing our hope in who He is and what He has done for us. The verses above reflect two of the most important aspects of this: Our spirit is made new through the cross, and our soul is made new through the word of God.

Jesus' Shed Blood

Blood is the life of the human creation. Life is taken when blood is shed. Modern medicine acknowledges the truth about life being in the blood. They often require blood transfusion to sustain the life of a very sick person, especially one who had recently lost lots of blood.

Since the Bible teaches us "the wages of sin is death" (Romans 6:23 NIV), every sin has to be reconciled by the death of something or someone. Throughout the Old Testament teachings, this was typically the blood of a sacrificial animal, often an unblemished lamb. At the end of the Old Testament, the practice of animal sacrifice was ended by the shedding of another's blood, but this time, one that would be the final sacrifice for all. John 1:29 (NLT) records John the Baptist saying about Jesus, "Look! The Lamb of God who takes away the sin of the world!"

On the cross, Jesus Christ paid for our sins by His own life. He gave His life by shedding His blood. We can have life not only today, but eternally, by that blood which He willingly shed for us. It's not the physical act of shedding blood that is significant. If so, Jesus could have just had a laceration somewhere on his body that shed blood for us all. No, shedding blood is a metaphor referring to the fact that **without death, there is no forgiveness of sins.**

So, our true transformation – a profound change from the inside out – is made possible only through the perfect sacrifice of Jesus on the cross. Here are several important elements of this gift that God offers us:

- **Jesus's shed blood provides complete forgiveness.** Within the Christian belief system, there is no forgiveness without the shedding of blood. An atonement is a payment, made on behalf of the one who has sinned, in order to redeem them from the penalty of their sins. This payment could not be made in any other way than the shedding of blood. We cannot replace this blood with our good works, praying without ceasing, helping and loving others, or even giving more money.

  "I have given you the blood on the altar to purify you, making you right with the Lord. It is the blood, given in exchange for a life, that makes purification possible" (Leviticus 17:11 NLT).

"...without the shedding of blood there is no forgiveness" (Hebrews 9:22 NLT).

- **Only Jesus could die for our sin.** Romans 3:23 (NIV) says, "all have sinned." Because every human being has come short of the glory of God, none is capable of atoning for his or her own sin or the sins of others. Therefore, there has to be Someone blameless who must do the job. He must be a human since He will atone for the sins of humans. He must also be God because that is the only way He would be the mediator between God and mankind. Jesus Christ is the only one who fits this description.

  > "For there is one God, and one mediator between God and men, the man Christ Jesus" (1 Timothy 2:5 NIV).

- **Shedding of blood was necessary.** Jesus Christ could have been drowned in water, He could have died of strangling, He could have died of a severe sickness, starvation, or any other means of death. None of these include the physical shedding of blood, though. That would not have been an acceptable atonement because the shedding of blood was required for the forgiveness of sin.

  > "For this is my blood of the new covenant, which is poured out for many for the forgiveness of sins" (Matthew 26:28 NIV).

  > "This is my blood of the covenant, which is poured out for many," He said to them" (Mark 14:24 NIV).

- **Redemption is possible only through Jesus Christ.** Redemption can only be attained through the blood of Jesus Christ. The blood of a lamb or goat or calf is no longer acceptable by God for the forgiveness of sins as it was prior to Jesus presence on the earth. The sacrifices of the Old Testament (which ended at the cross) were merely a foreshadowing of the cross. The animals that were sacrificed were symbolic of Christ to come.

> "… being justified as a gift by His grace through the redemption which is in Christ Jesus (Romans 3:24 NIV).

- **Redemption was planned from the beginning**. That Christ will shed His blood and die for the sin of the world was planned by God "from the foundation of the world." He has always had this as part of His plan. It wasn't what some have attempted to explain as God's "Plan B."

> "He (Jesus) was chosen before the creation of the world, but was revealed in these last times for your sake" (1 Peter 1:20 NIV).

- **God's plan had not been known by the world**. Although the cross was unknown to the world before it happened, the plan has always existed with God.

> "Yet when I am among mature believers, I do speak with words of wisdom, but not the kind of wisdom that belongs to this world or to the rulers of this world, who are soon forgotten. No, the wisdom we speak of is the mystery of God – His plan that was previously hidden, even though He made it for our ultimate glory before the world began. But the rulers of this world have not understood it; if they had, they would not have crucified (Jesus)" (1 Corinthians 2:6-8 NLT).

- **We must trust in the blood of Jesus.** From the day that Christ shed His blood on the cross, there came an end to any other sacrificial blood shed for sin. Therefore, *any of us who has not put* *our faith in the blood (sacrificial death) of Jesus is yet to receive the forgiveness of our sin.* Regardless of how religious or righteous we might be today, if we have not trusted in Christ's shed blood for the forgiveness of our sins, we're still an unforgiven sinner. What it means to trust in the blood is to admit we're a sinner who cannot save ourselves; believe that Christ has died in our place, shed His blood to fully pay the penalty of our sins; and that He was buried, and He rose again that we may be made right before God.

> "For everyone has sinned; we all fall short of God's glorious standard. Yet God, in His grace, freely makes us right in His sight. He did this through Christ Jesus when He freed us from the penalty for our sins. For God presented Jesus as the sacrifice for sin. People are made right with God when they believe that Jesus sacrificed His life, shedding His blood. This sacrifice shows that God was being fair when He held back and did not punish those who sinned in times past" (Romans 3:23-25 NLT).

- **Christ purchased us by His blood.** Christ redeemed us from being deserving of punishment to receiving the power to become the children of God. The price that He paid to accomplish this was His blood. Christ is to us the only source of righteousness, sanctification, and redemption.

> "For you know that it was not with perishable things such as silver or gold that you were redeemed from the empty way of life handed down to you from your ancestors, but with the precious blood of Christ, a lamb without blemish or defect" (1 Peter 1:18-19 NIV).

- **A sacrifice was made once and forever.** Christ's atonement is the only and last acceptable atonement (payment) for sin. It is referred to in the Bible as "one sacrifice forever." Once we're washed in the blood of Jesus, we're cleansed and forgiven once and for all – forever.

> "For Christ also suffered once for sins, the righteous for the unrighteous, to bring you to God. He was put to death in the body but made alive in the Spirit" (1 Peter 3:18 NIV).

Although God is certainly able to protect and heal His people physically, the blood of Jesus Christ was not shed merely to ensure our material prosperity or to miraculously remove our health conditions here on earth. His love for us is much, much greater than that.

The Word of God

God's word empowers us and enables us to go all the way in our pursuit of Jesus. In the passage from Romans, Chapter 2, nonconformity to the world does not simply mean avoidance of worldly behaviors. If that were the case, Jesus would have been affirming the Pharisees as opposed to challenging them. Certainly, behavior modification is important. It just is not the depth of transformation the Bible calls us to. We can use our willpower to avoid all sorts of unhealthy, ungodly, and un-Biblical choices in our lives, yet still not be transformed in Christ.

Further, true inner transformation is not merely switching from the to-do list of the world to the to-do list of the Bible. Rather, what happens to us occurs within our heart. When the apostle Paul in the Bible described how we are to replace the to-do list, he does not replace it with the works of the "law" (613 commands the Israelites of the Bible were expected to obey), but the fruit of the Spirit, found in Galatians 5:19-22-23 (NIV) – "love, joy, peace, forbearance, kindness, goodness, gentleness, faithfulness, and self-control."

These only become part of who we are when rooted in our hearts, not merely through the dedication of our mind and will. Our mind and our will provide the outward expression of what God is doing in our heart. They, themselves, are not the truest measure of who we are in Christ. Have you ever heard someone say, "Her heart wasn't in it" or "He is just going through the motions."?

The Christian alternative to immoral behaviors is not a new list of moral behaviors. It is a profound shift within us through faith in Jesus Christ.

> "He has enabled us to be ministers of His new covenant. This is a covenant not of written laws, but of the Spirit. The old written covenant ends in death; but under the new covenant, the Spirit gives life" (2 Corinthians 3:6 NLT).

So, true transformation is a radical change from the inside out, that unfolds as we read, study, believe, and submit to the truths and teachings of the Bible, and allow God's spirit to redefine our hearts in the process. We must surrender our heart to God's word, or what we learn will just become another set of unachievable rules and unreachable expectations in our lives. Here are several ways God uses His word to grow us and change us:

- **God's word guides us.** We don't stumble in darkness anymore. We have the Light. We follow His word, walk in His steps and are empowered to become more like Christ.

  > "Your word is a lamp to guide my feet and a light to illuminate my path" (Psalm 119:105 NLT).

- **God's word convicts us of sin and wrongdoing.** We don't wonder anymore if we're right or wrong. When we fill our hearts with God's word, we know when we fall short and ask for the grace to get up when we fall.

  > "For the word of God is alive and powerful. It is sharper than the sharpest two-edged sword, cutting between soul and spirit, between joint and marrow. It exposes our innermost thoughts and desires" (Hebrews 4:12 NLT).

- **God's word cleanses us and makes us holy.** God's desire for us is to become purified like gold. His word cleanses our minds and hearts. The more we study and apply God's word the more we become like Him.

  > "...to make her holy and clean, washed by the cleansing of God's word" (Ephesians 5:26 NLT).

- **God's word shows us who we have been created to be.** When we surrendered our heart to Jesus, we were instantly translated from darkness to light. He gave us a new identity – our true identity. However, we need to acquaint ourselves with this new life continually. We must be intentional and committed to live out the teachings of the Bible for true and lasting change to occur.

  > "For if you listen to the word and don't obey, it is like glancing at your face in a mirror. You see yourself, walk away, and forget what you look like" (James 1:23 NLT).

- **God's word rids our hearts of evil**. We can win the battle against sin by humbly accepting God's word into our lives. It has the power to renew us each day.

  > "So, get rid of all the filth and evil in your lives, and humbly accept the word God has planted in your hearts, for it has the power to save your souls" (James 1:21 NIV).

- **God's word instructs and corrects us.** The journey to renewing our minds is a daily one. The word of God sheds light on every difficult situation and every moral confrontation.

  > "All scripture is inspired by God and is useful to teach us what is true and to make us realize what is wrong in our lives. It corrects us when we

are wrong and teaches us to do what is right" (2
Timothy 3:16 NLT).

- **God's word makes our minds new.** We renew our minds by
  studying and living out God's Word. We ask Him to guide us
  as we dig into the Bible, and we commit to use the myriad of
  resources that are available to us.

  "Study this book of instruction continually.
  Meditate on it day and night so you will be sure
  to obey everything written in it. Only then will
  you prosper and succeed in all you do" (Joshua
  1:8 NLT).

Beauty from Ashes

Throughout the Bible, as well as ancient practices, ashes have been the
symbol of deep repentance and grief. Sometimes our lives have been
painful. Sometimes they've been difficult. And sometimes they've felt very
dark. Life leaves its mark on us, like ashes of grief, in the deepest parts of
our being, where no one but God can really see.

Our lives have been littered with shame and rejection and unmet need.
They haven't been easy, and many times our lives have felt really unfair.
In the middle of all this, we've often wondered where God was, why He
would have allowed such bad things to happen to us, and why He didn't
step into our painful situation and make it right.

God's Word Says He Was There in the Midst of It All

Even though we may have not always seen it, or felt it, or even understood
it, we can have certainty that God is, was, and will be with us through
every painful time in our lives. He reassures us in Isaiah 61:3 (NIV), "to
provide for those who grieve... to bestow on them a crown of beauty instead
of ashes."

God will never reject us or abandon us. His love for us is greater than we could ever imagine, even if we may have felt He was absent amid the messiness of the world we grew up in and now live in. Jesus reminds us in John 16:33 (NIV), "In this world you will have trouble, but take heart, for I have overcome the world."

Jesus Christ came to set us free, to redeem us, and to bring us hope. He came to give us beauty from the ashes of our lives.

> "The Spirit of the Sovereign Lord is on me, because the Lord has anointed me to proclaim good news to the **poor**. He has sent me to bind up the **brokenhearte**d, to proclaim freedom for the **captives** and release from darkness for the **prisoners**, to proclaim the year of the Lord's favor and the day of vengeance of our God, to comfort all who **mourn**, and provide for those who grieve in Zion – to bestow on them a crown of beauty instead of ashes, the oil of joy instead of mourning, and a garment of praise instead of a spirit of despair. They will be called oaks of righteousness, a planting of the Lord for the display of His splendor... Instead of your shame you will receive a double portion, and instead of disgrace you will rejoice in your inheritance" (Isaiah 61:1-3, 7 NIV).

God has no intention of letting us remain stuck in the shame of our past and the brokenness of our present. He provides hope and purpose amid every experience of darkness and despair (see Romans 8:28). The ashes will steadily fall away, and His unending grace and glory will shine beautifully through every broken place within us.

Questions from Dr. Dave

For personal reflection or group discussion of Chapter 9

In what ways has this chapter opened your eyes to the difference between the soul and spirit? Are you better able to understand how a person's heart remains self-focused and worldly unless our spirit is renewed by faith in Jesus Christ? Reflect on how God has given you assurance of His spirit's presence in you? If this is difficult for you, allow Him to examine your heart and reveal what might be standing in the way.

"It is ludicrous for us to think we can meaningfully change or improve our actions, decisions, feelings, or thoughts without examining and redefining the beliefs and environmental factors that influence them." This is a statement I made in this chapter. Consider the nature of the beliefs that might be at the root of your greatest inner battles. Are they true and in alignment with God's word and nature? Or are they false, built on faulty information? What beliefs is God wanting you to begin to let go of today?

Whether you already knew it, or if this was the first time you've ever considered it, true heart change can only occur through Jesus shed blood and the Word of God. Has this been the basis of your hope for a change life? If so, express your gratitude to God for what He has done for you and in you. But if this is new to you, invite Holy Spirit to lead you to a greater understanding of this magnificent gift.

"The renewing of our soul will extend no further than the honest acknowledgement of our inner brokenness."

Dr. Dave Ralston

CHAPTER 10

Jesus Makes Us New

Inner brokenness is demonstrated through the lives of human beings in an immeasurable number of ways. In authoring each of our life stories individually, God is fully aware of the generational legacies passed down to us by our families, the complexities of our real-life experiences, and the uniqueness of our inborn, God-given temperament. He alone is able to make our personal, unfolding life narrative distinct and beautiful -- not in spite of our brokenness, but built upon it.

Whether the origins of our brokenness were malicious or unintentional, physical or intangible, overtly obvious or imperceptible, the evidence of their existence cannot be denied.

Good News

These two corresponding passages in the Bible powerfully reflect how God lovingly and intentionality demonstrates His unconditional love amid our sin, shame, grief, and emptiness. No other scriptures exemplify how we can find hope to overcome our brokenness as these do.

I concluded Chapter 9 with the passage written by the prophet Isaiah to the people of Israel who had been taken captive by their oppressors. Now I want to explore that same text through a much more focused lens. So, please allow me to present this important passage again:

"The Spirit of the Sovereign Lord is on me, because the Lord has anointed me to proclaim good news to the poor. He has sent me to bind up the brokenhearted, to proclaim freedom for the captives and release from darkness for the prisoners, to proclaim the year of the Lord's favor and the day of vengeance of our God, to comfort all who mourn, and provide for those who grieve in Zion—to bestow on them a crown of beauty instead of ashes, the oil of joy instead of mourning, and a garment of praise instead of a spirit of despair. They will be called oaks of righteousness, a planting of the Lord for the display of His splendor... Instead of your shame you will receive a double portion, and instead of disgrace you will rejoice in your inheritance" (Isaiah 61:1-3, 7 NIV).

The Israelites in the eighth century BC undoubtedly found great optimism and comfort in this good news that God promised them through the words of the prophet. Their confidence, however, lacked the tangible hope that you and I have in the cross of Christ.

On their side of history – 800 years before the birth of Jesus in Bethlehem – the Messiah was only a promise passed down through Jewish prophecy and traditions.

On our side of history, however, where you and I are blessed to know the fullness of Christ through the Bible, we are able to establish our hope in a reality that is profoundly more absolute and certain than what the Israelites were only able to imagine conceptually. What centuries of prophecy had spoken of and written had finally been realized in the person Jesus Christ and His undeniably central role in human history.

This was powerfully recorded by Luke, the gospel writer, as he personally witnessed his friend Jesus stepping into His rightful place at the climax of centuries of foretold truth, and the fulfillment of all that the prophets had promised:

"He (Jesus) went to Nazareth, where He had been brought up, and on the Sabbath day He went into the synagogue, as was His custom. He stood up to read, and the scroll of the prophet Isaiah was handed to Him.

Unrolling it, He found the place where it is written: "The Spirit of the Lord is on <u>me</u>, because he has anointed <u>me</u> to proclaim good news to the poor. He has sent <u>me</u> to proclaim freedom to the prisoners and recovery of sight for the blind, to set the oppressed free, and to proclaim the year of the Lord's favor.

Then He rolled up the scroll, gave it back to the attendant and sat down. The eyes of everyone in the synagogue were fastened on Him. He began by saying to them, 'Today this scripture is fulfilled in your hearing'" (Luke 4:16-20 NIV).

This Good News Is for All of Us

The Bible illuminates seven realities within these passages. And when we humbly admit that each of these are actually characteristics of our own fallen nature, this revelation will completely turn our lives inside out, and radically shift our identity from the brokenness of our pasts to the hope and wholeness found only in Jesus.

Within these two passages, God outlined seven specific individuals who personified the fundamental nature of mankind's brokenness from sin and shame. Our temptation is to quickly envision these characterized in the physical world. But God wants us to consider them more deeply – in the realm of our soul and spirit.

Although we might be able to identify people who literally fit within these headings, God's appeal is for us to open our hearts and minds to the reality that each of these individuals is represented in us.

Whether we're willing to find ourselves in any or all of these characterizations or not, I believe that you and I have more examples than we could possibly count of instances when we have been judgmental or condemning of individuals whose lives had unfolded in these very ways. To call myself a follower of Jesus yet look down on others simply because their brokenness looks different than mine, makes me no better than a Pharisee.

In addressing the self-righteousness of the Pharisees, Jesus said to them,

"Woe to you, teachers of the law and Pharisees, you hypocrites! You clean the outside of the cup and dish, but inside they are full of greed and self-indulgence. Blind Pharisee! First clean the inside of the cup and dish, and then the outside also will be clean" (Matthew 23:25-26 NIV).

The *renewing of our soul* will extend no further than our honest acknowledgement of our inner brokenness.

The Poor

Physical poverty has existed in varying degrees since the beginning of time. There have always been those without food, water, shelter, clothing, and countless other needs.

But as troubling as this can be, God's inclusion of the term "poor" in this passage was intended to speak even more to those who faced poverty of spirit and soul. Our spirit defines our identity, our conscience, our morality, and the nature of our gods. Our human soul is the place within us where all of our beliefs, thoughts, experiences, memories, and emotions reside. Without the presence of Christ within us, the wellbeing of our spirit and soul – let alone our source of hope – can only be as great as what we've experienced in life up to that point in time.

Jesus not only came to proclaim the good news to the poor; He <u>is</u> the good news for the poor! "This poor man called, and the Lord heard him; He saved him out of all his troubles" (Psalm 34:6 NIV)

A large portion of my childhood was spent living with a single mom in an apartment in federally funded housing projects. Many aspects of those years caused feelings of embarrassment, inferiority, and poverty on multiple levels. Although my entire past has been redeemed by Jesus Christ, there have been times in my adult life where I have allowed myself to slip back into that poverty mindset, even though I know I have been adopted as a child of the King, and all of His lavish abundance is mine!

I feel pretty certain that some who are reading this know exactly what I'm saying.

The Brokenhearted

In the Bible, the brokenhearted are people who are deeply aware of their spiritual bankruptcy and helplessness, and long for someone or something to save them. Theologian Marjorie O'Rourke Boyle writes, "Broken hearts are embodied in the Hebrew scriptures as crippled legs that have walked deviant paths, stumbled, and fallen against the God's law."

Many times through the course of my life I have tried yet failed, pursued yet ended up disappointed in my pursuit of what I believed would satisfy the longings of my soul. Each time, God has been right there, as a loving Father, to pick me up, dust me off, and take me back home again.

Psalm 147:3 (NIV) says, "He heals the brokenhearted and binds up their wounds." And Psalm 34:18 (NIV) reads, "The Lord is close to the brokenhearted and saves those who are crushed in spirit."

The nearness of Holy Spirit while we're in the depths of our brokenness is the most comforting, caring, nurturing experience we can ever experience in life. Allow God into your darkness.

The Captives

To be taken captive implies that a force greater than ourselves has captured, ensnared, or brought harm to us, despite our having done nothing to deserve such treatment. Captors persuade us to believe what is not true, lead us to believe we deserve to be treated in this way, and strip us of our identity and dignity.

While some have encountered our captors through physical world experiences, others became introduced in other ways. Many who are reading this continue to be held captive in our souls to the memories and the shame perpetrated by a molester or abuser or someone who abandoned us in our past. Others are emotionally captive to a narcissistic spouse, parent, or relationship. Yet others continue to be bound to the emotional pain of rejection and abandonment from our childhoods. All are carrying a weight that is not ours to carry!

Jesus spoke these words to people just like us who had been taken captive by the perils of the first century world: "Come to Me, all you who are weary and burdened, and I will give you rest. Take My yoke upon you and learn from Me, for I am gentle and humble in heart, and you will find rest for your souls. For My yoke is easy and My burden is light" (Matthew 11:28-30 NIV).

And the apostle Paul tells us, "It is for freedom that Christ has set us free. Stand firm, then, and do not let yourselves be burdened again by a yoke of slavery" (Galatians 5:1 NIV).

Freedom from captivity is ours because of the accomplishment of Christ, not by anything of our own doing. Paul is not attempting to motivate us to fight or to try harder to be free. True freedom is not found through our efforts. Release of our soul from the painful grip of our captives has been given to us by Christ. It can be found in no other place.

The Imprisoned

Most of us probably never put much thought into the difference between a captive and a prisoner. A captive is held captive due to no fault or wrongdoing on their part, whereas a prisoner is imprisoned due to some sort of wrongdoing that fell outside the accepted laws.

Again, I'm very certain that some who are reading this book have actually been incarcerated for one reason or another. I have many close friends and acquaintances who have spent time in jail, prison, or penitentiary. In fact, I communicate often with a good friend who is serving out a twenty-five-year sentence in Texas.

However, this section is not written just for people who are currently or who have ever been behind bars. That is way too small of a subset of people than I believe Jesus is writing to in the Bible verses we're looking at. Jesus was speaking hope to every one of us who knows what it feels like to live in a prison of guilt, shame, and regret for something we have done or failed to do.

In John 8:36 (NIV) we read, "So if the Son (Jesus) sets you free, you will be free indeed." And we read in 1 Peter 2:16 (NIV), "Live as people who are free, not using your freedom as a cover-up for evil, but living as servants of God." Freedom from the bondage and shame of our own bad choices is found only in the blood of Jesus. His grace is greater than our greatest sin! **None of us, and nothing we could ever do in life, is beyond**

the reach of God's undeserved, unshakable grace! This may be exactly what some of us need to hear!

One of my all-time favorite movies is "Shawshank Redemption." Andy Defresne spoke a line in that movie that I've never forgotten: "I guess it comes down to a simple choice, really. Get busy living or get busy dying."

I'm pretty sure there was not much theological context to that statement he made. Nonetheless, I believe it is a slogan worth holding on to. While Andy was referring to living and dying in the physical sense, the quote becomes much more powerful when we allow it to become a motivator in the life and wellbeing of our spirit and soul.

Today I am free in Christ. The chains are gone. I've been set free. So, I need to get busy living!

The Mourning

In the Sermon on the Mount, the second Beatitude that Jesus spoke was, "Blessed are those who mourn, for they shall be comforted" (Matthew 3:4 NIV). The passage we're digging into from Isaiah 61 (NIV) tells us Jesus was sent to "comfort those who mourn." But do we fully understand the depth of how He wanted us to consider this word "mourn"?

Most certainly Jesus was speaking to people who had experienced the death of a dear loved one. His comfort is found during those times of loss as we draw near to God and feel His love drawing near to us (see James 4:8).

The Bible contains so many examples of Jesus speaking deeply spiritual things with words that, on the surface, could be assumed as only relevant to the physical world. For example, Jesus entirely reframed the teaching from the Ten Commandments regarding murder when He said, "Murder begins in the heart. You have heard that it was said to those of old, 'You shall not murder, and whoever murders will be in danger of the judgment.' But I say to you that whoever is angry with his brother without a cause shall be in danger of the judgment" (Matthew 5:21-22 NKJV).

In a like manner, I feel confident that when Jesus said that He "comforts those who mourn," He was not merely inferring that He comforts those who grieve the death of a loved one. Jesus had something much more visceral in mind.

There are nine words in the original languages of the Bible that we would translate as "mourn" in the English language. The strongest example is the word "pantheo" in the Greek, which denotes an aching or grieving deep within the human soul.

Author Troy Dobbs, in his book *The Blessed Life* – a book devoted entirely to unpacking each of the beatitudes – writes, "One bona fide mark of a follower of Jesus Christ is that they don't excuse, rationalize, trivialize, belittle, or ignore sin. Rather, they grieve over it, confess it, and repent of it… The right perspective on sin, in turn, prompts us to react and respond to our sin appropriately."

Further, Troy states, "Jesus is saying we miss the point when we mourn more over who or what we've lost than over what we've done. In 1 Samuel 15:24-25, the confession of Saul's mouth was faster than the contrition of his heart. He didn't genuinely grieve over his sin. He actually made an excuse for it… And that's true of a lot of people; they would rather get it over with than genuinely grieve it. We'd all rather get back to the party instead of getting right with God."

Puritan Thomas Watson stated, "A wicked man will say he is a sinner, but a child of God says, 'I have done this evil.'"

Jesus desires to bring comfort to the deepest, darkest places in our soul, where sin and shame from our past lay hidden. His comfort amidst our mourning. No judgement. Just comfort.

The Blind

"Satan, who is the god of this world, has blinded the minds of those who don't believe. They are unable to see the glorious light of the *good news*. They don't understand this message about the glory of Christ, who is the exact likeness of God" (2 Corinthians 4:4 NLT).

Blindness is a characteristic that needs little explanation. We all have experienced times where we lacked the ability to see, even if we might have 20/20 vision. Again, Jesus was certainly speaking hope to those who were literally blind, but more significantly was speaking to every one of us who has, at times, been blind to the truth and the realities of Jesus, His reckless love for us, and His desire to remove the blinders from our eyes.

At times in my own life, I have allowed "blind spots" to creep into my line of sight. Typically, these have consisted of unresolved conflict, an attitude of self-righteousness, unrepented sin, or chronic toxic shame from my past. When I've finally let down my guard to allow Holy Spirit to reveal these to me, God has been so kind and compassionate in how He has opened my eyes to help me see more clearly.

Jesus is willing and able to bring sight to even the very worst of our blindness. But first and foremost, we must be willing to admit we cannot see.

The Oppressed

The term "oppressed" in the Bible refers to those who have been crushed, bruised, taken advantage of, or are victims of abuse or violence. Jesus came to set free the oppressed. He doesn't offer the answer. Jesus is the answer for the shame and pain of oppression.

He came to set us free from oppression in a manner that doesn't ignore the reality of our situation. Jesus provides us hope and freedom in the midst of our situation. And for some reading this book, we may be unable to entirely remove ourselves from our oppressor. Even then, Jesus desires that we find freedom in our soul which no human oppressor can ever take from us!

Jesus reveals the God of perfect justice. Every judgement we make as human beings will be flawed because every human being is flawed. We can only see life through clouded lenses. We must humbly acknowledge that only the God of perfect justice is able to see things clearly and knows how to make all things right.

Don't miss Jesus's powerful words in Romans 12:19 (NIV): "Beloved, do not avenge yourselves, but rather give place to wrath; for it is written, 'Vengeance is Mine, I will repay,' says the Lord."

When we have been victims of oppression, we often become the perpetrators of oppression in another person's life. A worthy reminder: "Hurt people hurt people!" This is the very nature of generational sin and shame. We duplicate the very same destructive shame into our children that we experienced while we were children ourselves.

In the death of Jesus, we are able to completely see the justice and the mercy of God work in perfect harmony. Sin's penalty is paid. Sin's forgiveness is provided. Jesus is our substitute, taking the penalty that our sin deserved, so that He who is rich in mercy and grace offers us His undeserved love (see Ephesians 2:4-5).

This paradox of justice and mercy must guide us in our journey to freedom. Mercy in the form of complete forgiveness through Jesus is the key that frees us from our oppressors. When we choose to unconditionally forgive our oppressors in our hearts, we release ourselves from the grip of shame they put us in. When we trust Jesus's promise that He alone will avenge the wrongs others have done to us, we find an indescribable freedom in our souls. By trusting Jesus's promises of mercy for our souls and justice to our oppressors, we introduce a legacy of true freedom into a thousand generations that will come after us.

Making the Turn

I've sometimes felt that my journey of transformation has been like trying to turn the Titanic. Very intentional. Yet slow and methodical. More than three decades in fact.

The beauty of being transformed by Christ into the likeness of Christ is that it's all about the journey. There's really not a destination – at least not in this life there's not.

So, for those of us who are perfectionists or controlling or obsessive or compulsive or whatever else, you cannot do soul work incorrectly, quickly, or perfectly! I know that rocks the world for some. But trust me, it will be the imperfectness and the out-of-controlness and the incompleteness that will actually allow us to experience the new life we have always longed for. Another paradox. My life becomes perfect and under control and complete when I give up trying to make it that way. What a concept!

Step-By-Step

Our journey together will be made step-by-step. No, not like a step-by-step recipe in a cookbook that turns out pretty much the same every time. Put more succinctly, we're going to take all that God has shown us and allow it to make us new – one step at a time, one day at a time. Each of our journeys has been personalized and customized by our Creator. No two are alike.

Psalm 119:105 (NIV) says, "Your word is a lamp for my feet, and a light on my path." Picture with me that we're all standing outdoors in a dark place where we've never been before, with the moon not shining brightly enough for us to even see the path, if there is one. Then Jesus hands each of us a lantern. Not just any lantern. His lantern provides only enough brightness to illuminate the single step right in front of us.

Some of us might say, "Jesus, I need more light! I can't see where I'm going." Some maybe, "I don't feel safe if I can't see the entire path." Others, "We're not moving fast enough Jesus." A few might even say, "I know where we can get a better light." But I feel confident that, inside each of us, we'd be saying: "Jesus, I'm afraid to trust You."

If you're feeling that way, join the crowd. This entire book is written for broken people – the shamed and the shamer, the controlled and the controller, the fearful and the fear-causing, the weak-willed and the powerful, the captive and the captor – and all that are akin to these. There is not an expectation that we completely understand, or fully trust, or easily surrender, or readily follow. If we were able to muster that level of willpower, or clarity, or surrender, or confidence to "get it right," we probably wouldn't be reading this book to begin with!

I'm grateful that Jesus is fully aware that if He gave us more light, we'd either attempt to control what was ahead of us, or we would become so worried about how we're going to navigate it that we'd become paralyzed. If He told us where the path was leading us, we'd stubbornly dig our heels in and refuse to move, a lot like stubborn children defying their parents. If He picked up His pace to match our tempo, Jesus knows how many amazing things we would pass right by and miss entirely along the way. He also knows that if He were to let us provide the light or control how it's used, it would go out long before the journey had been fully experienced.

I think I'll just make a decision today to trust Him a little more than I did yesterday.

Let's all agree to this one rule, the only rule in the entire book:
NO PERFECT PEOPLE ALLOWED!

Prayer for Serenity by Reinhold Niebuhr

There is a great deal of history surrounding the nearly century-old Serenity Prayer, and I'm pretty well versed in much of it. Although some have questioned the Biblical integrity of this prayer, I personally believe that each of its six segments are substantial and worth committing to.

During the years I was on staff as Lead Pastor of Counseling & Restoration at a large church in Texas, I had the opportunity to preach an eight-part series on the "Biblical Foundations of the Serenity Prayer." This fourteen-line prayer took on entirely new meaning and power in my life, as well as the lives of countless others. Needless to say, I found nothing within this prayer that Jesus would not be pleased we had prayed. Allow me to focus on a section from the middle of the text:

- Living one day at a time, enjoying one moment at a time.
- Accepting hardships as the pathway to peace.
- Taking, as Jesus did, this sinful world as it is, not as I would have it.
- Trusting that He will make all things right if I surrender to His will.

Although we have learned that God and His word have provided the roadmap for our journey toward wholeness, I believe the Serenity Prayer offers meaningful road signs that serve as reminders along the way, and encouragement, as if throngs of people had lined up along both sides of the road, cheering for us every step along our journey:

- Take the journey one day at a time.
- Enjoy what God has prepared for you in each and every moment.
- Remember, hardships are the pathway, not obstacles, along your road to peace.
- Learn to accept this sinful world – and the diversity of people who live in it – as they are, not as you think they should be.
- Trust that Jesus will make whole all of the broken things in your life.
- Surrender yourself to Jesus every day.

"Therefore, since we are surrounded by such a huge crowd of witnesses to the life of faith, let us strip off every weight that slows us down, especially the sin that so easily trips us up. And let us run with endurance the race God has set before us" (Hebrews 12:1 NLT).

Questions from Dr. Dave

For personal reflection or group discussion of Chapter 10

Have you been pleasantly surprised by how much Jesus seemed to detest the self-righteous but lifted up the broken and sinful? What difference might it make in your life if you were to place your faith in this Jesus, not the version of Jesus the world makes Him out to be? What parts of you would you stop hiding if you knew there was zero risk of being rejected? Express those right now, wherever you are. Allow your heart to feel the depth of your newfound freedom. He hears you, fully knows you, and still unconditionally loves you.

As Jesus unrolled the scroll and read the words of the prophet Isaiah, He spoke His love and hope for seven specific people groups: the poor, the brokenhearted, the captives, the imprisoned, the mourning, the blind, and the oppressed. As you examine your own heart, do you identity personally with any of these? Has it been difficult to speak of these things in your past, for fear of what others might think? Hopefully this chapter has made it evident that Jesus favors the broken, not the righteous. Don't hold your shame in one more day. Tell your story to someone you trust. Experience the light of Jesus' love and grace in your darkest places.

The Serenity Prayer has been a constant at every twelve-step meeting across the world for nearly a century. As you read and studied it in this chapter, did it take on any new meaning or relevance to you? What parts stood out the most? I invite you to read this prayer aloud at least once every day. Commit yourself to the words you're speaking, and believe they are for you.

PIECE 4

Masterpiece: *From the Inside Out*

OCEANS

And I will call upon Your name.
And keep my eyes above the waves
My soul will rest in Your embrace
For I am Yours and You are mine

Your grace abounds in deepest waters
Your sovereign hand will be my guide
Where feet may fail, and fear surrounds me
You've never failed, and You won't start now

Hillsong Worship

CHAPTER 11

Passing Through the Desperate In-Between

As God moves us from the brokenness of our past to a future filled with His wholeness and purpose, we will unquestionably experience times of uncertainty, anxiousness, and fear. Gifted author Lysa TerQuerst, in her amazing book entitled *Uninvited*, describes this season as "moving through the desperate in-between. Look at this incredible excerpt from Lysa's book:

> If we place our hope and future in the hands of our unchanging, unflinching God who never leaves us or forsakes us, we'll find healing and freedom. We'll be able to see something on the other side of all the pain. Something good. Something we know will be worth whatever it takes to get well. So instead of running from the pain, we embrace it as necessary. We must feel the pain to heal the pain. If we never allow ourselves to feel it, we won't acknowledge it's there.
>
> Remember, the pain isn't the enemy. Pain is the indicator that brokenness exists. Pain is the reminder that the real enemy is trying to take us out and bring us down by keeping us stuck in broken places. Pain is the gift that motivates us to fight with brave tenacity and fierce determination knowing there is healing on the other side.
>
> And in the in-between? Pain is the invitation for God to move in and replace our faltering strength with His.

197

I'm not writing that to throw out spiritual platitudes that sound good; I write it from the depth of a heart that knows it's the only way. We must invite God into our pain to help us survive the desperate in-between.

We Must Become Comfortable with Being Uncomfortable

I can still remember back to 1988 when I asked my dear friend (the one who gave me the John Bradshaw book that started this whole amazing journey), "What can I do to speed this up? I don't like feeling all of these painful emotions and memories. How could this be helping me?" I was certain that there had to be a faster, easier, less painful way to get emotionally well.

Truthfully, there were many times I was ready to just throw in the towel. Especially in the early months and years of my soul work, there were days that I literally felt like I was in over my head, and sadness and aloneness were closing in around me. Emotions would come like tidal waves, oftentimes unexpectedly.

In the words of Peter Scazzero, in his book *Emotionally Healthy Spirituality,* "we must be willing to tolerate the discomfort necessary for growth."

Friends, such is this journey from shame and brokenness to hope, healing, and wholeness. We can't rush it. We can't force it. We can't perfect it. We can't breeze through it. We can't avoid the pain that is part of it.

We must compel ourselves to let go and trust God. Some days we'll feel like we're standing strong and taking confident steps forward. Yet other days, we'll lack the desire to get up and push the ball forward another day.

Trust me, this must be part of our journey. In fact, it's an essential and indispensable part of it. Part of our journey of life-change. Part of being made new, redefined **from the inside out.** In my personal experience, the days and seasons where I felt like I couldn't get up and I couldn't keep going might actually have been among the most valuable of them all.

It's in those moments of doubt and despair that our subconscious mind and heart begin to learn that we actually are worth it – worth getting up and taking more steps forward, worth creating boundaries despite what we might lose, worth letting go even when we can't see through the fog. For maybe the first time in our lives, we learned to comfort ourselves amidst our own emotional pain and realized that we didn't need to turn to a person, an indulgence, or a compulsion in order to make the pain go away. We truly believed that God was with us in our darkest, lowest moments, because we could actually feel His loving, tender presence within us as we sat on the rock at the bottom of our soul. Those times are very precious and deeply transformational!

Storms Strengthen the Root System

A few weeks ago, when I was mindlessly surfing the internet just to pass some time, I ran across a very insightful article that seemed to shed light on the necessary uncomfortableness of our journey of growth.

> A great experiment in the desert called the "biodome" created a living environment for human, plant, and animal life. A huge glass dome was constructed to house an artificial, controlled environment with purified air and water, healthy soil, and filtered light. The intent was to provide perfect growing conditions for trees, fruits and vegetables, as well as humans.
>
> People lived in the biodome for many months at a time, and everything seemed to do well, with one exception. When the trees grew to a certain height, they would topple over. It baffled scientists, until they realized they forgot to include the natural element of wind. Trees need wind to blow against them in order for their root systems to grow sufficiently deep and strong enough to support the tree as it grows taller.
>
> Who among us doesn't long for a perfect growing environment for ourselves, with no disruptions from outside influences? We strive to avoid the times of conflict and tension, when life's daily challenges push against us. When they do, the normal tendency is to curse them or

run from them. If trees could talk, would we hear them curse the wind each time they encountered a storm?

We can learn a great deal from nature's wisdom at work if we are open to the lesson. Watch how a tree bends and sways gracefully when the wind blows against it. It does not stand rigid, resisting the flow of energy. It does not push back. The tree accepts the strong wind as a blessing that helps it grow. Such experiences develop our character and deepen our spiritual roots. When we grow deep, we too, stand tall.

In-Between What?

In my counseling office here in Louisville, there are two doors on opposite sides of the room – one that leads out into the hallway, and one that leads into a small storage room. I'd guess that the distance from one door to the other is maybe twelve feet.

Metaphorically picture with me that the storage room door represents the things in our lives that are behind us – our past hurts and failures, performance and approval, shame and brokenness. The door to the hallway represents God's plans for us – "plans for good and not for disaster, to give us a future and a hope" (Jeremiah 29:11 NLT).

Despite what might seem to be the obvious, best choice, the familiarity and security of what's in the storage room – the life we've always known – tends to magnetically draw us back in that direction.

We Must Make a Choice

Every follower of Jesus – albeit every human being – has a pivotal decision to make. We stand individually in a room called life, with the opportunity to choose between two doors. One is cluttered with a life of hurt, loss, and brokenness; the other is filled with a new life in Christ. One is familiar but unfulfilling; the other is hope-filled but unknown.

Many of us hold tightly to the door that connects us to our past, while Jesus stands in the door of our future, inviting us to trust Him and commit to follow Him. Unfortunately, our arms won't reach far enough for us to hold onto both doors at the same time. We fear letting go of one before we can confidently grab hold of the other. As humans, we seem to have difficulty with this space in the middle where it feels like we're not holding on to anything.

Our journey toward wholeness demands that we let go of the one before we can step into the other. And the space where we're not holding on to either door we call "the desperate in-between" – that space between brokenness and wholeness.

Real, Authentic Faith in Jesus Christ

> "Faith shows the reality of what we hope for; it is the evidence of things we cannot see" (Hebrews 11:1 NLT).

Our decision to no longer live our lives as a continual expression of our past, and to fully let go and trust God with our future, demands what the Bible refers to as **faith**.

On this journey, faith calls for us to accept some wonderful new realities on our adventure from brokenness to wholeness:

- We will trust Jesus with our entire life.
- We will not know what our future will look like.
- We will not reach our ultimate destination while on this earth.
- We will frequently feel as though we're not in control.
- We will do many things we lack competence in doing.
- We will feel the pain of grief, loss, and disappointment.
- We will learn that being right might sometimes be wrong.
- We will realize that striving to be good is a disadvantage.
- We will have no one else to blame for our condition.
- We will become comfortable with being uncomfortable.
- We will realize no one can take this journey for us.
- We will experience true hope and wholeness.
- We will be deeply loved by Jesus.
- We will be completely forgiven by Jesus.

- We will be fully pleasing to Jesus.
- We will be totally acceptable to Jesus.
- We will be absolutely complete in Jesus.
- We will fully know and be fully known by Jesus.

The object of true, authentic Christian faith is Jesus! No one else. Nothing else. When we place our faith and trust solely in Him, we are trusting that He fully knows us, unconditionally loves us, and that He can be trusted with every aspect of our lives. When we cultivate this type of faith in our relationship with Jesus, we find real, lasting rest, peace, joy, contentment, and hope that is not dependent upon our circumstances, our relationships, or ourselves.

Landmarks Along Our Path

As our journey together draws to a close, it's important that we take a minute to really consider the actual implementation of the hundreds of concepts, principles, and truths we have learned through the preceding pages. In summarizing the meaningful landmarks we've encountered along our path, these stand out the most to me.

- The power of paradox.
- Life is about being, not about doing.
- Identity dependence robs us of our true identity.
- Toxic shame is the absence of healthy shame in childhood.
- Shame and sin are passed down through the generations.
- Our adulthood is an equal and opposite story of our past.
- We contribute to our shame by staying in an endless cycle.
- Each of us is born with unique, God-given temperament needs.
- Soul work requires identifying and grieving losses of our past.
- Jesus is the good news for every form of human brokenness.
- We must turn from toxic people, places, and things.
- We must uncover lies and false beliefs from our past.
- We must rediscover our true identity in Christ.
- We must nurture lasting hope in others.

- God gives us the power to live our lives from the inside out!
- We each are God's masterpiece!

Inside – Out

When I was a kid, I would get in trouble by my mom if I left my socks inside-out when I put them in the laundry basket. For some reason, it just seemed easier to leave them the way they were when I took them off.

The idea of something being inside-out carries with it the thought that something is backwards, not supposed to be that way. In a way, inside-out is a paradox – well, probably more of an oxymoron actually. How can something be both inside and out at the same time, right? Kind of like same difference – how can it be the same and different at the same time?

In 1989, probably less than a year after I was introduced to John Bradshaw and Melody Beattie's writings, I met (at least through his book) another amazing author – Dr. Larry Crabb – whose book was entitled, *Inside Out*. Dr. Crabb was a very successful Christian counselor, Director of the Institute of Biblical Counseling, and Professor of Biblical Counseling at Colorado Christian University.

His writing had an effect on me similar to what John Bradshaw's had just a year earlier. But this book was different. Bradshaw opened my eyes to the importance of soul work. Crabb introduced me to the concept of living the Christian life from the inside out. The coming together of these two was a beautiful collision.

Perspectives from Dr. Crabb

If we could look at my personal journey with Christ from a 30,000-foot view, we would see a handful of impactful moments when God moved my soul and spirit to a higher place. Studying *Inside Out* was one of those times. Come with me as I recapture some of the important elements from his teaching that I believe help crystalize all that we've learned through the previous chapters:

Certain groups of people come to my mind as I write. First, **those who are trying really hard to do what the Bible commands but feel frustrated**. You are doing all you know to do – not perfectly or course, but sincerely. And yet things just aren't right inside, and you know it. You feel more pressure than joy. God isn't changing either you or things in your world the way you ask Him to. You wonder if He listens to your prayers, or if He simply doesn't care about your struggles. My message to you is, **THERE IS HOPE!**

Second, I think of **those who are doing quite well** and feel content and happy most of the time. You really do love the Lord. You have proved Him faithful and real in hard times. Time in His word is often a rich experience. Prayer is far more than mere ritual in your life. You like your church, you're blessed with good friends and family, you feel satisfied with your work, and you enjoy your leisure time. Your life is not without tensions, but God gives you the strength to press on with confidence. By the grace of God, life is good. My message to you is, **THERE IS MORE!**

Third, I think of **those who are hardened**. Nothing has really gone your way. The promises of God you were taught don't seem to materialize, at least not in your life. Perhaps you've always felt different, never a good fit like your brother or sister. Your parents never held you up as the model for other kids to follow. My message for you is, **THERE IS LIFE!**

Fourth, I think of **those who are in positions of Christian leadership**. The pressure to model for others what maturity looks like can lead to breakdown or pride. You realize that others think of you as better than you know yourself to be. It's hard to maintain an image, but the pressure to encourage people by displaying what God can do in a life surrendered to Him makes you hide a few of the real struggles. My message for you is, **THERE IS LOVE!**

Is it possible to change at the core of our being? How much change can we really expect? This is about changing from the inside out, a process that begins with an honest look at whatever is happening in our life and continues without ever pretending things are better than they are. The courage to be honest is necessary if we are to experience the kind of change Jesus makes possible. **Real change requires an inside look.**

Can a woman molested as a child really learn to embrace her sexuality? Can men with homosexual urges ever really become heterosexual? Can people who worry too much about things, or a couple whose marriage is no more exciting than a television rerun, or folks with bad tempers really change?

Perhaps the most concerning question that emerges from a study of change from the inside out is how far inside do we have to look? Once we agree that an inside look is necessary for deep change, we enter the mouth of a dark cave that tunnels off in endless, uncharted directions. There will always be more to see. We could spend a lifetime (unnecessarily) exploring the winding caverns of our soul and never come out into sunlight.

There must be more to this journey than just more and more darkness. As Christ-followers, we are children of light. Even in the midst of darkness, we know where we are headed. We have a lamp that always reveals the next step, and a hope that keeps us moving even when the lamp seems dim. The Christian journey is not to be characterized by joyless confusion and morbid despair. And that's precisely what develops if we define the path to growth as merely an endless search for further awareness of all that's happening deep within us.

We must not mistake an intense, absorbing heaviness for spiritual growth. Spiritual depth frees us to be spontaneous in the midst of sadness. It enables us to press on in our involvement with people even when we stagger from blows of severe disappointment. A mature relationship with Christ is reflected in the capacity to hear whispers of assurance when discouragement is oppressive. And even when we're mishandling frustration by retreating into an anger or self-pity, mature depth won't let us escape the convicting awareness that we're designed to love, even in a situation like this.

The purpose of an inside look is to promote that kind of spiritual depth and soul health. The more deeply we sense our thirst, the more passionately we'll pursue water. The more clearly we recognize how we tend to dig our own wells in search of water, the more fully we can repent of our self-sufficiency and turn to God in loving, obedient trust.

An inside-out perspective is necessary if we are to move beyond superficial (behavioral) change to authentic (heart) change from the inside out.

I'll Close with This

As I've developed my own style of writing, teaching, and counseling through the decades, I've taken the liberty to integrate much of the very best of what I've learned throughout life and have attempted to present it in this book in a manner that is meaningful, practical, and life changing.

One final concept I would like to leave you with is what I refer to as the **Inside-Out Principle©.** In developing this, I have merged the teachings of the Inside Out model of Dr. Larry Crabb with the teachings of the Temperament model of Drs. Richard and Phyllis Arno. This combined perspective has become the passion of my personal mission on this earth.

In this one visual element, I've attempted to illustrate what I believe to be the culmination of everything I've conveyed through the hundreds of pages of this book: **God created our lives to be lived from the inside out!**

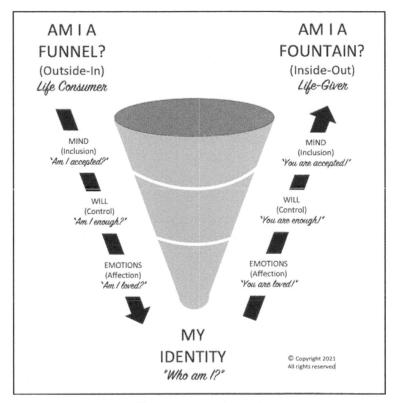

AM I A
FUNNEL?
(Outside-In)
Life Consumer

MIND
(Inclusion)
'Am I accepted?'

WILL
(Control)
'Am I enough?'

EMOTIONS
(Affection)
'Am I loved?'

AM I A
FOUNTAIN?
(Inside-Out)
Life-Giver

MIND
(Inclusion)
'You are accepted!'

WILL
(Control)
'You are enough!'

EMOTIONS
(Affection)
'You are loved!'

MY
IDENTITY
'Who am I?'

Fountain or Funnel

Am I a Funnel?

Lived from the outside in, our lives operate much like a funnel, gathering and consuming life from others around us in hopes of finding our identity through the acceptance, worth, and belonging the world provides. This is the natural way human beings live in our flesh – the part of us bent toward self. Either consciously or unconsciously, we consider life through the lens of "how is it affecting me?"

In doing so, the apex of the funnel (our identity defined by the world) is yearning for the things of this world to satisfy our soul needs and provide meaning to our lives. And when they don't, we either seek for more or better (pride), or we succumb to self-absorption and compulsivity (shame). God did not create us to live this way.

Or Am I a Fountain?

Lived from the inside out, our lives operate much like a fountain, giving life to everyone and everything around us, seeking to partner with God in meeting our "neighbor's" needs of body, soul, and spirit. We become a giver of belonging, worth, and acceptance of others. This is the natural way of living a life submitted to the spirit of Jesus within us – the nature focused on sharing the love of Jesus with others. Our purpose is defined by the question, "How can I be a giver of the love and hope of Jesus to those around me?"

Now the apex of the funnel (our identity in Christ) finds meaning and purpose through being God's hands and feet, bringing living water to those around us – both near and far (see John 4:14). When we live in this way, we discover the fruit of God's presence blossoming in our lives – love, joy, peace, patience, kindness, goodness, gentleness, faithfulness, and self-control. This is what God created us for!

Getting to The Inside

Human beings have a natural bent towards self. The result is, we place our identity, worth, and purpose in the hands of people, places, and things in the world around us. For certain, many are appealing to our humanness and seem to promise satisfaction to our souls. Nonetheless, we must learn that to place our hope in anyone or anything that can potentially fail us or leave us will ultimately end in hurt and disappointment.

We can't live from the inside if we're not there. We can't lead a person to places we've not reached on our own transformational journey. Attempting to present the depth and maturity inherent to an inside-out life when having stayed only in the shallow end of the pool, is analogous to attempting to display spiritual fruit in our life without our roots being solidly planted in the spirit of God.

Which We Choose Will Determine Our Purpose in Life

Are you a life-consuming funnel, living from the outside in? Or are you a life-giving fountain, living from the inside out?

My Gift to You

As I've written this book, I've attempted to introduce you to many of the wonderful, life-changing gems that God has blessed me with on my personal journey from brokenness to wholeness.

- Meaningful books I've read.
- Life-changing experiences I've had.
- Inspiring people I've met.
- Deep emotional pain I've felt.
- Tender comfort I've received
- Lasting hope I've found.
- Loving Jesus I've given my life to.

As I draw this wonderful book to a close, please allow me to give you a gift, a gift that was first given to me many years ago. When I received it, it came in all kinds of packages that arrived sporadically over many months and years.

But now, as I pass this gift along to you, I've put all of its parts into one package. In fact, it's already been put together for you. I made sure to include instruction on how to get optimal benefit from the gift. All I ask you to do is carefully open it, willingly receive it, and commit to love it and nurture it… one day at a time.

You Are God's Masterpiece!

The wonderful precious gift is **you**. The you that God intended from the beginning. The you that you've always wanted to know. The you that has begun to emerge as you've given yourself fully to Jesus.

For more than three decades, God has shined His light on the broken pieces of my life, encouraging me to scoop them up and surrender them to Him like an offering. My loving Father has taken every single element of my life that the enemy has told me was bad, and He has been intricately and perfectly crafting those pieces into a one-of-a-kind Masterpiece!

I pray you'll allow Him to do the same for you.

Turn your eyes upon Jesus.
Look full in His wonderful face.
And the things of earth will grow strangely dim.
In the light of His glory and grace.

Amen

SECTION 2

THE ROADMAP

PIECE 5

TURN: *I'm A New Creation!*

"Transformation requires turning."

Dr. Dave Ralston

CHAPTER 12

Turn

The part of our journey that we're about to embark on provides the opportunity to integrate into our own situations the countless truths, principles, and inspirations we've learned through Section 1. As I've heard it said back home, "This is where the rubber meets the road."

Several years ago, God inspired me to create an innovative and exclusive Christ-centered pathway to help others decisively turn from the brokenness of their past and turn toward wholeness that could only be found in Christ. The name of this model is **TURN**™.

The remainder of the book provides a clear roadmap that will guide us on our personal life-changing journey toward greater wholeness. One step at a time. One day at a time. TURNing our broken pieces into Masterpieces!

God Is the Author

My life as a Christian has certainly not been one that could be characterized as overly emotional, extreme, or radical. Quite the opposite actually. Some of that, I'm sure, is due to the steady nature of the family I come from. Some probably is an expression of my inborn temperament. And some may simply be from my having become wiser through having lived several decades on this earth.

Regardless, I'm about to share a very real and personal story that, needless to say, moved me way outside of anything I considered normal. I've included this story, in hopes of deflecting any accolades or praise that the publication of this book (and specifically the TURN model) might bring. God alone provided every element of vision, knowledge, reference, experience, perspective, and talent that went into the creation of this book.

John, known as the *disciple whom Jesus loved*, wrote in John 3:30 (NLT), "He must become greater and greater, and I must become less and less." I pray that will one day be said of me.

God-Sized Dreams

In 2013, on what seemed to be a very typical night at our home in Kentucky, my wife Ann and I were sound asleep. As usual, our Basset hound Nellie was snoring obnoxiously on the floor beside the bed. The house was dark and quiet. Everything was status quo. But what God had in store for me that night literally changed the trajectory of my life ever since. And I pray with great anticipation that it will have a profound effect on your lives as well!

At around 2:00 a.m., I began to have a dream. No big deal, right? Most of the dreams I had ever had either really didn't make much sense or were difficult for me to even remember once I woke up. This night was different.

In this dream I could clearly identify me and my wife Ann, as if it were happening today. We were standing in the middle of a huge shoulder-to-shoulder crowd of faceless people. But the remarkable part was that Jesus himself was walking in between me and Ann, and He had His arms around both of our backs, as if to make sure we didn't get separated from Him as the three of us moved through the crowd.

Then Jesus took His arms from around us and extended them straight out in front of Him, like if He was getting ready to say a blessing over the crowd. But instead of speaking over the masses, His words spoke over me and Ann. Jesus said, "Dave, Ann, anyone you touch I will touch." I get cold chills even now as I type this.

That dream was followed by another related dream. Even though I don't recall actually having seen Jesus's face in this second dream, I knew He was speaking to me – or at least in some way, God was telling me something important that He didn't want me to miss.

What was flooding through me was an intricate process for guiding people from years of inner brokenness to a future of wholeness in Christ.

Although Ann and I had been involved in our church's Celebrate Recovery© years earlier, the thought of something like this wasn't even remotely on my radar in 2013.

Prior to that night, if someone had attempted to tell me a similar story from their life, I very likely would have either considered them fanatical, or thought they were making it up to make themselves look more spiritual than they really were. I ask that you not think that of me.

After that night, my relationship with Jesus began unfolding into something very new and different. I stopped trying to put God in a box that would allow me to feel safe and in control. I began respecting other Christians' experiences with God, even if they didn't fit within a paradigm that I was familiar with. And I truly began to trust that God would do radical things in and through my life, often when I least expected it!

The Name Came First...

Somewhere in between dreaming and being awake, I began to realize this information was coming into my head faster than I could keep up with, and in greater detail than I would ever be able to remember. So, I woke up, got up and went into our kitchen, got a pen and paper, and sat down at the table. I know it sounds hard to believe, but thoughts just began rushing through my head. I could hardly write fast enough to keep up with them.

What I first wrote down was the name of the process God was showing me: **TURN**. An acronym that represented the four distinct phases our soul and spirit must progress through en route to maturity:

"T" represents "Turn away from toxic people, places, and things."
"U" represents "Uncover shame and false beliefs from our past."
"R" represents "Rediscover our true identity in Christ."
"N" represents "Nurture lasting hope in others."

... Then Lots of Details

Then I began to think/see/perceive (I'm not exactly sure which it was) much of the framework of the TURN process begin to emerge. The

TURN model would serve as a roadmap for an individual's personal journey from the hopelessness and emotional pain of their shame-based past, to lasting hope, wholeness, and freedom found only in Jesus. TURN would systematically guide individuals through a personal examination of twelve essentials of Christ-centered soul work that would culminate in offering to others the hope, healing, and wholeness they have found.

"Turn away from toxic people, places, and things."

- Denial
- God's Love
- Surrender

"Uncover shame and false beliefs from our past."

- Roles
- Family
- Shame

"Rediscover our true identity in Christ."

- Strongholds
- Restoration
- Forgiveness

"Nurture lasting hope in others."

- Boundaries
- Identity
- Purpose

It's probable that some of the pieces I scurried to write down that night may have subconsciously come from my experiences with Celebrate Recovery©, or even my participation in a twelve-step group nearly twenty-five years earlier. So, I certainly don't want to imply that TURN is the first of its kind, nor that 100 percent of its elements were of my innovation.

Millions of men's and women's lives have been renewed through these and other similar recovery programs.

Notwithstanding, the comprehensive, systematic design of TURN offers every participant a safe, proven platform where they can discover and develop their unique place for seeking, serving, shepherding, and shaping the lives of those around them. TURN is a process of being transformed from brokenness to wholeness, not a recovery group aimed only at maintaining sobriety or abstinence. TURN is a pattern for living a life of hope in Christ, not a program to be signed up for or joined. TURN is a vehicle for lasting heart-level change, not a set of principles to be memorized and learned in order to gain understanding of our problems and inner struggles. TURN is an intentional discovery and healing of the toxic shame within us, not a curriculum, that once completed, leads to a certificate suitable for framing. And most importantly, TURN is entirely Christ-centered, standing firmly on the truth that only Jesus is "the way, and the truth, and the life" (John 14:6 NIV).

In my saying all of this, please understand, TURN is a powerful, God-given tool that is much bigger than me and more life-changing than anything I've previously encountered. I certainly would not or could not have come up with all of this on my own – and especially not at 2:00 in the morning.

I'm Leaving Some Pieces in The Box

After God showed me the TURN model that night, I pondered it and talked to God about it off and on for a few weeks. It just didn't seem to have relevance at that point in my life. Eventually I transferred all of my notes into typed form, and filed them away on my computer, not knowing if any of it would every come to fruition.

A few short years later, Ann and I decided it would be good for us to move from operating a non-profit Christian counseling private practice, to serving in similar ministry role, except full time on staff at a church. After more than a year of resumes and networking, I was invited for an initial interview online with a large, thriving church in Texas. In the third online interview, I was asked if I had any sort of vision of what a large group "recovery" program might look like if I were to be offered the job. Enter TURN!

I shared the entire picture of what God had provided me for the TURN model a few years earlier. I followed that up by sending a lengthy document spelling out every detail. From that point forward, there became a shared enthusiasm of how God might use TURN in that church community.

Three or four months later, Ann and I were Texans, and both serving on staff at that church. My position was as lead pastor for Counseling & Restoration, and Ann's was as a Christian counselor on my team.

I feel certain God opened that door to allow the TURN approach to develop from merely theory on paper into a proven, life-changing program in the lives of men and women who needed exactly what TURN offered. When we arrived in Texas, obviously no TURN program existed. When TURN was fully launched five months later, God had formed a team of servant-leaders around us. By the time we left Texas, after TURN had been ongoing for eighteen months or so, more than 650 men and women had benefitted from the multiple elements of the TURN ministry. And there were now nearly seventy people on our team, serving God through greeting, hosting, setting up, providing refreshments, managing the resource table, leading small groups, teaching classes, lay counseling, and so much more.

In God's perfect time, He saw fit for that season to end. He then began to open doors for me to write this book and to share this wonderful, God-given model on a much grander scale.

Having said all of this, there will be many pieces of the comprehensive TURN model that will be left "in the box" during our journey through this book. They're important, but not necessary here. When combined, though, the numerous ingredients of TURN create a healing community, where men and women of all walks of life discover hope, healing, and wholeness through an upward spiral of spiritual growth and soul development. This is lived out in the context of a safe, accepting large group environment, topic-specific discussion groups, lay counseling for individuals and couples, and opportunities to seek, serve, shepherd, and shape lives - our own, as well as those who desperately need what we have found.

Credit Where Credit Is Due

The name and framework for TURN literally came to me in an amazing dream. However, I could not have included the detailed teaching elements of the TURN process had it not been for resources written by outstanding colleagues within the field.

I must bring special attention to the anointed work of Stephanie Tucker, Director of Family Programs at New Life Spirit Recovery, and author of *The Christian Codependence Recovery Workbook*. Stephanie has done extensive research, teaching, and writing on the topics of codependence, boundaries, and shame, and I am forever grateful to Stephanie for giving me her permission and blessing to include a considerable amount of her wisdom and words within the twelve components of the TURN process. Since authoring *The Christian Codependence Recovery Workbook,* Stephanie has hoped for her teachings to be adapted to reach an even broader audience. I sincerely pray that the TURN model has achieved that objective. Thank you, and God bless you, Stephanie.

God Makes the Crooked Straight

Not long after my wife and I moved into our first brand new home, I arranged for the local plant nursery to deliver and install a perfect weeping willow tree in our side yard. Ann had always wanted a beautiful, wispy tree that we could one day sit in the shade of, drink iced tea, and reminisce about our kids and grandkids.

Just a couple years after the tree was planted, all of Kentucky experienced the worst ice storm in over a century. Literally everything was covered with over an inch of solid ice – including our beautiful weeping willow. The weight of the ice caused our perfectly straight tree to bend to the point that its tip was actually touching the ground. And it stayed in this position for weeks.

Once the warm weather of spring melted off all the ice, the tree was finally able to stand back up on its own – but its trunk remained bent in the shape of a banana. Months and months of attempting to straighten and stake the tree could not fully correct its bent and wounded trunk.

Fast forward a few years to just a few months ago when Ann and I drove by our old house. Our fifteen-year-old weeping willow tree was now nearly thirty feet tall and fully grown. Yet upon closer examination, its trunk was still crooked, just as it had been for over a decade – physically mature yet developed in wrong directions.

God Turns Our Shame Inside Out

Toxic shame has had an effect in many of our lives that seems similar to what an ice storm had done to our weeping willow. We lived our childhoods immersed in emotional, relational, and internal storms, which together caused the framework of our souls to become bent, crooked, and dysfunctional. Much like the weeping willow, once we reached adulthood and became outwardly mature, our minds, wills, and emotions remained underdeveloped, misguided, and even childlike in some ways. But that's not the end of the story God has for each of us.

> "And I will bring the blind by a way that they know not; in paths that they know not will I lead them; I will make darkness light before them, and crooked places straight. These things will I do, and I will not forsake them" (Isaiah 42:16 NASB).

The next four chapters of *Addition By Subtraction* will provide all of the tools necessary to progressively move our lives from bent to upright, from crooked to straight, from broken to whole. Let's take our time and fully experience every moment of this amazing adventure, one day at a time.

Whatever it is, whatever has happened to us, whatever we have done, and whatever unfinished business we might have, our God is so awesome, so huge, so merciful, so intimate, and so gracious, that He desires to bring healing and release from our pasts.

God loves you. He loves each and every one of His children individually, completely, and unconditionally. Because of this love, He is gentle and careful to bring to our awareness only the things He knows we need to deal with or reconcile at that particular moment in time. If it's not in our conscious awareness, then we can trust that God isn't ready for us to face it yet, if ever at all.

Am I Too Broken Even for God?

Some reading this book might be saying to yourselves, "This all sounds well and good, but my brokenness is beyond even God's ability to fix." They may believe their sin is beyond God's willingness to forgive, or that they have lived too long for God to make new, or that they are too lost for God to ever find.

Fortunately, God is not like us, or our parents, abusers, or those who rejected and abandoned us. He is everything that our souls have longed for from the day we were born. And He offers us this intimate connection with Him through our relationship with Jesus. The Bible says that if we've seen Jesus, we've seen the Father. We can let go of our past, present, and future, and fully trust them in His loving hands!

> "For this is how God loved the world: He gave His one and only Son, so that everyone who believes in Him will not perish but have eternal life. God sent Jesus into the world not to condemn the world, but to save the world through Him" (John 3:16-17 NLT).

There's Only One Path That Leads to Heart Change

In an earlier chapter we examined how the shed blood of Jesus and the power of God's word make us right before a Holy God. That spiritual transformation is known as "justification," which miraculously occurs in our spirit at the very moment we place our faith in Jesus Christ alone. A good metaphor for justification could be that of a **wedding**, a moment in time when we made a lifelong commitment.

However, the bride and groom's relationship is about much more than just the wedding day. The beauty of the relationship is found in the journey the couple experiences together for the rest of their lives. God created **marriage** as a wonderful illustration of the growing relationship He desires with each of us. Every mature relationship -- including our life with Jesus – contains peaks and valleys, twists and turns, offenses and forgiveness, grief and new beginnings, grace and mercy.

In the context of our Christian faith, this deepening relationship with Jesus is called "sanctification" -- being transformed day-to-day from the person who has been defined by life in this fallen world, into the person created by God from the very beginning. To some, words like "sanctification" and "transformation" may seem like religious jargon. I certainly understand. I simply refer to this entire concept with the words "heart change."

By now you know that I enjoy connecting a real-life example to many of the deeper concepts I write about. There is a centuries-old story that I dearly love, and it provides a beautiful illustration of the process of change.

Tradition tells the story that Michelangelo, an Italian artist and sculptor in the fifteenth century, was carving an angel out of a large cube of marble. Day after day, month upon month, he would strive and chisel and brush. One day, a young girl asked him, "Without any form of drawings or patterns, how do you know what to remove and what to keep?" Michelangelo replied, "I can see the angel in the marble, and I simply carve until I set him free."

God is doing the same work in each of us. Chiseling away all of the shame, abandonment, pride, failure, rejection, and brokenness, and allowing our true identity to be revealed a little more each day we're with Him. The Bible refers to God as the potter and we are the clay (see Isaiah 64:9). Or maybe, He is the sculptor, we are the block of marble!

Action Steps

Authentic life change occurs within us only as we speak to God (pray) from our hearts -- honestly, vulnerably, and consistently. The Bible provides guidance as to the vital elements of our continual conversation with God:

- **Acknowledge** the specific nature of our sin, guilt, and shame.
- **Confess** our brokenness and wrongdoing openly to God.
- **Repent** by asking God to change our hearts to be more like His.
- **Trust** that we are fully forgiven, and that God has made us clean.
- **Experience freedom** from shame, guilt, and brokenness.

I believe I'm safe in assuming that every one of us reading this book has been affected in some way by toxic shaming at the hands of others. And, in turn, we have bruised, wounded, or broken countless others' souls as a result. Sanctification is not merely a means for us to be forgiven for the things we've thought, said, and done wrong, and how they may have contributed to us hurting others. It does not merely release us from the burden of our sin and shame. It is much, much deeper and more spiritual than that.

> "I acknowledged my sin to You, and my iniquity I did not hide; I said, 'I will confess my transgressions to the Lord'; and You forgave the guilt of my sin" (Psalm 32:5 NLT).

> "Repent, then, and turn to God, so that your sins may be wiped out, that times of refreshing may come from the Lord" (Acts 3:19 NIV).

> "For as high as the heavens are above the earth, so great is His love for those who fear Him; as far as the east is from the west, so far has He removed our transgressions from us" (Psalm 103:11-12 NIV).

God provided us this miraculous pathway in order for our soul (identity) to be progressively renewed: From our fallen human nature to the very nature and character of Jesus.

An Everyday Parable

These things I've been explaining can be pretty difficult to understand and even more challenging to fully believe. Nothing else in our lives looks quite like the paths and processes God has put in place for His children to be restored to Him.

As we examined in earlier chapters, Jesus often used parables -- everyday stories to illustrate God-sized principles. I'm going to give it my best shot to share a personal parable that will hopefully help us get our minds around these concepts.

When my two adult sons – Sean and Seth Ralston – were young, they were pretty much what I had always pictured boys being like: active, carefree, outgoing, aggressive, competitive, and so on. Even though our house was somewhat kid-proof, their mom always had lots and lots of crafts, accessories, and antiques displayed throughout the house.

On one occasion when she was vacuuming, she discovered that one of her treasures had been broken. As you might expect, I was pretty quick to explain how it couldn't have been me who did it. So, that left only the boys as the probable culprit or culprits.

I called the boys into the room, showed them what we had discovered, and asked them if they knew anything about how it may have happened. They were both quick to deny any wrongdoing. I reassured them they weren't in any trouble, but their mom and I just wanted to know how it had gotten broken.

For a couple days they both laid pretty low around me, reluctant to make eye contact. But finally, they broke. They came to me and admitted that the damaged item had been an important accessory in their basketball games played on the Jordan Jammer hoop in their bedroom.

The look on their faces made it obvious they were fearful to admit what had happened. I can still remember how scary situations like that felt when I was a kid. But, when I hugged them tight and told them they were forgiven, that there wouldn't be any punishment, and that their mom and I loved them very much, I could see a wave of relief came over both of their faces.

Although I can't tell you that they never broke anything else after that, I can assure you that their relationships with their dad and mom became a little different that day. From that day forward, they both knew they had the freedom to make mistakes, and even bad choices. They knew they were safe to admit when they had made a mistake or a bad choice. They were reminded that their parents were still their parents, and that we expected them to make better choices in the future. They experienced that we were on their side, not their enemies. And most importantly, they knew that no matter what, we loved them more than they could ever comprehend!

Allow God's Love to Become Personal

Hopefully this has helped you see how God loves you unconditionally, even though He knows <u>everything</u> about you. And He has already forgiven you even before you've confessed to Him.

I'm merely a human father. And if I could extend love and grace to my sons in this real-life example, then imagine how much Jesus wants you to experience HIS unconditional mercy, grace, and forgiveness – the love of your perfect heavenly Father.

We All Need an Advocate

The Bible makes it crystal clear that our heavenly Father wants His children to have an advocate while we're here on this earth. I found one particular definition online for the word "advocate" that I felt defined it really well: "one who promotes, supports, and defends another, regardless of the circumstances."

There's a pretty good possibility that many of us reading this book lacked a constant, loving advocate in our lives, especially when we were young. Some of us may have had to become our own (and only) advocate – fending for ourselves and being forced to grow up way too soon.

We needed someone to be proud of who we were, and to assure us that we were deeply loved, completely forgiven, fully pleasing, totally accepted, and absolutely complete.

These fundamental components of our identity may have been overlooked through our childhoods. Then as adults, we may have searched tirelessly for something or someone that would fill these voids.

God alone wants to be the final authority of our infinite worth and value, the most prominent voice our hearts listen to, and the advocate we constantly trust and depend on.

> "My dear children, I write this to you so that you will not sin. But if anybody does sin, we have an **advocate** with the Father—Jesus Christ, the Righteous One" (1 John 2:1 NIV).

"And I will ask the Father, and He will give you another **advocate** – the Holy Spirit – to help you and be with you forever" (John 14:16 NIV).

Jesus is our **advocate**. His Holy Spirit is our **advocate**, and He lives within us and will be with us forever. One day at a time and one moment at a time, we can trust that **God is our advocate**, constantly present with us, promoting, supporting, and defending us, regardless our circumstances.

In an earlier chapter, I illuminated the seven most prevalent forms of inner woundedness: the poor, the brokenhearted, the captives, the imprisoned, the mourning, the blind, and the oppressed. Every human being has a story. And God has been in the center of writing each one from the very beginning. To find Him, we must be willing to search for Him among the broken pieces of our lives. He is patiently waiting there -- ready to turn our ashes into beauty!

We can lean on God in every situation of life. He will never shame us, reject us, or abandon us. He is all-knowing, all-present, all-powerful, and all-loving. We can fully trust Him with every step of this beautiful adventure. He alone is our perfect **advocate**, and He alone can turn our broken pieces into masterpieces.

Questions from Dr. Dave

For personal reflection or group discussion of Chapter 12

Has there ever been a time in your life (possibly even today) when you believed that your sin and wrongdoing was beyond even God's ability or willingness to forgive? The enemy wants you to keep on believing that, in hopes of preventing you from experiencing God's unconditional love and freedom. Consider whether now is the time to tear down any walls of doubt and allow the love of Jesus into your most broken places.

God chose to supernaturally place TURN on my heart at a time when my mind was least able to over-think or under-trust it. Is God showing you how the TURN approach could very well be the pathway to hope that you've long been praying for? Which of the four TURN elements makes you the most eager? Which makes you the most anxious?

In the last section of this chapter, I defined the word "advocate" as: "one who promotes, supports, and defends another, regardless of the circumstances." Many of us have never had another human being be our trusted advocate. We've had to advocate entirely for ourselves. Or we've gone through seasons feeling entirely alone. As you ponder the truth that Jesus is and will be your unshakable advocate every moment of every day, what thoughts and emotions does this cause to bubble up in your heart? Is there anything keeping you from fully allowing Jesus to be this near to you?

"Repent, then, and turn to God, so that your sins may be wiped out, that times of refreshing may come from the Lord"

Acts 3:19 NIV

Turn from Brokenness to Wholeness in Christ

TWELVE FOUNDATIONAL TRUTHS OF THE TURN APPROACH

PHASE 1: T - Turn from Toxic People, Places, and Things

1. "When I refused to confess my sin, my body wasted away, and I groaned all day long. Day and night Your hand of discipline was heavy on me" (Psalm 32:3-4 NLT).

DENIAL – Turn my denial into awareness.

2. "For God so loved the world that He gave his one and only Son, that whoever believes in Him shall not perish but have eternal life. For God did not send His son into the world to condemn the world, but to save the world through Him" (John 3:16-17 NIV).

GOD'S LOVE – Turn toward the unconditional love of Jesus Christ.

3. "Trust in the Lord with all your heart and lean not on your own understanding; in all your ways submit to Him, and He will make your paths straight" (Proverbs 3:5-6 NIV).

SURRENDER – Turn over control to a loving God.

PHASE 2: U - Uncover the Lies and False Beliefs of My Past

4. "Throw off your old sinful nature and your former way of life, which is corrupted by lust and deception. Instead, let the spirit renew your thoughts and attitudes. Put on your new nature, created to be like God—truly righteous and holy" (Ephesians 4:22-24 NLT).

ROLES – Turn from my unhealthy false identity.

5. "I, the Lord your God, am a jealous God, punishing the children for the sins of their parents to the third and fourth generation of those who are disobedient to me, but showing love to a thousand generations of those who love me and keep my commandments" (Deuteronomy 5:9-10 NIV).

FAMILY – Turn from any dysfunctional influences of my family-of-origin.

6. "So now there is no condemnation for those who belong to Christ Jesus" (Romans 8:1 NLT).

SHAME – Turn from toxic shame to freedom in Christ.

PHASE 3: R - Rediscover My True Identity In Christ

7. "We demolish arguments and every pretension that sets itself up against the knowledge of God, and we take captive every thought to make it obedient to Christ" (2 Corinthians 10:5-6 NIV).

STRONGHOLDS – Turn loose of emotional strongholds.

8. "If we confess our sins, He is faithful and will forgive us our sins and purify us from all unrighteousness" (1 John 1:9 NIV).

RESTORATION – Turn to restoration from my sin and shame

9. "Make allowance for each other's faults and forgive anyone who offends you. Remember, the Lord forgave you, so you must forgive others" (Colossians 3:13 NLT).

FORGIVENESS – Turn resentments into forgiveness.

PHASE 4: N - Nurture Lasting Hope in Others

10. "Seldom set foot in your neighbor's house – too much of you, and they will come to hate you" (Proverbs 25:17 NIV).

BOUNDARIES – Turn walls of fear into healthy boundaries.

11. "Yet to all who did receive Him, to those who believed in His name, He gave the right to become children of God" (John 1:12 NIV).

IDENTITY – Turn toward my true identity in Christ.

12. "And we know that God causes everything to work together for the good of those who love Him and are called according to His purpose for them" (Romans 8:28 NLT).

PURPOSE – Turn from confusion to purpose.

The next four chapters will guide us through the four important phases of the T-U-R-N journey that has been outlined above. There are three Biblical truth topics within each of the four phases, totaling twelve lessons in all. These are outlined above and taught in subsequent chapters.

Please remember, there is no wrong way to work through this. The route you take is exactly the right one! Just keep moving forward one page at a time, one truth at a time, one chapter at a time, one day at a time. You're worth it!

CHAPTER 13

Phase 1: T – Turn from Toxic People, Places, and Things

"When I refused to confess my sin, my body wasted away, and I groaned all day long. Day and night Your hand of discipline was heavy on me."

Psalm 32:3-4 NLT

DENIAL

Turn My Denial into Awareness

Introduction

- The definition of denial is: "Refusal to admit the truth or reality of something; typically motivated by self-protection."
- The lies of our past blind us to things that really do exist, while at the same time causing us to see things that aren't there.
- The most difficult thing about recovery is seeing things as they really are... and were. This means pulling off the filter, peeling back the masks, and getting into the raw layers of what our experience up to this point has really been.
- While it may sound scary, it can be summed up in one word – TRUTH. Jesus said, "Then you will know the truth, and the truth will set you free" (John 8:32 NIV).
- We avoid the very truth that can bring the freedom we so desperately need. We often create a reality of how we wish things would be (a fantasy bond), or we cover over things through our skills of compensation (Equal and Opposite principle).
- The distortion of reality is a safety net that allows us to hide behind a façade that states, "Everything is fine." It creates an illusion, a false impression, which may seem to satisfy the approval of others, but leaves us barely hanging on.

- Denial blinds us from living the life God intends for us. Satan knows that as long as we don't believe (or admit) that a problem exists, we will never be able to find a solution. He will use whatever forces possible to keep us in denial.

Ways We Participate in Our Own Denial

- We deny the way others have hurt us.
- We deny who Christ says we really are.
- We deny the unhealthy behaviors of others.
- We deny our own sinful, hurtful behaviors.
- We deny our own feelings.
- We deny the imbalance of our relationships.

Freedom from Denial

Being able to expose and dispose of denial is a foundational and necessary ingredient for any change to take place and for freedom to be found. There comes a point when the issue must be addressed properly for healing to take place, and the only safe and effective way for this to occur is alongside Jesus. Certainly, a skilled human counselor can provide guidance, but only the True Counselor can extract those deeper and more traumatizing situations and uncover the true impact.

We are made in the image of our Creator. We have been formed and hand designed by Him, with uniqueness, giftedness, significance, and worth. God desires to remove the things keeping us from fully being that person. Going through the process restores us to our original design.

What God Says About You:

> "For I know the plans I have for you," says the Lord. "They are plans for good and not for harm, to give you a hope and a future" (Jeremiah 29:11 NIV).

"I knew you before I formed you in your mother's womb. Before you were born, I set you apart" (Jeremiah 1:5 NIV).

"O Lord, you have examined my heart and know everything about me. You know when I sit down or stand up. You know my thoughts even when I'm far away. You see me when I travel and when I rest at home. You know everything I do. You know what I am going to say even before I say it, Lord. You go before me and follow me. You place Your hand of blessing on my head" (Psalm 139:1-5 NLT).

Unmet Needs

Just as we need to uncover forms of denial that conceal the events and things that happened to us, we must also recognize the neglect of our God-given needs. People can hurt us by what they do to us; they can also hurt us by what they don't do. For many of us, a root of abandonment, neglect, and rejection is responsible for our wounds.

As human beings, our souls have three critical, yet basic, needs

Belonging. The need to be known and loved (the Affection element of the temperament).

Competence. The need to be accepted for what we do (the Control element of the temperament).

Acceptance. The need to have significance (the Inclusion element of the temperament).

Children who grew up in shame-based homes may never have had these needs met, or they were met in unhealthy, ungodly ways through false messages of what it meant to be loved, accepted, and significant. In some families, having your needs met is considered to be selfish. Children grow up to believe that their basic needs are wrong, causing them to learn to cope by themselves. This creates the cycle of denial that anything is actually going on.

How Do I Identity Unmet Needs in My Life?

Many times, our felt needs are far from actual needs. We need the guidance of the Holy Spirit to show us the difference. Let's explore some of the areas where we are prone to experience wounding or brokenness caused by the neglect of legitimate needs:

- **Genuine experience of love**. When relationships lack love, they are replaced by codependency and control.
- **Life nurturing and guidance**. By not nurturing a child yet expecting him or her to 'know life', parents send their children false messages about God-given, legitimate needs.
- **A sense of protection**. Children require the safety of healthy boundaries and protection from outside threats.
- **Healthy forms of discipline**. Discipline teaches proper boundaries and a sense that their actions have consequences to a child.
- **Nurturing of identity and gender role**. This distortion can lead us into many levels of toxic relationships and sexual identity problems.
- **Acceptance as a valuable and precious child**. Without this, the root of shame will be planted, and the child will continually try to prove worthiness or will simply give up.
- **The loss of a carefree and fun childhood.** Children aren't meant to carry adult problems. Children from these families have no understanding of the fun and carefree lifestyle a child was intended to live, and they tend to take life very seriously.
- **The instilling of self-esteem**. A healthy self-esteem ensures a child has an accurate and balanced perspective of self.
- **Encouragement**. If we never have anyone speak positively into our hearts in childhood, we have believed that nothing about us made us special or worthwhile.

When we've had unmet needs in childhood, we must recognize and grieve what we lost. Today we have new choices. We don't have to continue down destructive paths, trying to replace the things we lost or missed. By grieving over our losses (allowing ourselves to actually feel what we feel), we can move on in a healthy way and ask God to make up for our unmet needs. If we ignore and stay in denial of those needs, we unknowingly continue trying ineffectively to replace what was lost.

Self-Examination and Taking Personal Inventory

How do we know if we're in denial? How can we assess our unmet needs? Usually, all of us entering into this type of healing work may have many layers of denial. However, the scope of that denial can range immensely. That's why an honest assessment process is necessary.

We must set realistic expectations as we approach an inventory. At times, God may touch us and give us the ability to feel a supernatural healing instantly. But often in the healing process, God simply exposes lies that we have accepted as our form of truth.

He takes the truth of His word and makes it a reality within us, so we are walking in the light rather than in the darkness of the deceit and lies we've carried. A lengthy amount of time may be required to completely process the lies and false beliefs. So be patient – with God, and with yourself. Whatever your experience has been, be assured that the God who made you and loves you will walk with you through this process!

Breaking Free from Denial

Consider beginning an actual inventory of the issues in your life. Before beginning, spend time in prayer and meditation. Only God can reveal these things to us, and He must be present for this to be effective. Visualize yourself going hand-in-hand with Jesus as your guide. Ask Him to allow you to experience whatever senses are necessary to connect to the event or situation that He knows will move you toward greater wholeness in Him.

- **Ways you have been violated or sinned against.** Focus on the actual violation, not the person. It's important to see and face the violation and the effect it had on your life.
- **Immoral and sinful behaviors you committed**. Try to begin with the earliest memory and work your way forward to recent experiences. Consider specific, not general acts.

- **Painful and traumatic experiences.** These are typically major life issues, such as a parent's death, divorce, sexual assault, and so on.
- **Relationship patterns.** Recall relational patterns so you can understand where unhealthy dynamics exist. Include all-important relationships in the family of origin, and all-important adult relationships.
- **Unmet needs.** Explore things you needed and didn't receive, or things you once had and then lost. It is important to emotionally connect with these items, and at some point, go through an actual grieving process.

We look back only to emotionally connect with life experiences that have been repressed, disassociated, or not otherwise properly dealt with. In essence, we must "feel in order to heal." Our inability to feel has led us to compulsive or addictive behaviors in the first place.

Now, instead, we face those things we have hidden by learning to embrace and trust the True Comforter, Jesus Christ. By allowing ourselves to actually feel the pain of our past, we will begin to discover a new understanding of God who loves us infinitely more than we could even comprehend. He carries our grief. He is The Healer!

Prayer to Break Denial

Father God, denial is a scary word. It means I have been deceived somehow. I ask You right now to remove the blinders from my heart. Please show me anything that has kept me from being the real person You made me to be. If there are wounds of shame I need to address, please show me. If I have been locked up on the inside while living differently on the outside, please rescue me.

I believe, according to Your word, that You love me perfectly. And in that perfect love, I know I can face the things in my life that I need to face. Be with me Lord. Guide me. Expose the things that have held me in bondage, but please do so lovingly and graciously. In the name of Jesus, I pray against the tactics of the enemy. I know he would tempt me to feel shame. Instead, let me see how much You love me and desire to set me free from shame and brokenness. In Jesus name I pray, Amen.

"For God so loved the world that He gave His one and only Son, that whoever believes in Him shall not perish but have eternal life. For God did not send Jesus into the world to condemn the world, but to save the world through Him."

John 3:16-17 NIV

JESUS' LOVE

Turn Toward the Unconditional
Love of Jesus

Introduction

God created us with an inherent need for love. It is even more important than the air we breathe and the food we eat. Just as our physical body would eventually die without our physical needs being met, a lack of love will disrupt our ability to grow emotionally or spiritually.

- The very reason for our existence is carved out of love – we were designed to receive and give love as the basis for all relationships (see Mark 12: 29-31).
- Without love, we can never fulfill our God-given purpose. Furthermore, we will never be satisfied, emotionally healthy, or whole.
- God used our parents to provide this much needed love before we were able to know Him personally. They were our first examples of how we would learn to interpret, give, and receive love in relationships. The type and amount of love we received (or did not receive) in childhood will deeply affect our ability to love in adult relationships. If our need for love was not adequately met, we will go through our adult life with a need for love and an empty heart. We may also acquire countless false beliefs about love that will directly spill over into all our relationships.

What Is Love Anyway?

The Bible teaches us multiple different types of what we in our culture might call "love." God included all of these in His creation of humanity to exhibit the fullness of His nature. Yet when we as human beings introduce these into our relationships with other people, we often tend to miss the mark on what God intended.

- **Hesed – Inspiring Love.** Through Christ, this is defined by love and loyalty that inspires merciful and compassionate behavior toward another person. But in our hands, we sometimes make love and loyalty contingent upon the merciful and compassionate behavior of another person toward us.
- **Philia – Affectionate Love.** This form of love doesn't involve any passion or sexual impulse. It's more seen as love between good friends or goodwill between us and someone we respect or admire. It finds its energy in what two people share in common. But in our hands, once the common interest has faded, we tend to convey that we no longer need this relationship.
- **Eros – Romantic Love.** Although this Greek term does not appear in the Bible, it is clearly portrayed in multiple examples. God is very clear in His word when He defines this intense sexual desire that is to be shared exclusively by a husband and a wife. Obviously, we have found innumerous ways to distort the beauty of this special form of love God created.
- **Storge – Family Love.** This is the form of love that family members feel for each other. It is most recognized as the love a parent has for their child. It's a very strong bond that is not easily broken. But in our hands, this can either morph into unhealthy forms of enmeshment, or sometimes will end in the face of unresolved conflict.
- **Pragma – Enduring Love.** The Greek word "pragma" is where we get the English word "pragmatic." It's a practical kind of love that stands the test of time. As the opposite of eros where the passion burns white hot and fades quickly, pragma matures and grows over time into something truly special.

- **Philautia – Healthy Self-Love.** This type of love refers to a healthy self-esteem and feeling of inner self-worth. When we find our identity and worth in Jesus, our relationship to ourselves, to others, and to the world will be a reflection of His love. Oftentimes, however, we tend to turn healthy self-love into unhealthy self-focus, self-absorption, and self-indulgence – all at the expense of our relationships with others.

- **Ludas – Playful Love.** If you've ever been in love, you have no doubt felt this form of love. It is the butterflies in your stomach, the quickened heartbeat, the anxiety you feel when you're waiting for your loved one to walk through the door. It's the flirting and teasing and playing you do in the early stages of dating. The focus is usually more on fun rather than building the relationship.

- **Agape — Unconditional Love.** Agape is by far the most special and most respectful of all the Greek types of love. It is the kind of love Jesus refers to again and again throughout His ministry. It is the form of love that sets our Christian faith apart from all other faith and beliefs systems. It is a universal, unconditional, selfless love for others. It involves caring more for others than for yourself. To give agape love is to be like Jesus. However, our ability to give agape love to others cannot exceed our transformation experience of being loved by Jesus when we least deserved it.

Agape Love Is Jesus' Love

God intended for our lives to be immersed in agape love. The moment we were saved, or born again, the Holy Spirit indwelled us and we were connected with agape. But for many of us, an experience of this type of love has never occurred. Shame and past beliefs regarding love tend to block the ability to truly understand and experience God's love. We may be afraid of intimacy with God because we don't understand how He operates, or we fear He'll reject us, hurt us, or abandon us in the same way others we've been close to have. Sometimes we are filled with bitterness and unforgiveness that prevent the Holy Spirit's ability to gain access. His love is there, but we can't experience it due to unresolved shame in our lives.

The remarkable thing about Christ-centered soul work is that love is both the problem and the cure. The true power behind healing and recovery from the brokenness in your life is being able to connect at a deep level with the God who created you and loves you unconditionally. In that love, you will find peace, wholeness, and the ability to function in healthy relationships. This change doesn't happen immediately. It is a process, so don't lose faith. If you seek Him with all your heart, you will certainly find Him!

God's Love System

In scripture, God lays out His system of love. He gives us a clear pattern to follow. We have referenced this same passage form the Bible several times throughout the previous chapters, so it's probably becoming pretty familiar. As recorded in Mark 12: 28-31 (NIV), Jesus was asked what He considered the most important commandment in the entire Bible:

> "'The most important one,' answered Jesus, "is this: 'Love the Lord your God with all your heart and with all your soul and with all your mind and with all your strength.' The second is this: 'Love your neighbor as yourself. There is no commandment greater than these.'"

Above everyone and everything else, we are to pursue a growing agape relationship with God, through His son Jesus Christ. This means we must put Him first and seek Him most.

Second, our connectedness to Jesus' agape love will flow through us like a spring of living water. In John 4:14 (NIV), Jesus assured the woman at the well that, "Everyone who drinks this water (the type of love that life on this earth offers them) will be thirsty again, but whoever drinks the water I give them (the agape love of Christ) will never thirst. In fact, the water I give them will become in them a spring of water welling up to eternal life." **We can't give away something we don't possess!**

Third, we are to allow the agape love within us to flow naturally from us to others. If we are truly filled with the unconditional, agape love of Jesus, sharing it with others won't be what we do, but rather a reflection of who we are.

Loving God First

Receiving love without paying a cost is something some of us have a difficult time comprehending. We may believe love is something to work for or earn, much like a job with a paycheck. If we believe God requires us to do special things to earn love from Him, we become "performance based." We will be prone to thinking "God is mad at me," or "I'm reaping what I've sowed."

If we measure ourselves by His laws rather than by His grace, we will always see ourselves as failures. But the problem goes even deeper. When we are in a performance mode with God, our actions and behaviors try to win His approval to make ourselves feel acceptable. We don't give Him what He truly desires, which are our burdens, pain, and sin. Instead, we are too busy trying to make ourselves worthy of Him. Trying to earn His love would be like insisting on paying a dear friend for the birthday present they gave you. The reason this cycle of behavior is so dangerous is that God's love doesn't rest on our efforts or attempts to be acceptable. It isn't what we do that makes us worthy in His sight. It's what He did for us!

True restoration only happens when we embrace, understand, and allow God's love to flow through us. Our best efforts to produce anything close to agape will always fall short. Remember, true love – agape – is a resource of the Holy Spirit, and we can access it only through a relationship with Him.

The Nature of God's Love

Here are some of the wonderful characteristics of God's love:

- **Based on grace.** It is a free gift that we cannot earn and don't deserve (see Ephesians 2: 8-9).
- **Based on choice.** He doesn't demand or force us to love Him or to receive His love (see James 1:15; Deuteronomy 30:19; Matthew 6:24).
- **Given out of true sacrifice.** It cost Him dearly to show His love to us (see John 10:11, 15-18; John 15:13, 3:16; 1 John 3:16).

- **Is unconditional.** There is nothing you can do to take it away or change it (see 1 John 4:7-10; Romans 8:38-39).
- **Seeks our admission of sin** so He can forgive and restore areas of our lives (see Luke 16:15; Matthew 23:25-28; Isaiah 64:6; Romans 10:3).
- **Desires intimacy with the "real you,"** not a false, counterfeit version (see Psalm 139; Isaiah 43:4; 1 John 4:18).

Unhealthy Love Systems

As we look at the heart of God and discover He is filled with grace, love, and kindness toward us, it should move us to desire to love and serve Him more. Often this doesn't happen because deep down, we are still blocked by faulty belief systems regarding love. When our earthly experience has been unloving, we may find it difficult to understand God's love. God is our real Father! He is the one who made us, and therefore, His acceptance and love will conquer any and all negative earthly experiences!

We interpret our world through our own senses and experiences, and we unknowingly have inside of us thousands upon thousands of "messages." Children raised in emotionally healthy family systems may be able to replay messages in their minds to recall valuable lessons their parents taught them. But children raised in emotionally unhealthy family systems may have messages that tell them, "You aren't lovable," "Something is wrong with you," "You're stupid," "You're fat," "You aren't good enough."

These messages are terribly shaming and destructive. For the adult child (shame-based child who is now grown up) who heard these messages, these words have the power to damage his or her entire perspective of love and relationships for a lifetime.

As we begin to face the wounds of our past, it can become difficult to realize that some of our behaviors, even if filled with good intentions, result from responding to these dysfunctional, shame-based childhood messages rather than the healthy foundations we had hoped to create. As we've wrapped ourselves externally in a package that seems to be acceptable and filled with good works, it can be unbelievably painful to realize that our efforts to fix, help, and compensate are rooted in our own pain, unmet love needs, internalized shame, and fears.

Most of these outward behaviors are driven by inward brokenness that occurs at a subconscious level. That means we don't intentionally live from this flawed system of love; somehow it has been recorded in our mind as the appropriate way of functioning in relationships, and we do it by default.

Characteristics of Unhealthy Love Systems

Unhealthy love systems all stem from the four false beliefs we looked at in an earlier chapter. Bestselling author Robert McGee presented these in his book entitled *The Search for Significance.*

- **The Performance Trap:** "I must meet certain standards to feel good about myself."
- **The Approval Addict:** "I must be approved of by certain others to feel good about myself."
- **The Blame Game:** "Those who fail (including myself) are unworthy of love and deserve to be punished."
- **Toxic Shame:** "I am what I am. I cannot change. I am hopeless."

Consider the Source

Many of us have at least heard the statement "like begets like," which means a member of one species will give birth to an offspring belonging to the same species. A cat cannot have a dog as an offspring. Similarly, a human soul cannot create a spiritual reality – within ourselves, in relationships, or life in general.

Unhealthy love stems from individuals -- bound to the four primary false beliefs -- attempting to experience healthy, unconditional, Christ-like relationships from a source that consists only of unhealthy, conditional, human love.

> "That which is born of the flesh is flesh, and that which is born of the Spirit is spirit" (John 3:6 ESV).

Within unhealthy love systems there are common internal shame-based factors that define those relationships:

- **Proving our worth.** Part of the obsession is in striving to convince other people we have value, goodness, and worth. In essence, we're saying, "Something is wrong with me, but I'm going to try to prove (to myself and other)] that I'm okay." Workaholics often fall into this pattern. Individuals with the Melancholy or Choleric temperaments often tend to align with this pattern. These two temperaments find their identity, worth, and value through the performing of tasks.

- **People pleasing.** There is often a tendency to be driven to please people, especially people who seemingly hold a place of importance in our life. In doing this, we give a great deal of power to another person. We believe we are only acceptable and worthy if we can somehow earn their approval. And as a result, our identity can never exceed the other person's perceptions of us. Individuals with the Supine or Sanguine temperaments often tend to align with this pattern. These two temperaments find their identity, worth, and value through the approval and acceptance of others.

- **Perfectionism.** We are often perfectionistic and hold ourselves to an extraordinarily high standard and must convince others we have it all down perfectly. We may equate one mistake with total failure, and become embarrassed, ashamed, or humiliated when people witness us making a mistake at any level. We must be strong, never let anyone down, and cannot show any sign of weakness. All five temperament types often align with this pattern, but each for different reasons: Melancholy: perfectionism is the standard of competence; Choleric: perfectionism is the standard for success; Sanguine: perfectionism is the standard for you to approve of me; Supine: perfectionism is the standard for you to accept me and not abandon me; and Phlegmatic: perfectionism is the standard in which I stand on, to prove why I don't need to commit the energy necessary to change.

- **Disassociation.** We eventually learn how to present an outward façade -- a "false self" -- while our inward life leaves us with a sense of being unknown, unseen, and unheard. Trapped within our own skin, a separation occurs that leaves us acting one way on the outside while feeling something altogether different within. It has left us vulnerable to making poor choices, allowing people to mistreat us, and participating in unhealthy situations, all while claiming our actions were done "in the name of love." Much as we examined above with perfectionism, disassociation takes on different faces dependent upon the individual's temperament: Melancholy: disassociating my internal fear of rejection from my external need to appear competent; Choleric: disassociating my internal fear of failure from my external need to be in control; Sanguine: disassociating my internal fear of disapproval from my external need to be liked, approved of, and loved; Supine: disassociating my internal fear of abandonment from my external need to be accepted; and Phlegmatic: disassociating my internal need to conserve energy from my external need to identify and stand against what is not right or just.

Is Self-Love Selfish?

Most of us who are reading this book struggle with seeing ourselves negatively at a core level, whether or not we are even aware of it. While we may have trouble loving ourselves, we become exceedingly self-reliant. This is called "pride." It is always self-centered, never God-centered.

If we can be totally honest with ourselves, we are often motivated by the need to self-protect, to get emotional needs met, and to control expectations, outcomes, or other people's behavior. Those are all self-serving motives and survival strategies that are independent of God and have pride at the root.

Pride is simply, "It's all about me." It is not necessarily feeling puffed up about ourselves. Pride also makes us compare ourselves with others, leaving us either "better than" or "less than" them. Pride causes us to see everything in life from our point of view, our needs, and our desires, and how the situations of life affect us.

Pride often is displayed in two forms. Both are driven by lack of true identity and self-worth, fear, and control.

- Self-promotion
- Self-protection

Admitting our selfishness is a vital key toward genuine change. It can lead to a true sense of brokenness, and the realization of our need for God to operate in our lives at a foundational level. When we are finally able to get ourselves out of the way and let God fully in, we will experience the type of self-love that leads to healthy relationship skills. God will teach us how to see Him, the world around us, and ourselves through His perspective.

Peter Scazzero, in his wonderful book entitled *Emotionally Healthy Spirituality: Unleash a Revolution in Your Life In Christ*, said this regarding the nature of healthy self-love:

> Jesus was not SELFLESS. He did not live as if ONLY other people counted. He knew his value and worth. He had friends. He asked people to help him. At the same time Jesus was not SELFISH. He did not live as if nobody counted. He gave his life out of love for others. From a place of loving union with his Father, Jesus had a mature, healthy true self.

Not seeing our true value in who we are in Christ doesn't mean we're "humble." By doing this, we're actually allowing ourselves to stay in that self-centered mindset. Without a Christ-centered attitude, we can continue to replay the old messages in our minds of what our parents or friends told us. We become bound by trying to overcome those negative perceptions of ourselves and become consumed with self; thus, providing the energy for the unhealthy cycle to continue.

Healthy Self-Love	Selfishness and Pride
I have the ability to accept the person God made me to be, with all my strengths and weaknesses.	I focus on myself and all my insecurities and flaws and believe everyone else is focusing on them too.
Since I am forgiven by God, I have the ability to forgive myself. I understand that "who I am" and "what I do" are entirely separate.	Since I haven't fully grasped God's forgiveness for me, I am unable to forgive others or myself. I feel I must pay the price for my actions or attempt to undo them independently. I feel my actions, or the actions of others against me, justify my sense of worthlessness.
I am able to recognize and embrace my skills, abilities, and authentic identity, knowing that everything I am is to be used for God's glory.	I am attempting to measure myself by the people around me, constantly searching to see whether I have enough to offer. I often feel either "too good" in some situations (self-promotion), or "not good enough" in other situations (self-protection).
I understand I have inherent worth, value, and ability to love and be loved based on my righteous standing in Christ Jesus, only through His shed blood on the cross.	I try to measure my worth by the things I do, the sense of accomplishment I attain, my efforts to fix people, and my own attempts to be "a good person."
I am dependent on Jesus Christ and I can do all things through Him.	I am dependent on myself, and others are dependent on me too.

Giving and Receiving Love

How many times have we tried to make an imbalanced relationship work? How many efforts to change other people have failed? In doing this, many of us bypassed the first two ingredients of God's system of love: Putting God's love first and loving ourselves. Since that left us empty and with so many needs, when we enter into a relationship, we put an enormous number of expectations on the relationship, as well as on the person or persons in the relationship. Not only do we expect it to satisfy our need for love and acceptance, unknowingly we expect it to replace God!

We are only intended to be conduits of God's love, not consumers of it. We looked at this in great detail in an earlier chapter. We don't have the capability to produce love on our own since it is a byproduct of God's Spirit. His love in us nourishes us and allows us the ability to properly give love away! It is life-giving, not because of the vessel that transports it, but because of the source that provides it.

Interdependent, Not Identity Dependent

God designed relationships to be fulfilling, satisfying, and mutually beneficial. He designed us to need each other and love each other to a degree, meaning we are created to be "interdependent" with others. In interdependence, we are connected and even intimate with those around us, but at no point do we lose our own identity. In interdependent relationships, we are not in a state of needing, but one of giving. When we link with others who are willing and ready to meet our needs, harmony, wholeness, and true agape love bind our hearts together. Our needs actually give others around us the opportunity to pour into us. Their needs allow us the same opportunity to pour into them.

We can only become true givers when we have God's love in us. Then we become carriers of that love, not consumers. We can offer it to others who need the same love, hope, and acceptance that God has given us.

Love Can Sometimes Be Difficult to Receive

Being on the receiving end of love can be very difficult for some of us, at times even humiliating. Some might rather go without than to have someone help meet their need.

Internalized shame and our self-reliant nature (pride) often finds it humiliating to receive others' gestures of love. Oddly, at the same time, we can be overly needy in other relationships. We might look for people to meet the needs that only God can fill. One of the sweetest and most satisfying experiences in life is being the receiver of true expressions of agape love.

Encountering Real Love

The way you love others right now is a direct reflection of your current belief system regarding love. It also reflects your love of God. God doesn't require us to share with others anything He hasn't already provided to us. Therefore, you can only love with God's agape love, in its true form, by receiving it first. We must learn what it means to walk by grace. Moment by moment, day by day, we need to focus on how God loves us, meditate on His promises to us, and establish a new foundation based entirely and only on Him.

As Paul teaches in Philippians 3:7-10, we convert our unhealthy love system to the love system God intends in the following ways:

- We must have our hearts broken to self, including self-efforts, self-benefit, and self-focus.
- We must realize our deep need for God to love and accept us, live in us, and receive His grace and forgiveness.
- We must discard our outward acts by which we try to prove our worthiness to self, others, and God.
- We must adopt a new system where we find our worthiness in Christ alone.
- We must personally identify with Jesus Christ in order to "know Him" and "be one with Him," including His sufferings, His death, and His resurrection power.

The radical, life-changing result of this is:

- We experience the type of love that will suffer and sacrifice for the benefit of someone else in order to accomplish the will of God and for them to experience the agape love of Jesus.
- We are able to die to self, including the selfish intents of our heart. Rest assured, we don't die to the authentic person God created us to be. That is our unique, inborn temperament.
- We are anointed with the power of the Holy Spirit to live our life through Him – this is the same power that resurrected Jesus Christ from the dead.

The truth of God's love means little or nothing in itself if we never activate it in our lives. We must receive it and open it like a gift before we can use it. We need a personal encounter with Jesus where He reveals truth to us. Without this, it's nearly impossible for what we know in our minds to be translated into what we deeply believe in our hearts. Lysa TerKeurst, another of my favorite authors, says in her book *Uninvited*:

> Only when we seek to apply God's revelations to our situations will we experience transformation. In this transaction, we must be able to stand before God and realize we are empty handed, bringing our "empty cup" and acknowledging in His presence that we need His love, even though we have nothing to give Him for it. We ask Him to do for us what we cannot do for ourselves.

We simply stand in His presence, allowing Him to mentor, guide, teach, counsel, instruct, nurture, comfort, and heal us. We don't do anything other than simply make ourselves available to Him and learn to trust and obey Him. We find that in Him, we become His love. This is the mystery of God, and it is the longing we all have in our hearts. This love then translates and spills over into our relationship with others and within ourselves.

The Test of Love

How can we identify the presence of authentic, agape love in our life? The Bible tells us that when it is operating in our lives properly, it will be evident (see 1 John 3:16-19; 4:9-21). These remarkable scriptures tell us that love is action oriented, not feeling oriented. They explain that we are to love just as Christ loves us – sacrificially – even if it hurts or costs us. When we truly find God's love, it transforms our heart. It helps us properly see ourselves through God's perspective, and eventually pours itself out to others.

Prayer to Find Authentic Love in Christ

Dear Father, I realize I've focused on myself and what I can do for You and others in order to make my life work. I realize now that I have little to offer apart from You. I also know that my life is about what You did for me when you saved me. And that You want to use me and work through me to touch others. I realize I have not always loved from a pure heart. I realize I don't always love myself. And I realize I often do not love You first. Apart from You, I am completely powerless to change. I acknowledge, confess, and repent of any negative love systems I have created in order to survive. I am ready to allow You to love me deeply and heal where I wasn't loved properly or was hurt by others. I embrace and receive the truth of Your love for me from today and forever more. In Jesus' name I pray, amen.

"Trust in the Lord with all your heart and lean not on your own understanding. In all your ways submit to Him, and He will make your paths straight."

Proverbs 3:5-6 NIV

SURRENDER

Turn Over Control to A Loving God

Introduction

No concept is harder for people to grasp than what it means to surrender. As sad as it sounds, many (if not most) Christians have never truly experienced the brokenness that leads to true surrender. The pathway to surrender is the pathway to experiencing and receiving God's love.

Our willingness to be broken of self, to realize our need for God, to receive God's forgiveness, and to enter into a new relationship with Him based on grace (not our effort) is what surrender is all about. Surrender is the doorway to a life of freedom.

- Some think of surrender as "what I have to give up." We associate surrender with defeat or loss. Yet surrender is an act of receiving and being able to give love. We realize, as we walk through the death of self, that "self" was an imposter preventing us from being the person God intended us to be.
- While salvation determines our eternal destiny, surrender affects the intimacy and connectedness of our relationship with Jesus. We could choose to live our lives for ourselves and never truly surrender, and if we have truly placed our faith in Jesus Christ alone, God would accept us as His children, nonetheless. What we would lose, however, would be our true purpose and identity while here on earth.

- We don't go through the process of surrender for any reason other than to become aware, to be able to repent, and to ask God to give us the power to change what needs to be changed. God has a better plan. We aren't just survivors; we are children of the one true God. To hunger for what God has in store for us, we must be willing to walk out in faith and conform our minds to God's mind and our wills to God's will.

A Soul That Is Surrendered, Not Just Saved

- **Perspective.** They filter their perspective through what Christ has done for them – they never want to take credit for the good things in their life.
- **Inner Peace.** They have indescribable peace within.
- **Joy.** They seem to have joy in the midst of challenging circumstances, and praise and thank God despite those circumstances.
- **Intimacy.** They speak to God and about God in an intimate and personal way.
- **Love.** They speak to others with love, showing grace and mercy to people who are struggling or hurting.

Surrender Requires Being Broken...

I'm sure we've all caught on by now that the entire focus and purpose of this book has been to help each of us uncover the brokenness in our lives, and to discover the true hope for a life of wholeness, fullness, and purpose found only in Jesus Christ.

Arriving at this point truly requires divine intervention. We need to both become broken of self and made aware of how much God truly loves us and has a plan for our lives. Some of us have reached this place, only to find ourselves taking back control. Others of us never really learned how to let go in the first place.

God is a giver and respecter of free will. He will not force Himself on anyone, nor will He make us submit our will to His. All of us, by our sinful flesh, are programmed to want to live independently of God.

There can be a huge wall of separation between knowing we need to depend on God, and actually transferring our trust to Him. There are several reasons why we have difficulty trusting God:

- Tainted parental experience may have clouded our perception of God.
- The term "father" could carry negative and emotional implications.
- We may not have ever taken the time to nurture a personal relationship with God, and simply don't know Him, His nature, and His character.
- We may have learned about God in a religious sense, and still see Him as someone who cares more about how we are breaking rules than about what concerns our heart.
- We may blame God for allowing circumstances to happen in our life.

Because God operates by a system of free will, He doesn't always interfere with the consequences of a human being's sinful choices. A God who is in control in one sense yet operating by a free will on the other hand can be difficult to comprehend.

We can't even begin to understand the world from God's perspective, so all we can depend on is the purity, the love, and the goodness of His character. We can rely on His word and trust that it is true. Here are some important things God says to us about the benefits of trusting Him:

"Trust in the Lord with all you heart and lean not on your own understanding. Submit to Him in all your ways, and He will make your paths straight" (Proverbs 3:5-6 NIV)

"It is better to take refuge in the Lord than to trust in humans" (Psalm 118:8 NIV).

"I love You Lord; You are my strength. The Lord is my rock, my fortress, and my savior; my God is my rock, in whom I find protection. He is my shield, the power that saves me, and my place of safety. I called on the Lord, who is worthy of praise, and He saved me from my enemies" (Psalm 118:1-3 NLT).

"But when I am afraid, I will put my trust in You. I praise God for what He has promised. I trust in God, so why should I be afraid? What can mere mortals do to me?" (Psalm 56:3-4 NLT).

"We are confident of all this because of our great trust in God through Christ. It is not that we think we are qualified to do anything on our own. Our qualification comes from God" (2 Corinthians 3:4-5 NLT).

"The Lord is a shelter for the oppressed, a refuge in times of trouble. Those who know your name trust in You; for You, O Lord, do not abandon those who search for You" (Psalm 9:9-10 NLT).

"Taste and see that the Lord is good. Oh, the joys of those who take refuge in Him! Fear the Lord, you His godly people, for those who fear Him will have all they need" (Psalm 34:8-9 NLT).

"Trust in the Lord and do good. Then you will live safely in the land and prosper. Take delight in the Lord, and He will give you your heart's desires. Commit everything you do to the Lord. Trust him, and He will help you" (Psalm 37:3-5 NIV).

... And Surrender Requires Trusting

Trusting in a God we cannot see requires faith (see Hebrews 11:1). For most of us, people have let us down or hurt us. Our ability to trust people in our earthly experience has been shattered. How could we possibly trust in a God we can't even see? Yet, we can trust in God because He is mightier, more powerful, and above everything that has gone wrong in our lives.

He despises the wrongs committed against us, but He has promised us redemption. He grieves over the sin and bondage in our heart – but He has a method of deliverance for us.

Dependence and Control

All forms of unhealthy dependence and control are the direct result of not trusting God. Anything other than God that captures our dependence can only lead us into bondage and further shame.

Self-Protection

Ultimately, all dependencies circle back to us attempting to control the areas of our lives where we have internalized the greatest shame-based fears. This inevitably leads to a singular focus on ourselves, most often in the various forms of self-protection.

- **Self-Dependence.** We may have learned that we ultimately needed to care for our own situations in life because other people were unavailable or incapable. Unknowingly, our operating system, or person we placed our trust in was self. Trusting in self is such a normal way of living. Most of us are unaware that something is even wrong with it. Self-effort, self-strength, self-attempts, self-sufficiency, self-security seem natural ways to function in everyday life for many of us.
- **Self-Protection.** A need to defend myself and my children from irresponsible or abusive people in my life, feeling it's up to me to maintain peace, control, and sanity in my house.
- **Self-Sufficiency.** A need to hold everything together in my life because I can't depend on others to help me.
- **Self-Righteousness.** A belief that "my way is right" and people should see and conform to that standard.
- **Self-Reliance.** A need to handle problems on my own because I don't have a support system I can trust.

- **Self-Made.** A need to work hard to become a good person, being proud of my effort to live a moral life and feeling disgusted with people who don't live by the same standards.
- **Self-Justice.** A need to find a sense of justice, often feeling that life and the injustices of others aren't fair and need to be "settled" correctly.
- **Self-Willed.** A belief that with enough willpower and strength, I can get myself through difficult times.

If we have extremely self-sufficient tendencies, we may have a difficult time trusting in anyone. If people were perceived to be untrustworthy in our lives, self-sufficiency became a means of survival. Because we feel the need to manage life, we bear a tremendous amount of stress and pressure from basically believing we must pick up the slack where God is falling short.

We may suffer physical problems because we neglect self-care. We may have other addiction issues such as alcohol, eating disorders, perfectionism. All compulsive behaviors are a passionate, obsessive need to maintain control. A vicious cycle of self-expectation and survival techniques drives us to carry the weight of the world on our shoulders. At some point, if we will finally allow our "self" to die and Christ to reign in our lives, we will find the most tremendous relief from burdens we could imagine – namely, the sufficiency of Christ.

Unhealthy Dependencies

Every human being is created with a dependent need within their soul. Certainly, some temperament combinations lend themselves to being more dependent than others. But none of us is exempt from being born with an inner nature of dependency. Even those of us who might see ourselves as strong or in control are dependent upon people and circumstances aligning with our efforts to exert our will over them.

The real heart-level issue is not whether we are dependent or not. It is the question of whom we are placing our dependency on.

- **People Dependence.** Dependent people overly latch onto the significant people in their lives, believing their own security rests on those people. They go to great measures to find stability in those relationships, believing they will satisfy their craving for love, security, and other emotional needs. Oftentimes, this individual will want dependence to be mutual in the relationship. In other words, they don't just seek dependence in a person. They feel secure in relationships where that same person is dependent on them in return. Although individuals with any combination of temperaments can become people dependent, those with the Supine temperament (as well as Sanguines who have been very soul wounded) are most often associated with this form of dysfunctional dependence.

- **Identity Dependence.** In an earlier chapter, I went into great length as to the prevalence of Identity Dependence in today's society. Different than People Dependence, Identity Dependence is a one-sided relationship, where the individual who is identity dependent believes they can only find their identity, worth, and value in the happiness, success, and approval of another individual. The Identity Dependent person is often willing to give up everything (or believe they have), just to please the other person. Identity Dependence is a dysfunctional tendency of any person whose life has not well answered the question, "Who am I?" Obviously, those individuals who have given the most of themselves away will be more apt to fall into this category, and these tend to be Sanguines and Supines.

- **Independence.** Although the least obvious of all forms of dysfunctional dependence, Independence is still a very real obstacle to trusting God (or conversely, a very real result of our unwillingness to trust God). As opposed to having unhealthy needs to be dependent upon the connection or approval of others, as we see in People Dependence and Identity Dependence, individuals who struggle with Independence believe that they need no one for anything at any time. They tend to not even like people, unless they will contribute to the independent person's needs for accomplishment or achievement. The two temperaments most often associated with this form of dependence dysfunctions are the Melancholy (depend only on themselves for competence and accomplishment), and the Choleric (depend only on themselves for control and achievement.

We Are to Be Christ-Dependent

Where dependency on anything or anyone exists, the person or thing that meets the need of the dependent gains power over that person, and in a way, becomes the person's god.

In our relationships with God, dependency on Him places Him in the position of power. This is good – He should be granted that position of power and authority. Scripture teaches in the Ten Commandments that we should have no gods before (meaning above or in front of) the one true God (see Deuteronomy 5:6).

By allowing ourselves to become dependent upon someone or something other than God, we allow them to become an idol in our lives; taking the place on the throne that rightfully belongs to Jesus. Unknowingly, we are giving power to whoever holds that position to answer these three fundamental questions:

- Who am I?
- Am I acceptable?
- Am I enough?

We have conditioned ourselves to believe that whatever answer they communicate into our hearts and minds must be true. And we build and live our lives accordingly. No human being should have that power in our lives!

We often see this in the lives of shame-based adults who continue to allow the past (and sometimes present) words, actions, reactions, opinions, and perceptions of their parents to dominate their lives -- every moment of every day, year after year. By doing this, we are keeping our human parents on the "throne" of our lives, while keeping Jesus on the sideline. Anything or anyone other than Jesus whom we give the power to define our identity, worth, and purpose is considered an idol (see Exodus 20:3-4).

Ask God to give you the courage and inner security to "dethrone" your parents, and allow them to become real, ordinary, imperfect human beings just as we are. This is the only way to allow room for Jesus to be on the throne of our lives.

"Am I now trying to win the approval of human beings, or of God? Or am I trying to please people? If I were still trying to please people, I would not be a servant of Christ" (Galatians 1:10 NIV).

Dependence in Relationships

Some forms of dependence are appropriate. For example, children are to be dependent on parents until adulthood. In a similar way, husbands are to shepherd the needs of his wife and children. So where do we draw the line? How can we establish when healthy and authoritative dependence is in place, or when dependence has become unhealthy?

To answer this question, we must turn to God's word. First, we must look at how God relates to us, His children. We know He is in a position of authority yet continues to respect our free will. He wants a relationship with us based on mutual love and submission, not force, coercion, or control.

As each of us look at our own personal life situation, we have to evaluate the fruits of the dependent relationship in order to determine whether it is healthy or dysfunctional. It is very appropriate to **depend on** other human beings in our life. However, it becomes unhealthy when we are **dependent upon** another person. Dependence implies that our health and wholeness are in the hands of another individual. The exception to this is when an individual is limited by some form of emotional or physical condition, handicap, or disability that compels them to be dependent upon others for their wellbeing. Healthy dependent relationships reflect the love of Jesus and promote an environment that fosters the well-being of each individual's body, soul, and spirit.

Dysfunctional Independent/Dependent Relationships

Dysfunctional dependence will always be defined by "dichotomous" characteristics, which actually damage relationships and inhibit trust and connectedness. The term "dichotomous" basically identifies entities that exist in opposition, seemingly irreconcilable in their differences.

Although the traits of the "independent" and the "dependent" I've listed below can be understood through each individual's inborn temperament, those in healthy relationships refuse to allow their temperament needs, strengths, or weaknesses to become an excuse for their attitudes or behaviors that elevate themselves at the expense of others.

Independent	Dependent
Controlling	Feels controlled
Correct or right	Never or rarely right
Competent	Less than competent
Perfectionist	Imperfect
Social	Shy or backward
Stubborn	Rebellious
Proactive	Reactive
Decision-making	Weak-willed
Achieving	Procrastinator
Exciting	Boring
Responsible	Cautious

As we've discovered since the very first page of this book, intra- and inter-personal wellbeing is found within the paradox of two seemingly opposites, not in one extreme or the other. God wants us to pursue that uncertain place where a healthy tension/balance exists between two opposing positions. That is where His ways are found.

Control in Relationships

Unhealthy dependency and control go hand-in-hand. Most dependencies, by definition, have an ultra-need to control people and circumstances, both often being expressed subconsciously. Even if we are obviously and purposefully attempting to control people and circumstances, we may actually believe it's our job to do so! We may even be the recipient of someone else's harsh control over us and use our own control in much more subtle ways in an effort to cope and survive.

All forms to control apart from that of the Holy Spirit are tools

of the enemy. Control stands in complete opposition to the godly characteristics of free will. Whenever we use control to get people to respond or behave in a certain way, it is evidence that the relationship lacks the understanding of true agape love. In reality, our need to control seeks to satisfy self, and people become a means to that end, whatever it may be. Like a childhood playground bully, control is always a reflection of an inward feeling of low value and worth.

Regardless the person's specific motive behind the need to control, it is always a result of not trusting God above all else. Wherever control exists, relationships cannot grow or thrive. In fact, the interpersonal connection is destined to some form of death: emotional or spiritual.

The Cycle of Control

There is a cycle that inevitably emerges in relationships where control exists. It begins with "controlling influence," where one individual attempts to control the entire atmosphere. The person focuses on their own needs, and abusive behaviors – whether physical, mental, relational, emotional, or spiritual – typically dominate the home.

In response to the controlling influence, members of that family system respond through what author Stephanie Tucker refers to as "counter-controlling." This person learns to "read" or anticipate the needs and emotional problems of those around them so they can respond appropriately. This is typically either an attempt to protect self, to indirectly assure that their needs get met, or both. Since this became a normal pattern of survival in childhood, the individual doesn't know any other way. Therefore, this pattern is repeated in adult relationships. Life is governed by either feeling controlled by someone or counter-controlling to get what is needed to survive.

Passive, Subtle Forms of Control

- **Feelings**. Attempts to control someone else's feelings or protect someone from bad feelings. The faulty belief is that "I have the power to manage your feelings."

- **Perceptions.** Attempts to control the way a person perceives, likes, or responds to us. The faulty belief is that "I have the ability to control how you perceive me."
- **Righteousness.** Strictly follows rules and moral behavior in hopes of gaining a sense of goodness, thus feeling superior to people who are perceived as "bad." The faulty belief is that "I am better than you."
- **Judging.** Uses subtle comments that include backhanded comments, sarcasm, and guilt-giving statements. The faulty belief is that "If I make you feel bad about yourself, I can cause you to change."
- **Dishonesty.** Exaggerates or tells lies to maintain a reputation or be perceived more positively. The faulty belief is that "It's okay for me to not tell the whole truth if it causes you to think better of me or to not get angry with me."
- **Entitlement.** Uses flattery or gifts to buy the affection or approval of someone else. The faulty belief is that "I deserve your acceptance because of all that I've done for you."
- **Reciprocity.** Tries to earn love by doing anything they think would cause someone else to love them. The faulty belief is that "I can earn your love and approval by pleasing you with what I do and say."

Passive control is extremely difficult to recognize when it has been etched into a person's character from a young age. All passive forms of control are expressed through various forms of manipulation, which can be very artful and disguised. The use of guilt and shame specifically tends to be learned through the family of origin. Influencing people and getting them to act the way we want them to act becomes a learned relationship skill.

Prayer to Let Go and Trust God

Father, I realize that I struggle with trusting You. Please forgive me and change me. Your word contains endless descriptions of who You are and how much You love me. I am declaring these truths in Your word as the activating power in my life. I desire to be set free from anything and everything that I am clinging to other than You. Teach me, Lord, to believe what Your word says and to transfer my trust to You. Teach me, Father, to surrender to You. I want to live the life that You designed for me to live. I don't want to waste another minute clinging to anything that will not lead me toward that life.

Please, Lord, have your way in my life. I need You right now. I realize I cannot manage my life without you. I see my self-dependency and my dependency on other people. I have tried to change people and fix their problems. I have carried the weight of the world on my shoulders. I have tried to control and dominate my world. I realize now that it isn't my job, and the journey from here on out is determined by my willingness to let You change me -- my mind, will, and emotions.

I ask You, Lord, to reveal or remove anything that might be hindering me from coming to You. I want to become like a child, willing to be led by You. Parent me, nurture me, guide and keep me in Your care. Enter into my heart at any point of need right now. Be not only my Savior, but also the Master and Father over my life.

Please change me from the inside out! Heal me where I'm wounded and love me where I've been hurt, bruised, and broken. If I don't see or understand my needs right now, please patiently reveal them to me. Thank you for Your goodness and Your grace. I release my tight grasp on my life, and instead put my hand in Yours. In Jesus name I pray, Amen.

God's desire in your life is to restore you to the person He created you to be, and to teach you how to love others in the same way He loves you.

Questions from Dr. Dave

For personal reflection or group discussion of Chapter 13

In what ways did you enter adulthood with fundamental needs unmet within you? Have you been open and honest about these, or have you stuffed them away and remained in denial of the effect they may have had on you? How has this affected your ability to love and trust God? Has it caused you to struggle in creating meaningful, intimate relationships with others? In what areas of your life has denial of the shame or brokenness within you hindered your ability to love and accept yourself? Are you ready to work on this?

In this chapter, I explained many of the forms of love found in the Bible. Although every one of these are created by God and are good, only unconditional agape love reflects the true nature of Jesus. What about agape love is hard for you to get your mind around? Have you ever experienced a love like that? Are you willing to? What barriers exist in your heart and mind that may need removed to allow God's love to come in? Have you tried to love others with a love you don't possess yourself? Now is the time to change that. Commit to allow God's love to melt the walls of fear, shame, and brokenness that have hardened your heart in the past.

Surrender requires being broken – broken of our own mind, will, emotions, and beliefs. What do you fear when you consider letting go and trusting God fully? What do you most have to lose? to gain? Upon whom or what have you misplaced your dependence? Can you see now how lack of surrender and misplaced dependence have contributed to patterns of control in your life? Ask God to reveal what He specifically wants you to let go of.

CHAPTER 14

Phase 2: U – Uncover Lies and False Beliefs of My Past

"Throw off your old sinful nature and your former way of life, which is corrupted by lust and deception. Instead let the spirit renew your thoughts and attitudes. Put on your new nature, created to be like God – truly righteous and holy."

Ephesians 4:22-24 NLT

ROLES

Turn from My Unhealthy False Identity

Introduction

We all grew up with families, relationships, and experiences that played a part in our sense of identity and set rules for life that have remained with us throughout adulthood.

While growing up with these unique windows of perspective, we knew only what we were taught, and automatically assumed it was right and true.

- As children, we were born with a "fantasy bond" to our biological parents. We believed subconsciously that our parents represented the ideal for all areas of our lives.
- As we approached adulthood, we still lived our lives based on those acquired beliefs. What we did seemed to simply be a byproduct of who we had become, whether it was right or wrong.
- Some of us, though, reached a point where we realized that the foundational ways we believe, think, feel, behave, and live in our relationships are causing us pain.
- This common struggle affirms in us that we aren't alone, and that it is okay to step out and pursue this journey with God.

Responses to A Shame-Based Childhood

Having been raised in a shame-based family brings out certain behaviors and patterns that are very abnormal, but necessary for survival. Historically, the name for this has been "codependence." But, as presented in an earlier chapter, I have renamed this "identity dependence," which is much more reflective of its true meaning. When children of such a home become adults, they frequently feel worthless and have great difficulty with close, intimate relationships. The tremendous emotional scars inflicted upon children growing up in dysfunctional, shame-based homes lead directly to relationship discord, emotional depression, vocational instability, and overall life dissatisfaction in adulthood.

Characteristic behavior traits and attitudes plague these individuals. In Chapter 3, I outlined Identity Dependence in great detail, and have re-presented a number of the most common of these here. These dysfunctional tendencies begin in childhood and continue into adulthood, and might include:

- Difficulty knowing what "normal" is.
- Difficulty completing projects or tasks.
- Exaggerate or lie compulsively, even when there is no need to.
- Are overly critical of themselves.
- Take themselves too seriously, and have difficulty having fun.
- Struggle with intimate relationships.
- Have a great need for control in their lives and become frustrated or angry when this cannot be achieved.
- Have a lifelong need for approval and affirmation.
- Have a feeling of being different from other people.
- Are overly responsible or overly irresponsible, or possibly both at the same time.
- Have extreme loyalty, even when unwarranted.
- Have frequent impulsive behavior, which only aggravates the existing problems.
- Believe a relationship with a significant other will fill the inner longing for love.

- Depend on relationships with emotionally unavailable people to meet their needs.
- Bound in relationships by performance (what I do) rather than core value and worth (who I am).
- Overly caring for others at the neglect of self-needs.
- Have difficulty saying "no".
- Tolerate mistreatment from others, while justifying their behavior and defending them.
- Cover up for irresponsible people in life by lying or filling in their gaps.
- Do for others what they should be doing for themselves.
- Attempt to protect others from emotional pain or the consequences of their unhealthy behaviors.
- Attempt to fix, manage, or control another person's life, often with the best of intentions.
- Have an overwhelming need to please people.
- Drawn to people who need help, yet have difficulty receiving help form others.
- Compromise personal belief systems to please another person, or in hopes of getting personal needs met.
- Fear being alone, or withdraw out of fear of close relationships, or both.

Shame-Based Family Roles

Within "dysfunctional" families, there are several roles that typically emerge. No one signs up for these. Individuals just move into them during the course of life in this family. And usually in an attempt to emotionally survive the toxic environment.

These roles are generally not healthy, but are, in a sense, necessary for survival. Bradshaw describes this dynamic like a mobile, the childhood toy suspended over a baby's crib, with multiple characters circling around a central point. If one character is removed, the entire mobile becomes out of balance and disabled.

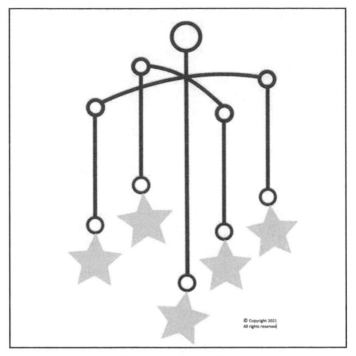

Child's Crib Mobile

Metaphorically, every member of a shame-based, dysfunctional system will do whatever necessary to exert his or her influence to restore normalcy back to the system. Consider these most common roles:

- **Dependent.** This individual is the one whom every other family member "dances" around. They are "dependent" on everyone else participating in their game, even though they may be the only one not aware that a game is even being played. They may be addicted, alcoholic, suffering from PTSD, angry, abusive, workaholic, manipulative, or just very strong-willed. They may be a parent or stepparent, or sometimes even a child. Regardless, they are the center point and creator of the emotional life of the entire home and family. Their life is motivated largely by a sense of shame and inadequacy. They tend to live in denial of the seriousness of their problem, denial of the impact their problems inflict on members of the family system, and denial of the inevitable downward course of their own lives and relationships.

- **Enabler.** A key member of the dependent's immediate family usually undertakes this role. Also sometimes referred to as the caretaker or rescuer, the enabler feels compelled to try, at all costs, to decrease the chaos and fear the dependent is producing. However, in doing so, this individual only helps perpetuate the dysfunction. Without the enabler, it would be difficult, if not impossible, for the dependent to continue in their role. There are four typical patterns enablers employ in an effort to cope with and control the behaviors of the dependent. The "sufferer" may suffer from many ailments, taking on the role of a victim or martyr, hoping to change the dependent's behavior by showing how much they are being hurt by them. The "punisher" may try to change the dependent by making their life absolutely miserable. The "controller" attempts to control the dependent's shaming behaviors by monitoring, supervising, and controlling every aspect of the dependent's life. And the "waverer" seems to ride a roller coaster in their relationship with the dependent: one moment attempting to control or force the dependent to change, then the very next moment totally giving up due to exhaustion in trying to bring about change.

- **Family Hero.** This is the individual who believes that somehow, directly or indirectly, he or she is responsible for the dependent's situation. By achieving, in whatever form, this individual believes they may help reverse the problems and make the dependent feel better (or love them, or come back home, or whatever). The characteristic behavior of this family member is overachievement.

- **Scapegoat.** The scapegoat in the shame-based family feels damaged or inferior, often recalling experiences of having been victimized or disadvantaged by other family members. Because of this, this person may decide that attention for being "bad" is better than no attention at all. The scapegoat's defense against emotional pain is in the form of substitution. This person will substitute almost anything that can be found as relief for the pain of believing they're "a loser," regardless how unhealthy that choice may be.

- **Lost Child.** This family member withdraws from the family in a quiet way, but not in an openly defiant way as the scapegoat does.

Loneliness is the most common feeling of the lost child, who is often quiet and passive. This individual is willing to "go with the flow" as a result of their feelings of powerlessness. They will resort to emotional and physical retreat as a defense against the painful events occurring in the home. They tend to create their own little world where tranquility can be enforced.

- **Mascot.** The mascot is the family clown or joker. They fear that the chaos at home will suddenly reach a boiling point and explode, the thought of which scares them to death. This uneasiness causes them to use humor and superficiality as a diversion to cheer up the dreary and depressing atmosphere. When carried into adulthood, this often results in emotional immaturity. They are loved by all but known by none!

- **Golden Child.** This individual is often found within families who have a parent or parents with narcissistic tendencies. The narcissist will tend to favor this child, as they represent all of the characteristics that parent loves about themselves. Despite being the "favorite," this child has difficulty finding their own identity separate from that of the narcissistic parent. They also may relate to others in the home in ways similar to the parent, in order to be seen on the "correct side" of situations.

Breaking the Cycle of Dysfunction

Through our own journey of restoration in Christ, we can alter the harmful ways we have engaged in these patterns. Breaking dysfunctional cycles doesn't always come easy. And when we begin this journey of life change, others may initially resent it and not understand. Remember, true change occurs only at the heart level. That's why just attempting to change external behaviors always eventually fails and leads to further frustration and discouragement.

In order for lasting heart change to occur, the key is to understand that our ultimate purpose is first to be in relationship with God, and then to have healthy and whole relationships with others. In that pursuit, the TURN process will guide us toward these objectives:

- Identify the key problems in our beliefs, thoughts, and actions.
- Explore the origins of our dysfunctions and trace them back to their root sources.
- Learn what God intended for our lives, both personally and in relationships.
- Overcome the negative effects of shame with the love of Jesus and the truth of God's word.
- Embrace the authentic purpose and identity for which we were created.

As you continue to diligently and faithfully work through this journey toward wholeness in Christ, you will begin to see these five elements realized in your life. As I've heard it said in many traditional recovery meetings, "It works if you work it!"

Prayer to Overcome Our False Identity and Dysfunctional Roles

Dear Father, I'm on this journey from brokenness to wholeness because I realize that something isn't working in my life. I often feel detached, broken, and empty, all the while seemingly being engaged and in a role of "helping" others, being under control, and having to hold things together. It's so confusing. It seems I'm doing the right thing, yet at the same time, something feels fundamentally wrong in my life and relationships. Please Lord, help me. Show me Your truth but offer it under the power and kindness of Your unconditional love toward me. Give me the faith and patience to allow You to make me new and offer me hope that this journey will lead me into Your abiding joy and peace. In Jesus name I pray, Amen.

"I, the Lord your God, am a jealous God, punishing the children for the sins of their parents to the third and fourth generation of those who are disobedient to me, but showing love to a thousand generations of those who love me and keep my commandments."

Deuteronomy 5:9-10 NIV

FAMILY

Turn from Any Dysfunctional Influences of My Family-Of-Origin

Introduction

Every one of us has been deeply influenced by our family system of origin. Whether they displayed healthy or unhealthy characteristics, the environment and people who raised us, as well as the experiences that occurred within that system, had an incredible effect on the formation of our character in adulthood.

We absorb the very patterns of behavior, belief systems, and relationship skills that were modeled to us, thus affecting every aspect of our adult lives.

- No matter what our earthly experience is or has been, we have a loving heavenly Father who seeks to "parent" us in His truth.
- Since He is the creator of the family system, He has the ability to supersede anything negative or toxic that we've experienced – if we allow Him to.

God's Intention for The Family

Just like human beings, God desired a family of His own to care for, love, and bestow His provisions and blessings upon. In fact, all of us were created for God's pleasure, to be loved, and to learn to give His love to others. The heart of God is depicted clearly through His creation of the family.

On earth, the purpose of the family was designed to provide a safe haven where love, security, and well-being allow for the healthy physical, emotional, mental, and spiritual growth of each member, especially the children. The family was intended to train its members for the "battlefield" of life. Children are to use the home, above any outside influence, to gain skills, to deal with emotions, to learn how to experience relationships, and to learn how to love. This special institution is meant to be a place of rest and safety amidst a world filled with troubles and pressures. It's a place where we are meant to experience intimacy and find acceptance.

Understanding the Very First Family

Before we seek to understand the family in our own life, it is important to know that we were at a disadvantage coming into the world. We inherited dysfunctional family skills from our forefathers, and we have been bound by their toxic results ever since. This simply means that, like it or not, our families will have imperfections.

The history of the first family helps us accurately identify our own challenges within our family systems. Eve's choice to disobey God's simple commandment that she was not to eat from one particular tree in the garden wasn't just a mistake. She chose to believe and trust that what Satan had told her was true, and that what God had told her was not. Not only that, but as she unseated God's position of authority in her life, she then opened the door for her husband to do the same. Adam's sin wasn't just that he disobeyed God, but that he allowed himself to be influenced by his wife through a lie that she had been told. In essence, Adam gave her permission to be in a position of authority over himself and God. His inability to stand up to her in the name of truth cost him dearly. Regardless of Eve's choices or actions, God held Adam responsible for the sin of them both because God had appointed Adam the leader of that family relationship.

The Consequences of Sin

We examined this very topic in great detail earlier in this book. But now, at this point -- where our journey is moving from general to personal – each of us has to look at ourselves in the mirror and consider sin through the lens of our own lives.

The fall in the garden meant that our fellowship with God had been broken, and the original plan for mankind was forever lost. Adam and Eve would now begin to seek to fill that void improperly, continually heeding other enticements. They would also no longer have the resources necessary to make their relationship work because those resources were based directly on their union with God.

Sin would leave a plague and bring pain to the family system from there on out. While not a popular teaching, God did in fact place a curse on the gender roles as consequences of the disobedience of Adam and Eve.

- **The male** was cursed to work the fields, which meant he would bear the burden of responsibility for working and financially supporting his family. This sense of responsibility would extend to more than just the material needs of the family. He would ultimately be responsible for creating an environment where all of their needs could be met: Spiritual, emotional, intellectual, physical, and social.

- **The female** was cursed to painful childbearing, and her now fallen nature would "desire" the love of her husband but would simultaneously resent his authority over her. As a result, she would place expectations on her male counterpart as a measurement of his "worthiness" to lead, and she would take the reins if he didn't measure up.

The irony of the two curses is that they portray the very heart of the breakdown we see occurring in many family systems in the twentieth and twenty-first century society that we've all lived in. The husband rebels against his gender role by being irresponsible and abandoning his family, or just the opposite, by working and being away from the family too much. The wife rebels against her gender role by trying to gain power over her husband, or by expecting him to ideally meet all her needs, or both.

As a result, children would inherit a fallen sin nature and be born in the world separated from God. As we've studied throughout this book (specifically in our key passage from Deuteronomy 5), the consequences of sin always extend to future generations. We inherited the curse of sin. Furthermore, we inherited the damage attached to the consequences of sin. This effect is called "toxic shame."

This means **we cannot possibly get it right or live without negative results, simply because we are human**. And our parents couldn't have either!

The Most Profound Paradox

You know by now how much I thoroughly enjoy examining things through the perspective of paradox -- two seemingly opposite or self-contradictory statements that, when further explored, carry greater substance than either statement would if standing alone. As we look at and seek to understand our own family systems, we must be consciously aware of the two juxtaposed realities:

- **Man's fallen nature**, inborn with the curse of sin.
- **God's redemption**, by grace through faith in Jesus Christ.

As each of us are able to deepen our understanding of the co-existent tension of these two realities, we will gain an entirely new perspective of:

- The beauty of how God perceives and loves us as His children.
- The humble view God wants us to have of ourselves.
- The heart of grace and mercy we extend to others.

> "The Lord has told you what is good, and this is what He requires of you: Do what is right, love mercy, and walk humbly with God" (Micah 6:8 NLT).

God's Intention for The Family

> "Unless the Lord builds the house, the work of the builders is wasted" (Psalm 127:1 NLT).

If we visualize God's perfect home, we will see a delightful place of rest, solace, love, peace and fulfillment. It will be comprised of individual family members working in their God-ordained positions to fulfill the purpose and plan for the family. If a home is operating in God's order, some distinct characteristics are bound to appear:

- **Jesus Christ** will be placed at the foundation as a real person who is given the ability to be sovereign and in control. Therefore, His love and power will affect all aspects of life.
- **Grace** will permeate the family's environment. Family members will be allowed to safely expose their faults and weaknesses without risk of rejection. Value, acceptance, and core worth will be instilled into all members as a result.
- **Unconditional love** will be present based on God's love working its way through each family member. This means there are no strings attached and no necessary tasks to perform to earn love.
- **The heart** will be emphasized more than behaviors. Children will be understood to be precious, valuable, and loved, no matter what they do, and despite any discipline that may be necessary. The governing values of the home will be grace and forgiveness, as opposed to performance and approval.
- **Roles and responsibilities** will be clearly defined and understood, allowing each family member to take responsibility for his or her own actions, and allowing others to take responsibility for theirs.
- **Boundaries** will be clearly stated, defining what is and what is not acceptable. When boundaries are broken, consequences will be enforced to make it clear that the breach of that boundary was unacceptable.
- **Communication** is real, open, and honest. All family members are allowed to express real feelings and share the challenges of life.
- **Consistency** will exist day to day, promoting a safe and secure environment for everyone.

When these characteristics are in place in a family system, several positive benefits will result, including:

- **Peace.** Security, peace, and joy are at the foundation.
- **Serving.** Family members genuinely desire to submit to and serve one another.
- **Freedom.** The home has a spirit of freedom that allows everyone the opportunity to succeed and fail.
- **Boundaries.** The development of healthy boundaries offers the opportunity to learn values of self-discipline and submission to authority.
- **Self-esteem.** Healthy self-esteem is formed where children are able to find their unique personalities, gifts, and identities in Christ.
- **Maturity.** The maturity process is nurtured, and healthy growth takes place spiritually, emotionally, and physically.

The purpose of understanding God's blueprint for the family isn't to evaluate how we may have failed, or how our parents may have failed us. It is actually to understand His design and purpose for the family – which are expressions of His heart. This means that above anything else, we can peer into our Heavenly Father's desire to relate to us.

Men's and Women's God-given Responsibilities to Their Family

We all come into the world helpless, dependent and needing love, worth, and belonging.

Since a family system is composed of individual members, we can trace a family's dysfunction back to the individual members of the family and the roles they perform within that system. Most important are the roles of the adults – the husband and the wife – and how they fulfill their roles in relation to their children as father and mother.

Men and women need to have an understanding of our God-given relational roles, regardless of our marital status. We are all married to God and are members of His family, so being healthy and whole within a love relationship and family system is an important element of soul health for every one of us.

The Biological Father

Every human being is born with an inner longing to be united with our heavenly Father. This is called a "father hunger," which exists at the deepest part of our human soul – the heart. To a child's heart, their earthly, biological father is the most real and accurate representation of the only one who can fill this God-shaped void within them.

Questions That Only Our Father Can Answer

The enormous array of life messages that our subconscious mind interprets cause our hearts to unknowingly answer these three foundational questions:

- **Identity** – "Who am I?"
- **Significance** – "Am I acceptable?"
- **Worth** – "Am I enough?"

Through childhood, whether our birth fathers are present or absent, Christian or atheist, loving or rejecting, aware or oblivious, they still communicate clear, indelible, life-altering answers to these profound questions within us.

A man who, for example, got the child's mother pregnant in a one-night stand, still communicated succinct answers to the questions in the child's soul. His glaring absence communicated to his child: "You're a mistake." "You're an accident." "I don't accept you." "You're not important enough for me to want to be your father."

Whether a child was raised without any father figure at all, or if a stepfather, foster father, or grandfather took the place of his father, his soul will always experience an incessant longing to be loved, accepted, and approved of by <u>his biological father</u>. Until this yearning is quenched by the unconditional love of the heavenly father, this adult-child will continue on their quest for their father's validation, even after the father is deceased.

Fantasy Bond with Father

The more painful the experience of abandonment (and re-abandonment), the more idealized the child's view of his would-be father becomes. This is called a "fantasy bond," which is a perfect illustration of the Equal and Opposite Principle we learned about in an earlier chapter.

Somewhat regrettably, I can still recall this from my own childhood. My parents divorced when I was just seven years old. In today's world that doesn't seem like such a huge thing. But in 1968, it was earth-shattering – and little-boy-shattering as well.

My dad moved away to another town (with another woman who became my stepmom) without telling me why he was leaving, where he was going, and what my future was going to look like without him.

Even as I'm writing this, I can still feel the sadness, loneliness, and longing for my dad. He made bad decisions. He divorced my mom. He abandoned my family. He left me to grow up in near-poverty without him. He missed every meaningful part of my growing-up years. But through all of that, he was somehow still my hero, and the one I longed to love me, accept me, and approve of me. I can't even begin to tell you the amount of time, effort, creativity, and energy I put into all types of "performing," all with the hope of somehow bringing my dad's love back to my heart. In some strange way, that quest continues even today, even though my dad has been deceased for several years.

As I experienced puberty and entered adolescence with the unresolved fantasy that my dad would someday "un-abandon" me, I unknowingly created a pattern of acting out in my relationship with my mom. In my mind I knew that she was the one who never left me, and continued to raise me, clothe me, feed me, and support me. Yet somewhere in my unawareness, my feelings toward her devolved to the point that, when I was in high school, I didn't really like to be with her. In my conscious mind, I very much loved her and appreciated her and respected her. But somewhere within me, I resented her and felt like she had stood between me and my dad.

Equal and Opposite: Abandonment | Enmeshment

In Greek mythology there is a centuries-old story of a young man named Oedipus. In the early 1900s, Sigmond Freud grabbed hold of this metaphorical example of an adolescent child's relationship with his parents and referred to it as the "Oedipus Complex."

Not one for secular psychology, or Greek mythology for that matter, it would be a stretch for me to agree with Freud's projection that this so-called complex is an actual dysfunction within a human's inborn nature. However, I do believe the story from ancient mythology can offer us a perspective on this unique parent-child relationship dynamic.

In the myth, the boy-become-young-man Oedipus, found himself in a quandary. Through his childhood, his mother had become overly dependent on him for her emotional needs. Unwittingly, Oedipus had become emotionally enmeshed to his mother as a woman, when what he really needed was to be maternally loved by her as his mother. In the absence of emotional intimacy with her husband, the mother's son Oedipus became a substitute for her emotional needs.

As Oedipus grew to manhood, he recognized his inner longing to be validated as a man by his father (as well as the other men). Yet he knew that to seek this would mean he would have to sever the unhealthy emotional connection with his mother.

Mythology would tell us that Oedipus ultimately killed his mother and pursued the affirmation and acceptance of his father. He entered manhood with his soul torn in two – carrying guilt for having "left" his mother, while experiencing a growing desire to be fully known by his father.

Many men in today's twenty-first century society were tragically over-mothered through their childhood. In some cases, this was due to unresolved shame-based fears within their mothers that caused them to cling to the love and intimacy of the boy they had birthed into this world. But in the majority of today's wounded men, it's not the mother's dysfunction, but the father's emotional or literal absence that leads to this unhealthy dynamic between mothers and their sons.

Regardless of the origin of the wound, God desires for men to find freedom for their souls to connect with their heavenly Father without them being bound to shame-based enmeshment with their mothers.

Father Wounds

We experience the **father wound** when our biological father communicates either unhealthy or insufficient answers to the three foundational questions above.

Through my years of counseling thousands of individuals, I've concluded that the complete absence of our birth father often leads to fewer and less traumatic soul wounds than does the ongoing presence of a toxic, shaming birth father in the child's life.

Regardless the reason for the birth father's complete absence – death, divorce, one-night stand, adoption, or death on the battlefield – the child-become-adult has some degree of finality (closure) in which to respond to emotionally.

In the case of a birth father who, to some degree, remains physically present throughout our childhood, an ongoing hope continues within us. We believe that if we could only perform in a way to gain his approval, our birth father would finally love us, accept us, and approve of us.

Re-Abandonment by Our Father

The repeated experience of abandonment by our father who is still in our lives leads to greater and greater compulsiveness. We are determined to do whatever it takes to one day gain his approval and acceptance. I call this phenomenon "re-abandonment," when the father moves in and out of the child's life either literally or emotionally.

Re-abandoning by our father can be experienced in many different ways, each causing us to internalize shame-based false beliefs. Our inborn temperament provides the lens in which each of us uniquely experiences the re-abandonment of our biological father. The way one child responds may be significantly different than the response of siblings.

Here are several common examples of the pain of re-abandonment. Although they are most shaming to a child, these same messages can also be internalized by the wife of a man who is emotionally and spiritually unhealthy. Simply substitute the word "husband" in place of the word "father" in these examples:

- **Neglect** – "I wish my father would see me and know me."
- **Workaholic** – "I must not be as important as my father's work."
- **Anger** – "My father is always angry because of me."
- **Abuse** – "I must deserve what my father is doing to me."
- **Criticism** – "I'm not good enough for my father."
- **Disapproval** – "I have to earn my father's approval."
- **Control** – "I'm powerless in my relationship with my father."
- **Withholding** – "I'm unworthy of my father's love."
- **Invalidation** – "It's because something is wrong with me."
- **Rejection** – "I'm not enough for my father."
- **Shamelessness** – "I want to be just like my father."

Bound by Performance and Approval

The uncertainly caused by our biological father's re-abandonment traps us in a perpetual "performance-abandonment" cycle that adds shame upon shame upon shame to the child's heart.

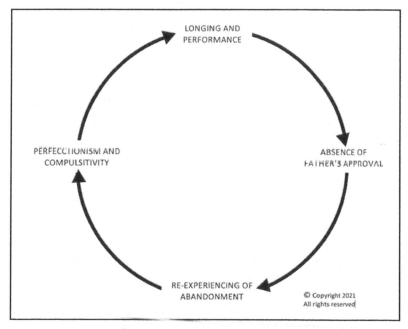

LONGING AND PERFORMANCE

ABSENCE OF FATHER'S APPROVAL

RE-EXPERIENCING OF ABANDONMENT

PERFECCTIONISM AND COMPULSITIVITY

Performance-Abandonment Cycle

The effect of father wounds always results in low self-esteem, a deep emotional pain inside, and a performance orientation that makes us a "human doing" rather than a "human being." While salvation in Christ makes us a new creation, it does not necessarily address the woundedness inside. Only our perfect heavenly Father has the ability to do that!

How Fathers Often Miss It

- **Love and affection**. Instead of focusing on loving his wife, he is on the receiving end of her love toward him, anticipating her to be the initiator and pursuer. Then he justifies his anger when she falls short in meeting his needs.
- **Protection.** Instead of protecting, he controls the members of his family in a dictatorial fashion, whereby he threatens them, abuses them, or instills fear in them. He becomes the one his family needs protected from.
- **Leadership**. Instead of leading, he avoids his responsibility and allows his wife to be in control and carry all the responsibility of the family. He becomes a little boy – another child – that his wife needs to "mother."
- **Provision**. Instead of being a provider, he looks to his wife or someone else (i.e., in-laws, welfare, church) to provide for the family. Or he may focus so much on materially providing that he is unavailable for anything else except his work, thus neglecting the other facets of his responsibility to his family.
- **Faithfulness.** Instead of being sexually faithful to his wife, he engages in relationships outside his marriage (either emotionally or physically) or escapes to the fantasy of pornography. The deeper his compulsion, the more authentic intimacy is lost with his wife.
- **Stability.** Instead of creating a consistent and stable infrastructure, he neglects and abandons the needs of his family. As a result, family members live in fear and insecurity, which many men have difficulty comprehending.

The Biological Mother

We all come into the world needing the tender presence of a mother's touch, nurture, care, guidance, and love. In fact, the mother's influence begins when we are in the womb.

Questions That Only Our Mother Can Answer

As with the father, our birth mother communicates profound answers to the questions that fulfill our innate need for nurture, comfort, and counsel.

- **Intimacy** – "Am I known?"
- **Belonging** – "Am I safe?"
- **Maturity** – "Am I whole?"

The Mother Wound

The absence of the intimate, safe, and mature maternal love of our birth mother creates a wound within us. This most often occurs in these ways:

- **Separated relationship** - Illness of our mother; our illness or extended hospitalization as a child; adoption; divorce; or death of our mother.
- **Painful relationship.** Neglect by our mother; any form of abuse; mental and emotional unhealthiness of our mother; or attempted abortion.

Shame-Based Patterns

When the most important emotional attachment in our childhood is traumatically interrupted, damaged, or absent, there is emotional pain that leads to very unhealthy shame within us. Many of these characteristics we carry into and throughout our adult life.

- Fear of abandonment
- Hunger for feminine touch
- Erotic fantasy
- Emotional dependencies
- Compulsions and addictions that bring comfort
- Fear and insecurity
- Emotional immaturity

Mother Wounds Contribute to Emotional Extremes

There are two opposite responses to a mother wound that affect our ability to achieve healthy friendships and healthy emotional intimacy within deep relationships and marriage. Our inborn temperament – specifically the type we are in the Affection area of our temperament – contributes greatly to which of these responses we might most likely experience.

- **Detachment.** Emotional detachment, wall-building, and extreme independence. Individuals who are Melancholy or Choleric in the Affection area of their temperament tend to respond in this manner. They often create walls that protect their hearts from further feelings of rejection or abandonment. These walls can be in the form of creating physical distance from our mother, or in the form of remaining physically present yet emotionally absent.
- **Enmeshment.** Emotional and identity dependence. Individuals who are Sanguine or Supine in the Affection area of their temperament tend to respond in this manner. They often allow or accept "false intimacy" in their relationships with others, in hopes of soothing their craving caused by the lack of deep approval and affection of their mother during childhood.

The mother wound has very different effects in the lives of women than it does men. The scope of this book does not allow us to go into much greater detail on this subject. I've chosen to simply provide a sampling of the most typical gender-specific effects of the mother wound.

- **Women.** Internalized low view of women; addictive, emotional and romantic dependencies; unhealthy desires for emotional connection with women; sexual confusion related to physical human touch.
- **Men.** Emotional indifference towards women; fixate on women as objects of desire to fill the deprivation of maternal love; either painfully detach or remain emotionally enmeshed in an unhealthy connection with mother; sexual confusion related to physical human touch.
- **Women and Men.** Separation anxiety that leads to striving, passivity, and depression; fantasies and fetishes involving women; self-eroticism; attachment to self; emotional drama in hopes of meeting unmet emotional needs of mother; weak sense of being.

Mother Wound Indicators

Allow yourself to ponder your childhood. Try to recall what the child version of you experienced. If you are unable to bring these memories into your conscious mind, trust that God is not ready for you to work through them yet. But if you are able to recall childhood feelings, consider them through this list of common childhood situations:

- Your mother just wasn't there for you on an emotional level.
- You were reluctant to turn to your mother for comfort or security.
- You doubted you had your mother's approval, so you were always trying to be perfect, or to justify when you weren't.
- You felt nervous, fearful, or frightened around your mother.
- Your mother expected you to take care of her physical or emotional needs.
- You were more of an adult than she was.
- You grew up way too fast.

Lasting Effects of The Mother Wound

God has the desire and the ability to heal every wound within us. As we studied in depth in an earlier chapter, the blood of Jesus and the word of God provide all that we need to be made whole, clean, and new in Christ.

Some who are reading this, though, have not yet experienced newness in Christ, and may still remain bound to some or all of the effects of our mother wounds.

- **Low self-esteem.** Secure attachment makes a child feel that they matter. Without this basic belief in themselves, children struggle to get a sense of self and to believe in themselves.
- **Lack of emotional awareness.** A mother who is emotionally present for their child is able to mirror their child's feelings, label those feelings, and help them to manage the feelings. The child doesn't need to suppress negative feelings, because they have a safe, effective way to manage them.
- **Inability to self-comfort.** Without the awareness of how to manage their feelings, children (and later adults) don't develop the ability to self-soothe. Instead, they turn to things outside of themselves for comfort. These things could include numbing activities like alcohol, drugs, pornography, and so on.
- **Relationship difficulties.** Adults with the mother wound have difficulty forming and maintaining the positive relationships that we all crave, because they've never learned to trust another human being fully. As a result, emotional vulnerability and intimacy feel unsafe or unnecessary.

Healing Our Father and Mother Wounds

Healing from our parent woundedness is a balance between acknowledging our negative feelings toward that parent and recognizing that Jesus wants us to forgive them. While remaining mired in the negative feelings may make us feel temporarily "right," we're actually only punishing ourselves.

It Takes a Lifetime

Our relationships with our biological birth father and mother are unlike any other relationship in our lives. The foundational blocks in the development of our soul were laid – knowingly or unknowingly – by these two adults. Everything else in our lives is then built upon those foundations.

We must choose to care for ourselves and allow God to renew our foundations. The old must go so the new may come.

- **Invite Jesus into our woundedness.** Knowing that Jesus wants to heal all who are broken-hearted, invite Jesus to enter into the place of your brokenness. "Though my father and mother forsake me, the Lord will receive me" (Psalm 27:10 NIV). "As a mother comforts her child, so I will comfort you" (Isaiah 66:13 NIV).

- **Express our pain.** It is necessary to express the pain of being or feeling unloved, ignored, shunned, ridiculed, and even victimized. James 5:16 (NLT) says, "Confess your sins to each other and pray for each other so that you may be healed. The earnest prayer of a righteous person has great power and produces wonderful results." Other helpful forms of expressing inner pain may include journaling, singing, writing poetry or music, or verbalizing our pain to God through worship. The more we externalize our pain, the less it remains toxically internalized within us.

- **Release our painful memories to Jesus.** Ask Jesus to take away the pain in each painful memory and replace it with His love. In His own ways, Jesus will creatively remove our pain, and transform the memory with His love and truth.

- **Forgive our parents.** We must choose, as an act of our free will, to forgive our father and mother and let go of all the resentment, bitterness, and anger we've held within us. Jesus' transforming love will change the perspective of both the experiences and the shame, and free us to accept the circumstances with grace and mercy. Forgiveness allows us to release ourselves from the one who wounded us, whereas reconciliation leads us to restore our relationship with the other individual. God commands us to forgive; He desires for us to be reconciled. He does not expect us or require us to be reconciled to a parent with whom we are not physically or emotionally safe to reconnect.

- **Love and accept ourselves.** Our concept of self was defined through our interactions with our father and nurtured through the way our mother interacted with us. We need to realize that the fact that our father or mother were unavailable, ill-equipped, or unable to build our self-image in a positive way was not our fault. We must release ourselves from this shame before we can allow God to love us, define us, and teach us to love and accept ourselves.

- **Strengthen our true identity in Christ**. Ask Jesus to reveal the truth about who we are. As Jesus affirms our sense of being, He provides an assurance of our worth and helps us know the true self that He created.

- **Develop self-awareness**. Without our mother's guidance and feedback, we didn't have the reinforcement needed to develop healthy self-awareness. We need to learn how to get in touch with our emotions – to feel what we actually feel. Naming our feelings is the first step to coping with the feeling.

- **Parent ourselves**. We can also learn how to parent ourselves, to advocate for ourselves, and give ourselves all the developmental, necessary things we may not have received as a child. Self-care of our soul and spirit isn't selfish or prideful. It is necessary that we be responsible to take care of our needs. We must believe that we do matter and that we're worth it! We must allow Jesus to become the Father our heart has always longed for. And we must allow His spirit to bring soothing nurture, comfort, and counsel into the hurt and woundedness of our soul.

- **Ongoing forgiveness**. Acknowledging our own feelings and grieving over what we never received as a child creates the emotional space needed to move towards deep forgiveness. We must continually grieve our deepest losses in order for God to turn our wounds into scars, our ashes into beauty.

- **Be our true, authentic selves**. As we connect with Jesus' profound love for us, the need for others to meet our emotional needs will diminish. This allows us to look outward at loving relationships with others. Living with our new self and being open to affirmation will free us to grow in our own story instead of constantly striving to satisfy the father and mother wounds within us.

Wounds Will Become Scars

Parenting is hard work. If you're a parent, you already know that. And sometimes parents get things wrong. Even very wrong. If we can recognize our father and mother for who they are, and not dwell on who we'd like them to be (past or present), we can move toward understanding and accepting them and all of their human weaknesses.

In some of our situations it could be possible to rebuild a damaged, broken, or absent relationship with our wounding parent. We must set firm, healthy boundaries before entering into that. If God is showing us that He wants us to build (or rebuild) some sort of relationship with our parent, He will open the doors, give us the words to say, and protect us on that journey.

In some of our situations, though, we may have had a neglectful or abusive parent that we may be attempting to forgive but cannot even consider actual reconciliation with them. God sometimes shows us that any form of reconnection with that individual would be unsafe or unhealthy to our soul and spirit. In such cases, it may be best for us to work through those hard feelings of shame and abandonment in our private, quiet times with Jesus. The rest is not our responsibility. Let go and let God be God!

Regardless which direction God leads each of us, the objective remains the same: Allow God to turn our wounds into scars, our brokenness into wholeness.

Identifying Possible Father Wounds and Mother Wounds

Identifying your emotional injuries and deficits is an important step to healing. Once the nature of our father and mother wounds is acknowledged, our healing journey can become much more focused as we move forward.

Below are two lists, each containing emotional wounds we may have experienced in our relationships with either our biological father or our biological mother. I encourage you to "score" each entry on a scale of 1-5, with 5 indicating the statement is "very true," and 1 indicating the statement is "not true."

This is not intended to serve as any form of diagnostic tool, but merely a guide for each of us to evaluate the impact of our childhood relationships with our parents. We can use this information to clarify the areas of our lives that may need the greatest attention on our journey from brokenness to wholeness in Christ.

Portions of this content are excerpts from a wonderful article by Bill Gaultiere entitled *Inventory of Emotional Wounds from Your Mother or Father.*

Father Wounds
[Please answer each question specific to your relationship with your father]

_____ 1. I did not receive enough holding, hugs, and loving touches.
_____ 2. I was rarely or never told, "I love you."
_____ 3. I did not receive patient listening and empathy.
_____ 4. I was told I was too sensitive, too emotional, or too needy.
_____ 5. When I was sick, I did not receive special care.
_____ 6. I was not joyfully celebrated on my birthday.
_____ 7. I was judged harshly.
_____ 8. I had to perform well in school or activities to be accepted.
_____ 9. I had to be good in order to be accepted.
_____ 10. My parent never or rarely played with me.
_____ 11. My parent never or rarely prayed with me.
_____ 12. I was not introduced to a personal relationship with God.
_____ 13. My parent abused me.
_____ 14. My parents divorced when I was a child.
_____ 15. My parent died when I was a child.
_____ 16. My parent had an addiction.
_____ 17. My parent had an anger problem.
_____ 18. My parent became very depressed.
_____ 19. My parent had low self-esteem.
_____ 20. My parent was not glad to see me or be with me.
_____ 21. My parent was over-stressed or anxious.
_____ 22. My parent left the family or abandoned me.
_____ 23. My parent did not protect me.
_____ 24. I was not protected from abuse and mistreatment by others.

_____ 25. My parent did not work to resolve issues and repair my hurts.

_____ 26. If I got angry, I was punished or rejected.

_____ 27. My gender identity and sexuality weren't affirmed and blessed.

_____ 28. My opposite gender parent didn't respect same gender parent.

_____ 29. I did not respect and admire my parent.

_____ 30. I was not encouraged to use my gifts.

_____ 30. As I got older, I was not trusted to make my own decisions.

_____ 31. I felt pressure to please my parent.

_____ 32. I felt overwhelmed by the emotions and needs of my parent.

_____ 33. I received a lot less attention and care than one of my siblings.

_____ 34. I often felt alone.

_____ 35. My family did not share in meals and activities very often.

_____ 36. I did not enjoy being with my family.

_____ Total Score / 36 = _____ Father Woundedness Score

[4-5 = Significant] [3-4 = Moderate] [2-3 = Mild] [1-2 = Slight]

Mother Wounds

[Please answer each question specific to your relationship with your mother]

_____ 1. I did not receive enough holding, hugs, and loving touches.

_____ 2. I was rarely or never told, "I love you."

_____ 3. I did not receive patient listening and empathy.

_____ 4. I was told I was too sensitive, too emotional, or too needy.

_____ 5. When I was sick, I did not receive special care.

_____ 6. I was not joyfully celebrated on my birthday.

_____ 7. I was judged harshly.

_____ 8. I had to perform well in school or activities to be accepted.

_____ 9. I had to be good in order to be accepted.

_____ 10. My parent never or rarely played with me.

_____ 11. My parent never or rarely prayed with me.

_____ 12. I was not introduced to a personal relationship with God.

_____ 13. I was abused physically, sexually, verbally, or emotionally.

_____ 14. My parents divorced when I was a child.

_____ 15. My parent died when I was a child.

_____ 16. My parent had an addiction.

_____   17. My parent had an anger problem.

_____   18. My parent became very depressed.

_____   19. My parent had low self-esteem.

_____   20. My parent was not glad to see me or be with me.

_____   21. My parent was over-stressed or anxious.

_____   22. My parent left the family or abandoned me.

_____   23. My parent did not protect me.

_____   24. I was not protected from abuse and mistreatment by others.

_____   25. My parent did not work to resolve issues and repair my hurts.

_____   26. If I got angry, I was punished or rejected.

_____   27. My gender identity and sexuality weren't affirmed and blessed.

_____   28. My opposite gender parent didn't respect same gender parent.

_____   29. I did not respect and admire my parent.

_____   30. I was not encouraged to use my gifts.

_____   30. As I got older, I was not trusted to make my own decisions.

_____   31. I felt pressure to please my parent.

_____   32. I felt overwhelmed by the emotions and needs of my parent.

_____   33. I received a lot less attention and care than one of my siblings.

_____   34. I often felt alone.

_____   35. My family did not share in meals and activities very often.

_____   36. I did not enjoy being with my family.

_____   Total Score / 36 = _____ Mother Woundedness Score
[4-5 = Significant] [3-4 = Moderate] [2-3 = Mild] [1-2 = Slight]

A Home That Breaks Down

Now that we've examined our unique relationships with our birth father and mother, it's important that we widen the lens and look at how the hearts of our parents directly contributed to the function or dysfunction of our family-of-origin.

Whenever the family system falls short, that system is no longer operating as God intended, thus it becomes "dysfunctional." I've often heard people say, "Isn't every family dysfunctional?" I explain that a family's dysfunction is not merely a reflection of issues within the family system or family members. True dysfunction lies in the family's unwillingness or inability to acknowledge their shame-based dysfunctions, to allow these to be openly talked about, to allow family members to receive validation of their true feelings, and to seek God's solutions for the dysfunctions. Shame-based secrets – not merely the apparent "dysfunction" – are what makes a family truly unhealthy and dysfunctional. We call these secrets "the elephant in the room."

The family is intended to be a representation of the ways God loves us. When it is damaged or dysfunctional, it can cut right to the heart of our perceptions and understandings of God Himself. The very purpose of the home is to be a safe haven and shelter. A home that has suffered shame-based damage is functioning outside its purpose. In fact, rather than protecting, it often puts its own occupants in danger. We would think it was insane to occupy a physical house that looks as though it could crumble; yet considering the wellbeing of each individual's soul and spirit, many of us have occupied that very type of "house" in our own lives.

Shame-Based Family Culture

A family that does not place Jesus in its center, and is governed by the three shame-based dysfunctional family rules that we discussed at length earlier in the book – DON'T TALK, DON'T TRUST, DON'T FEEL – will predictably be defined by these characteristics:

- The entire family is driven by the selfish needs and nature of a particular family member.
- Love is conditional and based on performance.
- The home environment is covered by guilt, shame, and fear.
- Individual family roles are undefined, unclear, and chaotic.
- Proper and necessary boundaries have not been established.
- Lack of consequences and discipline enable bad behavior.
- Lack of honest communication leads to the inability to communicate true, sincere thoughts and feelings.
- Everyone is playing a dysfunctional, shame-based role in an unending drama.

- Children in these homes are learning unhealthy patterns of relating and communicating that last a lifetime.
- Emotions are repressed and shamed, which drives every family member to unhealthy compulsions and addictive behaviors.

Shame-Based Feelings

- A sense of shame, insecurity, fear, and anger.
- The need for family members to rebel, overcompensate, or feel compelled to hold things together.
- Poor personal boundaries.
- Lack of control and a feeling of powerlessness.
- A sense of feeling trapped.
- Poor self-esteem and a false identity.
- Emotional and spiritual immaturity.
- Inability to have healthy relationships.
- Identity dependence.
- People pleasing.

God Heals and Restores

The good news comes as we realize that just as God cursed Adam and Eve, He also provided a pathway of redemption and renewal from that curse. **The curse was not the end of the story**. Along with the empty void and loss of fellowship with Him, God also introduced a plan of redemption. **His name is Jesus!** The plan that God provided for our salvation would allow all people to individually find their way back to Him. Not only would individual transformation occur, but families would have the chance to be made new and generationally changed as well.

Through Jesus Christ, the very heart of marriage would be exemplified through God's plan – giving it the opportunity to be healed, restored, and renewed. In fact, the very purpose of marriage would portray the relationship Christ has with His church. In fulfilling this, both spouses could come together in pursuit of spiritual maturity, wholeness, and intimacy with God – the ultimate and most fulfilling aspect of marriage.

Jesus Is the Foundation

Jesus Christ is the foundation upon which the home is to be built. When Jesus redeemed the human race, He undid the curse that had fallen on Adam and Eve. This means that those who surrender their lives to Him do not need to live in light of mankind's fall, but in light of God's grace. This puts our roles and responsibilities in an entirely different perspective.

Throughout the scripture, we see that Jesus Christ is the central theme. With Him at the center, the husband and wife love each other through Him and for Him. Christian marriages that aren't working properly aren't just a result of living under a curse, but they are an indication that the couple has not given Jesus Christ full dominion over their lives.

Many marriages can be imbalanced spiritually, where one spouse loves God while the other doesn't walk or live by Christian principles. The Bible tells us if we are married to an unbeliever, we should stay in that marriage if our spouse desires to do so. But if the spouse wants to leave, we are to let that happen, and proceed with our own lives and future marriage relationships.

"To the rest I say this (I, not the Lord): If any brother has a wife who is not a believer and she is willing to live with him, he must not divorce her. And if a woman has a husband who is not a believer and he is willing to live with her, she must not divorce him. For the unbelieving husband has been sanctified through his wife, and the unbelieving wife has been sanctified through her believing husband. Otherwise, your children would be unclean, but as it is, they are holy. But if the unbeliever leaves, let it be so. The brother or the sister is not bound in such circumstances; God has called us to live in peace" (1 Corinthians 7: 12-15 NIV).

When our marriage relationship is lopsided, we must be diligent to fulfill our responsibility as if we were serving Christ directly. We must learn to allow Him, not our spouse, to meet our needs Himself and go to Him as the source of anything that might be lacking in our marriage. The purpose of our own life and the purpose of marriage is to know and love God first! Through Christ, we can still find wholeness in our lives despite what our partner chooses to do.

To the degree we align ourselves to our identity and purpose in Christ Jesus, we will be able to appreciate our beautiful design as a male or a female.

God can and does make up for absent or disinterested spouses, but He is also capable of changing them from the inside out. Change has to start with one person, and we can be that incredible godly influence on our spouse simply by demonstrating an intimate relationship with the perfect, unfailing love of Jesus Christ, and taking that responsibility off of them.

Prayer for Freedom from Our Family's Dysfunction

Father God, my family life has been far from perfect. I don't want to dwell on or blame the dynamics of my past or current family, but I do want to understand Your will and purpose in my life. Give me the ability to see what I need to see in order to be set free from any damaging belief systems or toxic shame I may have acquired. Be my perfect Father right now and lead and guide me into all truth according to Your will at work in my life.

I am so grateful to know that You are the source of truth. As painful as it can be to see how my own family life has fallen short of this plan You provide, I have so much hope that You are already in the process of restoring that which has been broken. Teach me, Father, how to end generational patterns of sin and cycles of behavior that are harmful. Help me to fulfill the role You uniquely designed for me.

I am grateful that You already see me as Your perfect child. Change my heart, not merely my outward actions. Lead me into the life You intend and show me anything and everything that is not of You so it can be made whole.

I also pray for my family members, both in my current family, as well as my family-of-origin. Lord, I lift them up to You. You alone have the ability to restore my family and each individual member. Thank you, God. You are in control. You are a good, good father. In Jesus name I pray, Amen."

"So now there is no condemnation for those who belong to Christ Jesus."

Romans 8:1 NLT

SHAME

Turn from Toxic Shame to Freedom in Christ

Introduction

God is in the business of making broken things whole. It is through the life of His spirit that we are brought back to wholeness. Nothing that has occurred in our past is allowed to have sovereign reign in our life when we summon the God of the universe for assistance.

Those parts of our life that have been broken, emptied, or invalidated are precious to God.

- The word of God tells us how God is intimately involved with our pain: "You keep track of all my sorrows. You have collected all my tears in your bottle. You have recorded each one in your book" (Psalm 56:8 NLT). How amazing to know that God has His own inventory of each one of our burdens and emotions!
- He records our tears, not our wrongdoings! It is with that understanding of God's mercy and compassion that we are able to deal with the issues in our life. God's love toward us enables us to step out in faith and seek redemption.
- We are promised that nothing can separate us from God's love or take it away – nothing in the past, present, or future – including all the experiences we have had (see Romans 8:38-39).

- As we continue down the pathway toward healing, we must be willing to face the very things that caused us so much pain. We must also face our own wrongful behaviors.
- If we are courageous enough to move through this process, we won't be disappointed. It leads us into God's peace – a place where we can abide and rest in Him, despite anything that occurs externally around us. But to get there, we must be willing to remove the turbulence that has created so much conflict. We must be willing to face the shame within us.

Shame: The Poison of the Soul

Shame is the most lethal and toxic enemy of the soul because it prevents us from knowing and experiencing the love and grace of God. It operates by the realization that we missed the mark, we failed, or we somehow didn't measure up to a standard. Shame disrupts a sense of normalcy and wreaks havoc with our ability to be healthy and whole.

Satan will work hard to accuse, torment, and make us believe we don't measure up to God's standard, creating within us feelings of worthlessness, hopelessness, grief, depression, and chronic anxiety. When Satan captures our minds in these ways, he in essence has control over our lives.

The word of God deals very specifically with shame. In fact, Jesus didn't just come to remove our sin; He also came to remove the harmful effects of shame. In the context of our journey from brokenness, we believe that in order to be renewed, we must bring to light the very things we've tried for years to hide. By exposing these issues, the Holy Spirit seeks to cover us with God's grace. It is in this transaction that shame loses all power over us as we are covered in the reality of God's forgiveness, freedom, and acceptance.

Identifying Shame Messages

Identifying the shame in our lives may not come easily for some of us. Even if we begin to see events, sins, trauma, abuse, and other issues, we may be unable to see how shame took root. We often think that shame is a direct result of things we have done, or things that have been done to us. That is not necessarily the case. Shame is also a byproduct of the way others have imposed standards on us.

When we have been violated, neglected, or had painful words spoken into us – especially in childhood – they sent a message directly into our heart. The act itself was bad, but the message it sent had the potential to affect us for the rest of our life.

Shameful messages can also say, "You're bad, you're stupid, you're fat, you're ugly," and much more. And these internalized messages typically result in some form of obsessive thinking and/or compulsive behavior.

The one who spoke the shameful message planted the seed. The one who received the message experienced the message taking root, allowing it to control their thoughts, feeling, and behaviors to some degree.

Does that mean it is the fault of the one who spoke it? Not exactly. The problem is that as children we often automatically believe what our parents or trusted adults tell us. Eventually we might reject those messages. But in our early years, we accept them as fully true, and don't realize we have an option to do otherwise.

And further, when we carry shame, we unknowingly superimpose it on others. Shame is often passed from one generation to the next, as we've looked at in great detail in an earlier chapter.

How Does Shame Enter Our Life?

Toxic shame is a tactic of Satan. God does not use shame. He uses conviction in the life of the believer, never condemnation. Therefore, all toxic shame is dangerous and needs to be dealt with decisively. Here are the three ways shame enters into a person's life:

- **Not measuring up to standards**. We are born into a family and a world that is filled with expectations and pressures. We learn to measure ourselves by a certain level or standard. Shame is produced when we feel unable to live up to our own standards or the standards of those around us, especially our parents. This effort to live up to standards can lead to identity dependence and people pleasing, or living life based on a determination to "follow the rules."

- o **Self-Imposed Standards**. Through our life experiences, upbringing, and other acquired beliefs, we build an ideal in our own mind for the standards we should attain. Sometimes these are unrealistic or are based on standards of the world around us and the people in our life. It is in our broken, human nature to impose the same standards on others that we impose on ourselves. Therefore, when we or others don't measure up, we often become critical, judgmental, or even demeaning.

- o **Other People's Standards**. We often feel shame when rejected, criticized, or put down by others if we don't fit their arbitrary criteria of what is "acceptable." We often don't realize that failing to measure up to another person's particular set of standards doesn't necessarily mean we have done something wrong. Just the same, we can feel good about ourselves when we do succeed at measuring up to those standards (which can lead to pride and arrogance), and we can be devastated when we fail to measure up to others' standards (which can expose shame and brokenness).

- o **Family System Standards**. In every family, spoken and unspoken rules dictate acceptable standards. The standards may be extremely dysfunctional, skewed, or exceedingly unrealistic. If we've lived by toxic family standards, we'll be bound to feel shame as a result.

- o **Cultural Standards**. We are born with a desire to be accepted by the larger population around us. Therefore, if we don't measure up to what the world or society presents as acceptable, we can carry a sense of shame. Since culture shifts from generation to generation on what is acceptable, we may feel shame for having things in our life that are not currently (or no longer) accepted, trendy, or popular.

- o **Religious Standards**. A church or groups of "Christians" can promote a set of standards for conduct that emphasizes outward behaviors – rule following, appearance, religiousness – more than the heart. They can present a form of God that leaves us thinking we are unacceptable to Him unless we can be what those people say we should be. When we don't live up to those standards, we can feel rejected by that group and thus feel we are being rejected by God.

We must learn we can't judge ourselves in accordance with the standards of self or others. We need to judge ourselves by the standards of Christ. In 2 Corinthians 10:12 (NLT), Paul says this:

> "Oh, don't worry; we wouldn't dare say that we are as wonderful as these other men who tell you how important they are! But they are only comparing themselves with each other, using themselves as the standard of measurement. How ignorant!"

God measures us through the standard of Jesus Christ when we come into a relationship with Him. He doesn't compare us to Jesus. He sees Jesus righteousness when He looks upon us as His followers!

Our ability to comply with God's system and standards doesn't depend on our own effort, but on our relationship with Christ. Paul says in 2 Corinthians 5:21 (NLT), "God made Christ, who never sinned, to be the offering for our sin, so that we could be made right with God through Christ." Through this transaction, we are made perfectly acceptable to God, no matter what we've done. God's system overrides all other systems and standards and is the only basis of Truth!

- **Not dealing with our sin Biblically.** We can feel the guilt and shame of what we've done as evidence that something within us is inherently wrong. We often hang onto sin issues, feeling the need to continually be punished for the ways we've not lived up to a standard. As children of God, we have already been forgiven. The blood of Jesus took all our sins – past, present, and future – and paid the price to have them removed from our ledger. But sadly, we can continue to live in the shame of that sin rather than in the freedom of God's grace and forgiveness. Several things can prevent us from being able to experience freedom from our past violations:

o **Guilt**: A sense that we violated someone or something either by what we did or did not do.
o **Shame**: A sense of worthlessness whereby we feel we are unacceptable to God and others.
o **Condemnation**: A sense of being damaged, flawed, or rejected.

It stands in complete opposition to salvation. If we experience these, they are real issues we need to deal with. The enemy tries to produce in us a sense of God's judgment rather than God's love and grace. He will point out how unworthy we may be and try to bring us to a place where we hide from God in fear. There is a tremendous difference between the enemy's messages of guilt and shame, and the conviction of the Holy Spirit when we have issues in our life that really do need dealt with.

God's Conviction	Enemy's Guilt and Shame
Woos us in loving correction	Tears us down and points out what a failure we are
Focuses on the solution	Focuses on the problem
Reminds us of our true identity despite the things we do	Wants us to think our behavior defines our core value and worth
Encourages us to draw closer to God and His grace and mercy	Encourages us to move away from God, thinking He is angry
Offers forgiveness for our wrongdoings if we humbly confess to God	Holds us in bondage, unable to experience forgiveness

- **Through acts of violation committed against us.** We experience shame when people sin against us. Through violations, abuse, molestation, or shameful words, shame is placed on us and cuts to the very core of our self-worth. Abuse occurs when someone enters an area of our lives without permission in a way that violates or hurts us. Some abuse can occur when people neglect to fulfill a responsibility in our relationship with them. Any time a violating act is committed against us, shame can be introduced into our lives.

No matter our attempts, we feel we can't rid ourselves of this sense of dirtiness. It is a byproduct of the act itself. Despite our best efforts to forget about it or to cover it up with something that looked outwardly good, the shame continues to deliver toxic messages.

Are we destined to remain a victim of abuse forever? Thank God the answer is no! There is a cleansing remedy and a process to rid us of this shame. It is only through the precious blood of Jesus Christ as the cleansing power to eradicate both the shame imposed on us through our own behaviors and the shame imposed by others.

Types of Abuse

- **Physical abuse.** When someone hits, touches, or hurts our physical body, our nature and God-given boundaries have been violated. Sometimes victims of physical abuse have been told, "You deserve this." A human being, let alone a child of God, never deserves physical abuse!

- **Sexual abuse.** Any time we are touched by a person inappropriately in a sexual way without our consent, it could be considered sexual abuse. Sexual abuse is unbelievably damaging because it enters our deepest, most sacred and most intimate place – a place so precious it was reserved only for the covenant of marriage. Violations in this area shatter the sense of preciousness, purity, and sanctity. More than any other form of abuse, it will deeply affect the individual's ability to bond and trust in future relationships. Even when we willingly participate in sexual acts outside the context of marriage, we are participating in the sexual abuse of our own body. "Flee from sexual immorality. All other sins a person commits are outside the body, but whoever sins sexually, sins against their own body" (1 Corinthians 6:18 NIV).

319

- **Mental abuse.** When someone attempts to enter our minds or manipulate what we think or believe in order to hurt us, we can experience mental abuse. In some relationships, the victim is actually made to feel as though they are the instigator, thus justifying the perpetrator's actions.
- **Emotional abuse.** Emotional abuse feeds on our vulnerabilities and weaknesses. It can use fear, shame, guilt, or rejection to gain power over us. The perpetrator will use words as emotional weapons in an attempt to change another person's behavior. This is cruel, unloving, and unfair.
- **Spiritual abuse.** Parents and other authority figures can use the Bible (or words from the Bible) to frighten and scare others. Spiritual abuse uses the things of God to exercise human control over others. While God is powerful, He never attempts to force us to do anything. He never shames us but convicts us and desires to set us free.
- **Abuse by neglect.** We can be abused by not having physical or emotional needs met. When a parent withdraws necessities from a child (love, attention, or nurturing), or fails to meet other legitimate needs, actually abuse is occurring. Often this form of abuse is not intentional, but a projection of the parents' unresolved shame. Nonetheless, it can be very abusive in nature.

Abused? Or Abuser?

Two people participate in acts of violation: a victim (the abused) and a perpetrator (the abuser).

- **The victim.** The person on the receiving end of abusive behaviors is the victim. The victim is prone to be captured by the message the actual abuse sends. Essentially, in being the recipient of an act of abuse, a tainted and skewed perspective of God, self, and others can develop. Here are some ways victims can wrongly adapt:

  o **Believe abuse is deserved.** Some victims will get so broken-down, they will actually feel entirely responsible for the abuse.

No matter how hard they try, they replay a message in their mind that says, "I did something to deserve this."

o **The cycle of enablement.** Victims often feel the need to defend the person who committed the very acts of abuse that hurt them. They may believe the abuser couldn't help it, or they may justify the acts because they want to earn the abuser's love. This skewed form of protection actually encourages the abuse to continue.

o **The "I'm a victim" mentality.** Some victims who do not deal with the issues appropriately will develop dysfunctional relationship skills where they tend to always have to be in a "victim" situation. They will not be able to see themselves or others accurately and will participate in behaviors that either encourage bad behavior or falsely set people up to be perpetrators. This sort of victim actually feels most safe when in the role of victim.

- **The perpetrator.** An abuser or perpetrator is an unhealthy person. Everyone who lives in a fleshly body is subject to being led astray by the enemy in various ways. As human beings, the spirit realm around us is influencing us. People influenced by biblical truth will manifest behaviors that reflect that truth. People influenced by toxic surroundings or evil spirits will manifest other behaviors. God's objective for our lives is to give us life. Satan's objectives are to kill, steal, and destroy (see John 10:10). God uses people as vessels. Satan also uses people as vessels. Understanding this perspective is critical as we face the violations of a perpetrator, because it helps us identify the real enemy: Satan. A perpetrator is a carrier of shame. Instead of Biblically dealing with shame, the perpetrator acts out an emotional pain or demonic influence. Sadly, the behaviors they inflict on others typically stem from shame imposed on them through someone else's sin. Our culture tries to blame genetics for the emotional and behavioral challenges we face; but in the spiritual realm, the shame of sin is passed along form one person to the next, one generation to the next (see Deuteronomy 5:9-10).

o   What would make a person cross the line to become a perpetrator? People learn to cope and deal with life in different ways. For the darker and more evil forms of abuse, the person who becomes a perpetrator has developed a hardened heart. They have listened to the enemy rather than to God's principles, and now act out their anger, shame, fear, or powerlessness by hurting others. While we are allowed by God to hate the perpetrator's acts, it's important to remember that he or she needs grace as much as any other member of society. Even more humbling is to realize that every one of us could have been, or could become, a perpetrator in some way.

Prayer to Break the Shame Caused by Unhealthy Standards

Father, I ask for Your wisdom to know how You would have me see, hear, and respond to situations in my life. Show me Your heart and give me Your hands so I don't run people over by my harsh and unfair judgments or walk in shame of never feeling that I'm good enough. Place in me the spirit of grace and give me the delight and pleasure of resting in the truth that, as Your child, I already measure up to Your standard. As I receive and walk in that truth, God, give me the ability to share that same grace with those around me, walking only by the standard of Your love and not the standards of man.

As I look at the violations that have occurred in my life, I confess that, at times, I have minimized them. Other times, I've felt like a victim of circumstances. I may have even been mad or angry at You as a result. Please help me understand the reality of the shame and the messages that shame has imposed on me and prepare my heart as I seek you as the remedy to the pain and shame in my heart.

Thank you for healing me and making me whole, that I might be fully used for Your purposes. In Jesus name I pray, Amen.

Questions from Dr. Dave

For personal reflection or group discussion of Chapter 14

Were there any particular dysfunctional family roles you carried during your childhood? What may have been some of the factors that pigeon-holed you into that role? Has that role carried into your adult relationships in any ways? What pressures (either externally or internally) try to keep you from giving up that unnecessary, unhealthy role? Consider whether God wants you to continue to be defined by that dysfunctional role, or if He prefers you surrender that to Him.

In reading about God's original design for family, what emotions begin to arise within you? What's the connection between these emotions and the reality of your childhood family culture? Do you perceive that you experienced either father or mother wounding as a child? See how those wounds may connect with specific emotional struggles in your life today. Are you able to make a connection between your childhood wounds and your adult view of God? Allow God to convict your heart of what you need to bring to Him in repentance.

Have you ever considered that the people who created the standards that your performance, approval, and self-worth have been measured by are just as sinful, fallen, and unworthy as you are? In what ways has this book motivated you to stop living a life of performance and approval, and begin an exciting life defined by the grace, mercy, and forgiveness of Jesus? What steps can you take toward that right now?

CHAPTER 15

Phase 3: R – Rediscover My True Identity in Christ

"We demolish arguments and every pretension that sets itself up against the knowledge of God, and we take captive every thought to make it obedient to Christ."

2 Corinthians 10:5-6 NIV

STRONGHOLDS

Turn Loose of Emotional Strongholds

Introduction

Many of us have reached a point where the emotional pain in our lives has driven us to seek help. At the beginning of this journey, we are often filled with so many negative emotions that we don't even know where to begin. Like taking a medication for a headache, we are looking for the quickest fix possible that can take the pain away. For many of us, this means turning to our pattern of compulsion, addiction, or codependency as we have always done.

As difficult as this can seem, emotions really do have a very positive purpose. As we learn to properly identify them, we can gain some perspective, thus losing the power and intensity they have held in our lives.

- Allowing the Holy Spirit to comfort and nurture us during times of emotional pain brings healing to the deepest places in our soul and draws us into greater intimacy with Jesus Christ.

The Purpose of Emotions

We may have been taught that emotions are wrong or something we aren't supposed to experience or express. We have learned to cover them over or conceal them. We may have even been taught that emotions are not good.

Since we are created in the image of God, we should first understand that emotions are simply part of what makes us human. God gave us emotions so we could feel, be passionate, and experience the fullness of life. God also exhibited emotions (see Psalm 33:5; 95:10; Isaiah 49:15-16; 61:8; Zephaniah 3:17). If God Himself has emotions, clearly, they cannot always be wrong in and of themselves.

However, just like anything else God created for good, our emotions can get twisted and skewed. When we are living apart from God's plan, there are many negative consequences. Emotional pain is one of those consequences.

Emotions are like the check engine light in a vehicle. When emotions signal us, we must understand that something is happening and needs tended to. Emotions are warning signs. Our emotions are not the issue. They are merely an indicator of the real issue.

Imagine life if we didn't feel. And for some of us, that has become our reality. Yet for others, we can be completely imprisoned by our emotions. When we've lost control of our emotions, we no longer understand or identify the issues that drive them. We only experience the emotions connected to the real issues, and we allow them to reign and rule in our lives.

The Origin of Negative Emotions

Most negative emotions come from false beliefs and faulty thinking. Any belief that is rooted in our flesh – Satan's lies or the philosophies and systems of the world – leads to faulty thinking.

Robert McGee, in his book *The Search for Significance*, provides a clear perspective on how the false beliefs we internalized through childhood have a direct correlation to our behaviors and decisions in adulthood.

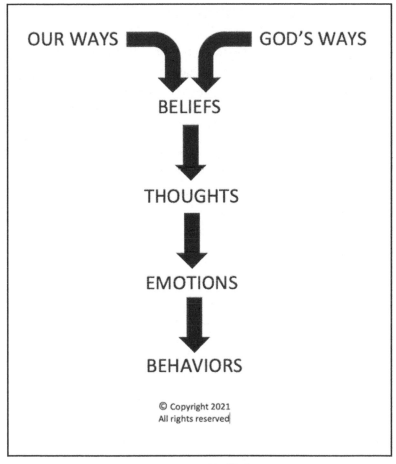

My Voice vs. God's Voice

Beliefs – Thoughts – Emotions – Behaviors

It is important to understand that while our thoughts and beliefs are choices based on our free will, emotions are irrational. If someone tells you to "stop feeling that way," you would not be able to. In order to stop feeling that way, you would have to first stop believing and thinking that way. If your emotions are causing you continual pain and suffering, it is important that you learn more about them, what might be driving them, and what God has provided for you to effectively manage them.

Negative Emotions Can Cripple Us

Every human being has a myriad of emotions within them – some healthy and productive, some not so much. Some emotions (we call these secondary emotions) are layered upon deeper primary emotions. As you move forward in your healing journey, you will learn to examine whether an emotion is truly the issue. Or is it simply an outward manifestation of a deeper, primary emotion? Although there are countless human emotions, we'll only be exploring five that are the most common.

- Anger
- Rejection
- Fear
- Loneliness
- Powerlessness

Anger

Anger is a defensive emotion that arises when we feel our boundaries and sense of rights have somehow been violated. Anger tends to arise when we are desperate to:

- Hold on to what we have.
- Validate who we are.
- Protect what we feel entitled to.
- Fight back when our sense of self-worth is threatened.
- Control when our basic needs are not adequately met.
- Defend when our beliefs are under attack.

Anger is often a response to the following types of negative life circumstances:

- We feel ignored.
- We feel worthless.
- We feel powerless.
- We feel our safety is being threatened.

- We feel that our basic needs won't be met.
- We feel unloved.
- We feel rejected.
- We feel unappreciated.
- We feel violated.
- We feel disrespected for our moral beliefs.
- We feel we aren't being taken seriously.
- We feel we are being ridiculed or criticized.
- We feel abandoned.
- We feel used.

Is It Okay for A Christian to Be Angry?

When anger is managed properly, it doesn't create a problem. God's word says, "And don't sin by letting anger control you. Don't let the sun go down while you are still angry, for anger gives a foothold to the devil" (Ephesians 4:26-27 NIV).

When we feel angry, it is comforting to know that God also displayed this emotion. God clearly was angry at evil. He hated it, and we are allowed to hate it too. But we are not allowed to be angry with people to the point where our hearts are filled with bitterness and resentment. The clear distinction between righteous anger and the type of anger that leads to many levels of sinful behavior is the ability to separate what a person had done from who a person is. Since most of us have difficulty doing this, at least initially, unrighteous anger tends to take over.

Using anger to defend and protect ourselves is unhealthy. It can become a wrong method of coping with our pain and is connected to the need to dominate or control others, or to not be dominated or controlled by others. Anger can literally cause our heart to harden and assume a combative or defensive position.

Destructive anger must be removed if there is any hope of life change. While anger can sound ugly, just like anything else we have learned about on this journey, anger has a purpose, an explanation, and a solution. Anger is usually connected with many other emotions. Often, we have to find the raw emotion that tends to trigger the anger.

Rejection

Being rejected by someone is perhaps the most painful things we can experience. Yet rejection is a reality of life. If we've experienced a painful childhood with a lot of rejection, facing rejection in adulthood can be that much more difficult. A root of rejection can cause much pain and lead to all sorts of dysfunctional thinking, feeling, and behaving. At the core, the person with the root of rejection has actually come to the belief that, "I'm not good enough. I'm not acceptable. Who could love me?" Whenever a life situation reinforces those negative beliefs, the feeling of rejection is triggered and the old shame messages begin playing in our head.

Rejection and Anger

Since rejection is often too painful to cope with, many people go directly from feeling rejected to feeling angry. When we experience rejection, we often counter it with a need to blame or find fault in the person or circumstances that cause it. We may not even realize that when we do this, we are actually in the defensive mode of anger.

Rejection and People Pleasing

Other times, rejection can drive us to compulsively find a way to be more acceptable. This leads to the behaviors of identity dependence and people pleasing. We begin to believe that the person who rejected us is right and therefore we need to adjust, compensate, or change to get that person to accept us.

It is important to know that when we embrace this type of system in coping with rejection, we have adopted an external reference point to determine who we are, rather than being internally defined through Jesus' spirit within us. Essentially, this means we use another person as our guiding influence. We have placed that person in God's position. The Bible calls this idolatry.

Dealing with Rejection

As we deal with rejection, we must first ask ourselves a difficult question: "Am I doing anything or behaving in any way that might be considered unacceptable?" Why should we ask ourselves this question? Because what we perceive as rejection may in fact be an appropriate response by others to something I am doing or representing. When this is the case, it is our behavior that is being brought into question, not our character, personhood, or identity. We must learn to separate who we are from what we do. And not be so sensitive to when we are corrected or called out for our actions, as if our personhood is being threatened.

Unlike the unhealthy patterns we've learned and implemented when we experience rejection, we can choose to create new ways of dealing with our shame-based rejection messages when they occur.

- **Identify the situation:** What is the nature of the rejection? Is it based on reality?
- **Identify the other person:** What is the level of their credibility in my life? Do they deserve the amount of power I've given them?
- **Identify ourselves:** Could I have done something to contribute to the rejection? Am I judging myself for what I did? Is my judgment too harsh in light of the situation?
- **Identify God's perspective:** What does God's word say about who I am? Am I trusting the approval of God? Or of others? What will it take for me to embrace God's perspective and to let go of my false beliefs related to the situation?

We are not responsible for how other people choose to see us! And, like it or not, not everyone is going to like us. We must stand firm in knowing who we are!

Fear

Fear comes from a threat of danger and a sense of insecurity. Sometimes fear is real, such as a storm about to hit our home. But oftentimes fear is irrational, meaning it has no basis in fact or truth. We can be afraid of people, circumstances, and events that will never hurt us.

Sometimes even our memories can produce irrational fears. These are typically tied to our inborn temperament in some way.

- **Melancholy.** Fear of not appearing competent; fear of rejection.
- **Choleric.** Fear of failure; fear of not being in control or under control.
- **Sanguine.** Fear of disapproval; fear of the absence of approval.
- **Supine.** Fear of abandonment; fear of being excluded or left out.
- **Phlegmatic.** Fear of expending unnecessary energy; fear of over-obligation of energy.

We can fear failure and never try anything new. We can fear rejection and never pursue satisfying relationships. People who are fear-based most likely didn't experience security and safety in childhood, and possibly even in adulthood. They perhaps didn't feel a sense of protection and the hope and assurance of support when a dangerous or less than comfortable situation arose.

God's Love Conquers Our Fears

People who are fear-based don't have the proper understanding of God or don't know how He relates to us as the perfect Father, Provider, Protector, Lover, and Giver.

Fear can completely paralyze us at times. A person bound by fear is a person who doesn't feel safe to do much of anything or to take reasonable risks. They literally hide under a shell, relationally detached and withdrawn.

Fear also has the ability to drive identity dependence. The fear of rejection can provoke the same negative feelings as if actual rejection had occurred. If we are rejected, we need to face that reality with a Christ-centered, Biblical perspective. But if we only fear being rejected, the event has not yet happened.

The Bible tells us there is no acceptable fear except the "fear of the Lord." We also learn in the Bible that "perfect love casts out all fear" (1 John 4:8 NIV). Therefore, it is safe to conclude that when we are fearful, we have a need to allow more of the love of God into our lives.

It is important to realize the need to place a higher priority on our relationship with Jesus. We must seek Him, look to Him, and believe He is our Protector and Defender in all ways and in all situations. We are reminded hundreds of times in God's word not to fear. We must choose to believe and live God's truth rather than the false beliefs that we've known for much of our lives. Unlike other emotions, fear is always illegitimate.

Loneliness

Loneliness isn't necessarily about being alone. It means we feel isolated and disconnected from others, for some, even when we're in a crowd. Loneliness says, "I am the only person going through this. No one would understand or care." Many people go through life lonely yet are never able to identify loneliness as the problem. They fill their lives with things, busy activities, social calendars, yet are left still feeling that void and discontentment.

God created us to be in relationships, but they were designed in such a way that He would come first, above everything and everyone in our lives. Any time we feel disconnected from others, we must first look at the health of our intimate relationship with Jesus.

Loneliness can lead to anger, fear, and even depression. Choosing to seek help and engage in community to overcome loneliness can be difficult. Often this journey of transformation that we're on together can feel lonely, as we give up relationships that are no longer healthy, or our own family members who don't understand what we're going through. It is essential to connect with people who can encourage us and who understand the path we've chosen to take in our lives. We need to surround ourselves with people who understand where we are, and don't cause us to feel judged, condemned, or unacceptable.

A Journey of Connecting

In reality, this journey from brokenness to wholeness is one of connecting. First, God wants to repair our broken or absent connection to Him. Ultimately that connection will give us the ability to connect to others in healthy ways.

Even so, we must be willing to accept loneliness as a part of being human. Sometimes we'll just feel lonely and need to use those times for solitude with God rather than isolating ourselves from others. By beginning to identify our loneliness, we can learn to hand over that feeling to God. We can use those times for prayer, reading God's word, and simply just being in His presence. As we focus on Him, we find the sweetness of His presence engulfs us. Rather than feeling alone, we feel connected to Him. Jesus said, "I will never abandon or reject you" (Hebrews 13:5 NLT).

Powerlessness

When we believe we are powerless, we are unable to help ourselves. We are unable to change our circumstances because something more powerful than ourselves overtakes us. It can be frightening to be powerless in a negative situation – particularly when there is a direct need or dependency concerning the person involved (spouse, family member, employer). Powerlessness can also happen when someone violates us or maliciously attacks our character. It can be felt in childhood when we have unhealthy or controlling families. If we have experienced a lot of powerlessness in our lives, a defensive reaction may occur almost immediately when we are put into any circumstances that are remotely similar as adults.

Powerlessness is at the core of many anger issues. When we feel unable to help ourselves or change our circumstances, we may protect ourselves through anger. We may also attempt to control things through our own efforts, directly or indirectly. Many times, in powerless situations we try even harder.

For some of us, the absence of healthy human limits (healthy shame) contributes to our inability to know where our will, responsibility, and capabilities end, and where God's begin. Without these boundaries in our lives, we can feel that we are powerless, while in reality we are just not as powerful as shame has convinced us we are supposed to be. John Bradshaw refers to this as "grandiosity" – believing we have the power to will the unwillable and to control the uncontrollable things in life.

The way we deal with our feelings of powerlessness can either add further feelings of shame, or it can turn our mind and will to God, the only One who truly has power and control to begin with.

Our own efforts, our angry and vengeful reactions, and our depression can't change a thing. When we learn to identify the emotion of powerlessness, we can come to a point of true surrender to God. There needs to be the attitude that God is more powerful than whatever obstacle we face. Instead of trying so hard, the ability to surrender to Him is where we find victory. In the midst of the pain and strain of feeling so out of control, we can rest in this stabilizing truth: "For I can do everything through Christ, who gives me strength" (Philippians 4:13 NLT).

Overcoming Painful Emotions

Dealing with painful emotions can be the most difficult challenge we face in our healing journey. Simply "getting over them" (as some may have told us to do) is difficult, if not impossible. True Christ-centered healing begins with learning how to stabilize our emotions and submitting them to the Lord, that He might bring us comfort, healing, and wisdom.

- **Remember that emotions are indicators, not facts.** Emotions reflect what is happening in our heart. They should not be ignored, nor should they be taken as factual truth. Understanding they are essentially a response and not the actual problem can help us put things in proper perspective. People who try to repress and deny emotions wind up with bigger problems. However, as we move through our emotions and accept the underlying event as it is, we give ourselves the chance to continue living an emotionally healthy life. We can reflect on the realities of what occurred and find hope in what we have learned. If we continually focus on the negative emotion without moving toward healing and acceptance, we become imprisoned or even paralyzed by it. This disrupts our ability to live a life of joy and peace, or to be able to experience all of God's blessings in our lives. The emotion has moved from being a healthy, normal human response, to now being a form of bondage.

- **Identify the belief system that drove the emotion.** When emotions become intense, we need to take a step back and identify the origin of the circumstance, thought, idea, or belief that triggered the emotion. Oftentimes there are false beliefs or messages attached to emotions that must be explored. It is not uncommon for a person to build an entire belief system about life, love, faith, and relationships upon a false message. These messages must be challenged by the truth of God's word and replaced in our hearts and minds. God's greatest work is done when we are honest with ourselves, recognize where we have been off track, and allow Him to do amazing things in our lives.

- **Identify when we transfer responsibility.** We must realize that another person is not responsible for how we feel. Emotions are influenced by our own thoughts and beliefs. If we continually see ourselves as a victim of others, we will never be able to experience true healing in our inner soul. That doesn't negate the fact that people can genuinely hurt us. However, by owning our emotions, we can begin to deflect negative messages. As long as we are humble about it, we can choose to refuse to allow others' negative words to penetrate our hearts.

- **Recognize Satan's part.** We can't discount the element of spiritual attack in our emotional challenges. Satan can't make us "feel" anything, be he does know where we are vulnerable. Those will be the places he will target his attacks. He tries to tempt us into thinking false things about others, and ourselves, knowing if we begin to accept his lies, we will wind up in bondage to our emotions and sinful reactions. The Bible teaches us about the weapons of spiritual warfare in the removal of strongholds: "For though we live in the world, we do not wage war as the world does. The weapons we fight with are not the weapons of the world. On the contrary, they have divine power to demolish strongholds. We demolish arguments and every pretension that sets itself up against the knowledge of God, and we take captive every thought to make it obedient to Christ" (2 Corinthians 10:3-5 NIV).

- **Claim God's promises to defeat negative emotions**. Whenever we feel a negative emotion, we can find a solution to resolve that emotion in the word of God. Claiming a promise against the emotion doesn't change the circumstance. We need to address the situation for what it is. But choosing to believe a promise against the emotion means that instead of dwelling on the pain that provoked the emotion, we are going to dwell on God's glorious provision to meet our need, whatever it might be. Learning to respond to painful emotions Biblically is a growth process, so, depending on our maturity level, it may take time before we see significant change. Eventually, as we learn to respond to our negative emotions in a healthy way, they are put in their proper place. As we practice this discipline in all areas of our lives, eventually our thinking, feeling, and behaving will be radically changed!

"If we confess our sins, He is faithful and will forgive us our sins and purify us from all unrighteousness."

1 John 1:9 NIV

RESTORATION

Turn to Restoration from My Sin and Shame

Introduction

Shame is a tool the enemy uses in the believer's life that robs us of the freedom and power God intended us to have. If our lives are filled with shame, we are in desperate need of an authentic and long-term remedy.

All of our coping skills and survival strategies were attempts to overcome shame. Little did we know that those efforts offered no possible means of a solution and, in fact, worsened the problem.

- We could think of each sin (and the accompanying shame) we carry within us as a chain that we are bound to. Those chains keep us living with a sense of guilt, compelling us to drag ourselves through life heavy hearted and filled with pain.
- We could also think of the acts of violation committed against us as an actual wound inside our heart. We have been medicating that wound for years, trying to soothe it with anything we hope will take the pain away. This is often in the form of addictions, compulsions, perfectionism, control, manipulation, and so on.
- As we move toward applying the actual solution and removing the shame, the first remedy is the ability to receive forgiveness for our sins. While it sounds simple enough, many of us don't realize how

difficult it might be. We are usually prone to thinking one of two extremes: 1) We don't need forgiveness at all, or 2) We don't believe we "deserve" to be forgiven, so we must work for it or earn it.

- When it comes to receiving God's forgiveness, there is an actual process and set of criteria. Anything outside those bounds will hold us in bondage and never offer us the power to overcome the shame within.

How Jesus Dealt with Sin

The Bible tells us that Jesus Christ identified with our grief and personal sin, including all the acts that were committed against us, and the things we, ourselves, did wrong. He felt the piercing reality of our transgressions, since they were placed directly onto His own body on the cross:

> "Yet it was our weaknesses he carried; it was our sorrows that weighed Him down. And we thought His troubles were a punishment from God, a punishment for his own sins! But he was pierced for our rebellion, crushed for our sins. He was beaten so we could be whole. He was whipped so we could be healed" (Isaiah 53:4-5 NLT)

When Jesus hung on the cross, He was exposed to an inconceivable act of shame. He was spit upon, laughed at, cast aside, and murdered – having done nothing wrong to deserve it. If anyone had the right to claim being a victim, it was Jesus. Instead, everything He did was mission oriented from a loving heart. He simply remained steadfast to the central mission: to forgive and restore the human race's connection with the Father.

What Jesus understood is something we all struggle to comprehend. He knew that all evil behaviors – within us and within society – are generated by the work of Satan, and that the only way to overcome the horrible reality of the sinful human heart is to conquer it through love and forgiveness. **Love and forgiveness were in fact the weapons used by God to destroy the power of Satan.** By offering this love to people, Jesus Christ took on the punishment that the sinful act itself deserved. Jesus didn't make people His enemies. He had only one true enemy – Satan and his army of demons.

This same dynamic applies in our lives as well. Since God provided a redemptive pathway back to Him, He desires that we receive it rather than live under sin's condemnation. He also calls us to forgive others, understanding that people who commit acts of violation are in need of redemption too.

Barriers to Experiencing God's Forgiveness

When we gain access to the real power behind forgiveness, we discover it is the doorway to a new beginning, offering us the way to be set free from every issue of sin and shame in our lives. Only forgiveness gives us the opportunity to be emotionally and spiritually healed and made whole. It can undo and repair the damage done and restore what was lost. It can turn our broken pieces into masterpieces.

But there are barriers that cause some of us find it difficult to receive this type of love:

- **Anger.** We are angry with God and blame Him for allowing things into our lives.
- **Unworthiness.** We feel unworthy to receive forgiveness for our own wrongdoings.
- **Pride.** We believe we don't need forgiveness since we aren't that bad.
- **Blame.** We believe it is "someone else's fault."

Anger at God

If God is so powerful and really loves us the way the Bible says He does, why are there so many terrible things in our lives? Many people ask this very question. In essence, some people are bitter toward God, as if He was the one who deliberately willed those things to happen. God's being all-powerful doesn't make Him directly responsible for the behaviors of sinful mankind and the evil in the world. Anything that is not perfect in this world is a byproduct of the reality of the fallen world and fallen mankind, not an act of God's doing. God is the author of free will. He allows people the freedom to make choices, even if they are wrong. We can be victimized by people and circumstances that are unfair. We can have painful childhoods. God knows this. And we can rest assured, it hurts Him too. At the same time, God will use all things together for good.

> "And we know that God causes everything to work together for the good of those who love Him and are called according to His purpose for them" (Romans 8:28 NLT).

Prayer to Overcome Anger at God

Father God, I admit that I'm angry and disappointed by You. I don't understand why You allowed me to suffer. I don't understand why You allowed these circumstances in my life. At the same time, I know You are a God of love, grace, and redemption. This means that my struggle with anger is something I need to deal with, and it is based on a lie that I've believed about Your character. Please reveal in my relationship with You and Your word how You love me and desire to restore and resolve the wounds and brokenness in my life. Please take my willing heart as the first step toward learning how to love You more and feel less angry toward You. In Jesus name I pray, Amen.

Unworthiness

We can be bound by a sense of guilt, shame, and condemnation that seems to justify why we believe we can't be forgiven (or why we shouldn't forgive ourselves). We need to come to understand that the very essence of forgiveness is that it is unmerited and undeserved. Although it may be difficult, we need to see Jesus' forgiveness as a gift, and in spite of the reality of our sin, simply open and receive the gift of forgiveness He offers us. God's forgiveness is a free gift based on His grace.

"For it is by grace you have been saved, through faith — and this is not from yourselves, it is the gift of God — not by works, so that no one can boast" (Ephesians 2:8-9 NIV).

Receiving this gift with no strings attached goes against our human nature, and especially against our identity dependent false beliefs. We are faced with a choice when we feel unworthy of forgiveness. Either the grace of Jesus is sufficient for us, or it is not. Which belief we choose to live by will determine our future. How foolish that we would reject a gift that God already bought for us, one that took something so precious as Jesus to purchase. **The truth is, we aren't worthy.** God offers us His gift not because we are worthy, but because He loves us unconditionally as His children!

Accepting and Receiving God's Forgiveness

In an earlier chapter, I provided great detail explaining God's process for us to turn from the brokenness of sin and shame in our lives, to the forgiveness and freedom of His love and mercy. Let's look at that again here as we implement it – right now – into our personal situation.

- **Confess.** Because we may have the impression that God is looking to us to be perfect, we may tend to want to bring Him the good rather than the bad in our lives. Actually, God wants us to admit to Him, agreeing with what He already knows about the sins and shame we carry. "If we claim we have no sin, we are only fooling ourselves and not living in the truth" (1 John 1:8 NLT). We don't just admit that sin is there. God requires that we actually speak and tell Him specifically what our sin is and how it occurred. "But if we confess our sins to Him, He is faithful and just to forgive us our sins and cleanse us from all unrighteousness" (1 John 1:9 NIV). We must stop trying to cover it up and striving to make things right in our human efforts. In this moment – right now – come to Him as you are, telling Him what's not right in your life.
- **Repent.** Repentance indicates a turn in direction. It's not just an outward change in our behavior. In fact, if we get legalistic and

focus on the outward appearance, we'll miss the entire point. Real repentance comes when our heart and mind are able to recognize the truth of God rather than the lies we've believed. We see things from His perspective and realize how we didn't measure up and where we went wrong. If we did anything or believed anything that opposed the word of God, we will need to repent. "Now repent of your sins and turn to God, so that your sins may be wiped away. Then times of refreshment will come from the presence of the Lord" (Acts 3:19-20 NIV). What a wonderful promise that, as we repent, not only will God forgive us our sins, but He'll also bring us renewal of our nearness to Him.

- **Accepting God's forgiveness**. Receiving is the most difficult step in this process for many of us. God's forgiveness is always a gift. He does require something on our part, but the forgiveness itself is free. We may continually push aside forgiveness in order to invoke our own form of punishment on ourselves. We may even feel this is a noble and responsible thing to do by declining it, but how this grieves God's heart! On the cross, Jesus paid the price for our sin. Therefore, when we reject His forgiveness, we essentially reject the finished work He did on our behalf.

Prayer to Trust God's Love

Father God, I don't feel worthy of forgiveness for some of the things I have done. I know Your forgiveness is free, but the things I've done don't seem to fit the criteria. Yet I must face the truth that You bled and died on that cross on my behalf. Why would I deny You that in my life? Please help me, Lord. Fill me with Your truth. Create in me a clean heart and remove everything in me that is not of You. In Jesus name I pray. Amen.

Believing We Don't Need Forgiveness

When considering a serious inventory of our sin, if we find ourselves saying, "I'm not that bad compared to…" there is a major barrier in our lives that will inhibit our further growth and freedom. Simply put, we won't receive the remedy if we can't see that a problem exists. Many times, we fool ourselves into believing that our own efforts and sense of goodness override any sinful acts we have committed. But this is so untrue. We can also use a personal justification system that says, "When I'm better than everyone else around me, I'm not really that bad of a sinner." This is extraordinarily false because in God's eyes, sin is sin.

We all have sin issues. We all fall short. It's a normal part of being human. Furthermore, we can't do much about it apart from a true transformation of our heart. Acts of morality can be done by anyone. Human beings, by nature, are capable of doing good things. But the only acts that please God are those done through Him, through the life of His spirit residing within.

> "We are all infected and impure with sin. When we display our righteous deeds, they are nothing but filthy rags" (Isaiah 64:6 NLT).

As innocent and harmless as it might seem, when we live before God with a checklist of the ways we believe we are good, we are living by a sense of our own righteousness. We cannot be forgiven in this condition. Not that God doesn't love us or is unable to forgive us, but we can only experience God's forgiveness to the degree we understand our need to be forgiven by Him. If you struggle with the inability to recognize your own sin, you might want to pray this prayer:

Prayer to Remove Self-Righteousness

Father God, I have lived my life believing I was a good person, and that my goodness made me acceptable to You. It's hard for me to think that I have believed something that actually contradicts and opposes You and the truth of the Bible. I turn from the lies I have believed about my own sense of righteousness and ask that You please break me to the point where I can see myself accurately. I know You love me and want to rescue me from this destructive mindset. Please forgive me and change me. I thank you for what you have done for me. In Jesus name I pray. Amen.

Truth Statements

Sometimes we need help applying God's remedy to our own personal sin issues. An aid in helping us grow in this area is referred to as "Truth Statements." These statements require us to name our sin for what it is, to acknowledge who we have harmed or adversely affected, and to consider the effects of our sinfulness. Here is a suggested pattern:

- **Identify and name** aloud the specific sin(s) I committed through my attitude, thoughts, words, or actions.
- **Acknowledge** who this sin has affected – another human being? God? Myself?
- **Consider** the harmful effects my sin has had on that person or persons, myself, and my relationship with Jesus.
- **Thank** Jesus, that He has already felt, suffered, and paid the penalty for this specific sin, making forgiveness possible and available to me.
- **Rest** in the Bible's assurance that, if I confess and repent of my sins, God will give me the gift of forgiveness.

Prayer for Forgiveness

Dear Father, I acknowledge that I sinned against You, and that my choices harmed or negatively affected another human being. I was wrong. I take complete responsibility for my choices. I truly am sorry. Please bless the person or people that I harmed. Please forgive me and release me from that debt. Please help me to fully trust that my sin is gone and that I have been fully forgiven. Please show me, in your perfect timing, if I need to make amends with the other person(s), or if I should simply release the situation to You. I thank You that Your grace is sufficient to cover my sin. Thank you for loving me the way You do. In Jesus name I pray. Amen.

Identifying False Guilt

While we may have legitimate sin issues in our lives that Satan plays on, sometimes we experience false guilt. False guilt is based entirely on a lie. It tells us we are to blame for something that was not our fault or that we played no part in. When we allow false guilt into our lives, it may lead to erratic behaviors to try to overcome it.

When we accept false guilt, we can also feel the need to constantly apologize and explain ourselves. It is as if we are responding to accusations all the time, often over things no one even said to us. The enemy is the accuser, and often this sense of guilt is a direct attack in the spiritual realm. Regardless of its origin, when we perceive people to be judging us, we can tend to respond in unhealthy ways:

- Becoming defensive and assuming people are accusing us of wrongdoing, even when there is no reason to assume this.
- Pointing out other people's faults or wrongdoing to move people down to a level "below" us so we feel acceptable.
- Point to our "goodness" in an attempt to protect ourselves.

The problem with these defensive measures is that often, not only is the guilt not for us to own, but now we create problems through our shame-based reactions to others. False guilt hurts relationships and takes away our peace and sense of righteousness in Christ Jesus.

> "So now there is no condemnation for those who belong to Christ Jesus. And because you belong to Him, the power of the life-giving Spirit has freed you from the power of sin that leads to death" (Romans 8:1-2 NLT).

If we struggle with feeling guilty all the time, it is important to pinpoint and identify the false messages. We must also learn to speak rational, Biblical truth back to those messages.

God uses conviction to make us aware of our need for change, so we can't discount our conscience when we are doing something that opposes the things of God. We must never lose sight of the reality that God loves each of us. Everything He does in our lives, including His conviction, is to lead us toward freedom. How liberating it is to know that in Jesus Christ we never have to be defensive. We only need to offer ourselves up with honesty and vulnerability. While our natural inclination might be to defend ourselves, we must learn to stand in the shelter and protection of God's word and declare, "I am who God says I am." As we learn to believe this statement in our hearts, guilt will no longer hold any power over our lives.

The Power of Forgiveness

Most of us find it difficult to face failure in our lives. Failure isn't the same as sin. As human beings, we constantly fail, fall short, and make mistakes. It is normal and necessary to fail in order to learn and grow. Even the moral failure of sin can still be a learning tool in our lives if we see it in the proper perspective and allow God to grow us through it. God sees us as His little children, and He understands that we are trying to take steps toward maturity. He's not screaming at us – He's encouraging us to get up, dust ourselves off, and go again.

In truth, God gives us plenty of room to make mistakes. He uses our mistakes to teach and train us. Even if people do reject us when we fail, God will never reject us (see Hebrews 13:5). We can find shelter under His grace while we are in the process of learning. And in that grace, we are fully loved, accepted, and approved of.

Receiving forgiveness opens the doorway to all future growth and healing in our soul and spirit. It also leads to an indescribable feeling of gratitude.

Have I Truly Experienced God's Forgiveness?

Several things will become evident in our heart when we have genuinely experienced God's forgiveness.

- **Gratitude.** We will thank Him, and truly understand that without God's forgiveness we would be hopelessly lost.

- **Intimacy.** We will desire to move closer to Him and not run from Him. The shame of our sin made us hide from God; forgiveness draws us close to Him.
- **Acceptance.** We will know in our heart that we are completely accepted and will no longer feel as though He is in any way rejecting us.

If we're not yet at this place in our relationship with Jesus, don't be discouraged. Diligently seek Him through faith. God's entire process of turning our brokenness into wholeness in each of our lives rests on our willingness and ability to receive His forgiveness.

Prayer to Truly Experience God's Forgiveness

Father, I have heard that I need Your forgiveness over and over. But sometimes I struggle "feeling" forgiven. I pray that every barrier and obstacle that might keep me from fully embracing Your forgiveness – including my self-righteousness or self-condemnation – be removed from my heart. Please help me God. I thank you that Your forgiveness is my freedom, and that You desire to turn my broken pieces into masterpieces. In Jesus name I pray. Amen.

"Make allowance for each other's faults and forgive anyone who offends you. Remember, the Lord forgave you, so you must forgive others"

Colossians 3:13 NLT

FORGIVENESS

Turn Resentments into Forgiveness

Introduction

The biggest miracle we will ever experience is receiving God's forgiveness and entering into a relationship with Him based on His grace, not our efforts.

From there the Christian life calls us to do things we couldn't (or wouldn't) otherwise do. He invites us to walk alongside Him, where He supernaturally enables us to live this life. We can keep running ahead of Him, feeling exhausted by our own efforts. Or we can accept His invitation and learn the peace of resting in Him, where we move through Him into deeper levels of freedom (see John 15:5).

- As we continue on this journey, we come upon tasks and challenges that go beyond our human capabilities. These challenges are actually opportunities for us to learn how to access God's power rather than rely on our own strength.
- One of the most difficult things God requires of us is to forgive others who have hurt us. It is a responsibility we are given as Christians, yet one that challenges our humanness at every level. We need God's power working in us to be able to forgive when our flesh nature says otherwise.

Hate Behavior, Not People

As we approach forgiveness, it is reassuring to acknowledge that the wrongs people committed against us were not okay. Jesus is not minimizing the harmful and horrible effects of what you've experienced. When we look at the list of ways people have sinned against us, we have every right to hate what's on those lists. Trying to go through life forgetting and getting over it will not change the effect those sinful behaviors have had on us, or the gaping wounds they inflicted on our heart.

It goes deeper than that. The effects of those violations sent a message deep within us. If those messages influenced us, they essentially have gained some degree of ownership in our lives. We need to not only get rid of the sin itself, be we also need to permanently remove the shame messages imposed on us as well.

Why We Must Forgive

God requires we forgive those who hurt us. Forgiveness is a powerful remedy against the very damage that sin and toxic shame imposed. It has the power to set us free from the harm it caused. Just as the blood of Jesus Christ was shed on our behalf to overcome the power of sin and death in our lives, we can apply that same remedy against the shaming effects of the violations that occurred to us. Forgiveness will conquer the violation!

When we learn to forgive people – not just their behaviors – the blood of Jesus is placed on the wound within us that the sinful act caused.

This doesn't mean that we are immediately and entirely set free from the damaging consequences of that sin. But through the act of forgiveness, the dirtiness of shame itself is removed, thus making it possible for the wound to be healed. Only a scar – a remembrance of God's healing power – will remain.

When We Don't Want to Forgive

Forgiveness is a choice of our will, not necessarily something we emotionally desire or feel. We may not want to forgive, but that doesn't mean it isn't the right and best thing to do as a Christ-follower. Forgiveness and bitterness are some of the results of not Biblically dealing with past violations and unmet needs in our lives. Nothing in our human nature will want to forgive people, especially when we believe they don't deserve it.

God makes it clear in His word that in order to live in His will, we must forgive those who hurt us.

> "If you forgive those who sin against you, your heavenly Father will forgive you. But if you refuse to forgive others, your Father will not forgive your sins" (Matthew 6:14-15 NLT).

Furthermore, when we choose unforgiveness, we stay bound to the pain, shame, and toxic effects of that violation. That means we won't be able to heal. Forgiveness is the master key to unlock healing in a wounded heart!

God's Way of Forgiving

When we get in touch with the heart of God, we discover that His methods of operation are entirely different from our own ways (see Isaiah 55:8-9). In fact, God tells us in His word that we are actually to get revenge on our enemies by showing them love and forgiving them. God calls us to a lifestyle of love and forgiveness that reflects His nature and character.

> "Get rid of all bitterness, rage, anger, harsh words, and slander, as well as all types of evil behavior. Instead, be kind to each other, tenderhearted, forgiving one another, just as God through Christ has forgiven you" (Ephesians 4:31-32 NIV)

Does this mean we allow people to hurt us and walk on us "like a doormat?" Absolutely not! In fact, there are times when people commit wrongs against us in such a way that there needs to be a consequence. That is something altogether different.

When we choose to deal with our pain independently of God's prescribed methods, there will be a consequence in our lives. Not only. will we have to deal with the shame that sin imposed upon us, but we'll also live life outside God's blessings that forgiveness brings. When we choose to be obedient to God's word and respond to violations through love, we will experience the blessings He has for us.

> "Don't' repay evil for evil. Don't retaliate with insults when people insult you. Instead, pay them back with a blessing. That is what God has called you to do, and He will bless you for it". (1 Peter 3:9 NLT)

A Bitter Spirit

If we remain bitter over a particular event or person, we can eventually develop a spirit of bitterness. It becomes an entirely polluted way of looking at life through chronically negative perspectives. We oftentimes develop a resentment "bank." As we overly help others, we simultaneously experience a sense of victimization. While emphasizing our own acts of service, we continue to build up a bank of resentment that says, "Look at all I've done for you. And you did this to me?"

Some temperaments (especially various blends of the Supine and Sanguine) tend to have a need to be needed. And they feel satisfaction when helping or pleasing others. This oftentimes leads to the feeling of being used and underappreciated, which can also lead to a spirit of bitterness.

Acknowledging we have a bitter spirit is the first step toward freedom. God asks that we release people and situations to Him for judgment. He only asks that we offer a willingness to forgive others, just as He is willing to forgive us. Recognize that complete forgiveness can take time. It is often a process, not merely something we "start doing." So, we can't let the enemy try to condemn us because we haven't forgiven someone completely or perfectly. God knows our hearts, and if we sincerely desire to forgive a person; or just the opposite, if we struggle with a bitter spirit, God can meet us right where we are. However, if we stubbornly refuse to consider forgiveness or to deal with our bitterness, there will be a snowballing of negative effects in our lives and relationships.

God doesn't force us to forgive people. We really don't have to forgive if we choose not to. But what we can lose is the ability to experience freedom and the supernatural ability to experience our relationship with Jesus in an intimate way. Unresolved sin and shame stand in the way. No matter how bad the act was, and no matter how undeserving the person is of our forgiveness, **our willingness to forgive a person will truly set us free!**

A Process for Applying Forgiveness

Talking about forgiving people is one thing. But facing those sins on an individual basis – and fully connecting with the emotions, the damage, and the consequences – is entirely different. Most of us inappropriately deal with the way others have hurt us. We don't understand the significance or the effects, so we think it will just go away in time.

The purpose of this process is to fully recall and work through each event that occurred that either you hold continued resentment toward or that remains toxic in your life. Don't get caught up in the process but recognize that it is more important to evaluate and pray over the violations so you might identity which ones need to be dealt with. God must be the one who directs the process. And it must be covered in prayer.

- **Process Feelings**. The ability to connect emotionally is an important aspect of healing. Here are important aspects of recalling past violations. We need to ask ourselves, "Can I acknowledge that the act was wrong and that as a human being I had certain rights that were violated? Can I identify with how the act made me feel? Have I been able to connect emotionally with what happened? Have I ever cried, grieved, or expressed hurt as a result? If our answer was "no" to items on this list, it is possible we are still protecting the painful event through some form of denial, whether intentionally or not. Only the power of the Holy Spirit can "breakthrough" your denial. If you trust God, ask Him to reveal where you may be wounded and broken, yet consciously unaware. Remember, He may know that you're not ready to deal with this issue yet, so don't put pressure on yourself.

It's certainly ok to move on for now and focus on something else. Just remember to continue to pray for God's guidance and power, not allowing the spirit of denial to take root.

- **Acknowledge the Truth.** If we were able to answer yes to the questions above, then we can begin to write and speak truth statements about the act. We need to find a place where we can be completely alone and speak the words audibly that have been revealed to our hearts privately. We are going to declare this to ourselves, to God, and to the enemy.

- **Willingness.** The final step in the process is a willingness to forgive the person who committed the act against us. Some important things to remember:

  o Forgiveness is **a choice of the will**, not a feeling or emotion.

  o Forgiveness **opposes our human nature**. Therefore, we'll need God's divine power to do it for us.

  o Forgiveness **begins with a small willingness**, not necessarily a strong desire.

  o Whatever violation was committed against us, Jesus felt and bore it personally Himself. Therefore, **we don't need to go through this alone.** He has already gone through it with us and for us.

  o As we deal with forgiving others, we aren't necessarily going to ever be in a relationship with them again. **Forgiveness is not reconciliation**. We can only be reconciled with those who have realized their part in the situation, are emotionally (and physically) safe to encounter, and are willing to make amends to us.

Write It Down

There is something about the human will that seems to be more concrete when we write it down and sign our name to it. Knowing this, I've provided a simple "worksheet" for us to put our feelings and thoughts in writing.

- Name the **violator or perpetrator** _____
  _____

- Name the **violation or hurt** done to you: _____
  _____

- Ponder your **heart's responses** to these questions:
  - Can I acknowledge that the act was wrong, and that as a human being I had certain rights that were violated?
  - Can I identify with how that act made me feel?
  - Have I allowed myself to fully connect emotionally with what happened?
  - Have I ever cried, grieved, or expressed hurt as a result?
- Speak this **declaration against sin**:
  - It was not okay that this violation or hurt occurred in my life.
  - I refuse it and the message it sent into my mind and heart.
  - It caused me to feel _____.
  - It caused me to see myself as _____.
  - As a result, I continue to believe that I am _____.
- Speak this **truth statement** into your heart:
  - While the violation or hurt told me a lie, I choose to accept the truth of God that I am deeply loved, completely forgiven, fully pleasing, totally accepted, absolutely complete in Christ.
- Speak to Jesus your **willingness to forgive** the violator:
  - Jesus, as difficult as it is, I realize that I must forgive this person as an act of my will.
  - I cannot do this on my own.
  - Please take it for me.

Action Points

As God slowly heals your heart, consider taking these additional steps toward freedom and wholeness from the brokenness of having been hurt or violated:

- **No-send letter.** Write the violator a letter that expresses how they made you feel, and then the choice you made to forgive them. You don't need to ever send the letter unless you feel compelled by God to do so. The purpose of writing it is for you to purge and express your raw emotions about the act, and the result of what was done to you.

- **Renounce.** In the name of Jesus, speak strongly against that sin and its shameful effects it had in your life.
- **Pray.** Here is a sample of a prayer you might consider using:

"Father God, I was really hurt by _____. But today, I choose to begin the process of forgiving them. I ask that you please forgive them for sinning against You and for violating or hurting me by _____ that they did do me. I pray that You would meet them at their point of need, as I know you are going to do with me as well. I release this person from my human judgment and ask that You place them under your righteous judgment. I renounce the sin and every damaging effect and message it imposed on my life. I ask that you give back to this individual any toxic shame that was placed upon me by them. And I pray that you would restore fully to me anything that You intended for me to have, but that they took from me through their sinful actions. I ask that you close the door between me and this individual, and seal it, in the spiritual realm, with Jesus' blood, never to be opened again. I pray earnestly that what Satan meant for evil, You will absolutely use for good. Thank you, Jesus, for setting me free. In Jesus name I pray. Amen."

The <u>Gift</u> of Brokenness

What may have happened to us in our past will become a part of our life story. But **as our wounds are healed and the broken pieces begin to come together in God's hands, they become a testimony to God's great power and love in our life**. As God administers His great truth into our lives, He takes away the deceptions and lies the enemy has spoken to us, day after day for many years. Although God is able to heal our wounds, we will never completely forget the pain, and don't need to. It will serve as a scar – a reminder of the healing work of Jesus Christ on our behalf – that we can reflect on when God gives us opportunities to encourage, support, and help others who are hurting.

As we encounter the power of the blood of Jesus Christ and His remarkable love and grace, we will become carriers of hope rather than generators of shame. We will possess tangible proof of the miracle of what God can do inside the heart of a human being who has been hurt and wounded. We can carry the message of God's love and power to others who are struggling. This means that at the very place and point where Satan attempted to destroy us, God will restore us and use that experience to further His kingdom.

Learning to Grieve What We've Lost

While forgiveness allows us the opportunity to remove the toxins of an injustice committed against us, we must also deal with those wounds that stem from neglect in our early lives, that we learned about early in this book. What people didn't or couldn't do for us can create just as much (if not more) shame as those violations that were perpetrated against us. If we don't effectively deal with these shame-based messages, we can go through life trying to satisfy those unmet needs in unhealthy or ungodly ways. Based upon our inborn temperament combination, this pursuit will take on a multitude of forms.

Much of the important work involved in the early stages of life transformation and restoration includes **grief.** We need to deal with those losses we weren't able to face before (or maybe didn't realized the importance of facing them). We will also find current losses in our lives for which we need to grieve. Examples might be the pain felt due to an absent spouse or the distant relationship of an adult child.

Grieving takes time. And it can't be rushed. Grief has a purpose and a season, but its goal is to move us to a point of healing and wholeness, rather than keeping us bound to things that continue to dominate and destroy our lives.

Steps to Grieving Your Childhood

- **Identify** the loss for what it really is. Create a written list of what you lost in your childhood, or maybe never even had to begin with. Be sure to include who it is you feel failed you in this way. Try to start with your earliest memories you can recall and work forward to the present. The perceived needs you have today may be skewed due to an undercurrent of unfinished business from your past. You may be expecting people to meet needs in your current life that actually stem from unmet needs in your childhood. To allow this healing work to be most effective, trust your perceptions. Although others may have experienced or perceived these things differently, your soul responded to them as you perceived them. And that's what matters here.

- **Legitimize** the needs you have listed. We spend most of our lives trying to minimize our needs. We must do the opposite if we hope to experience healing and a life of forgiveness. Consider saying something similar to this: "I needed you to _____ (love me, nurture me, protect me), but you didn't. I know you had your own reasons and issues, but it didn't change the fact that I truly needed this from you."

- **Connect** emotionally to the pain of not having something you needed. This may include your temperament needs not being acknowledged by someone important in your life. You may have had it at one point, and then eventually lost it. This could be the death or separation of someone close to you. It may have been the loss of the opportunity to just be a child. If you are still in denial or trapped behind anger, you may not have allowed yourself to actually feel the raw emotions connected to these experiences. Remember, "God won't heal what you don't feel." Consider saying something like this: "When you _____ (their hurtful act), I felt _____ (my emotional response)."

- **Acknowledge** where we have blamed others. Often when our needs aren't met, we begin to blame people and grow bitter and angry. We may blame our parents for how they raised us. We may blame a family member or spouse for not meeting our needs. We may blame God. Understanding our blame helps us see why we've been hindered from moving on.

- **Admit** our powerlessness. We must come to a place where we simply recognize that we are powerless over the person and their inability to meet our need. Or that we can do nothing to change the fact that they left us or failed us or rejected us or hurt us. From that place of powerlessness, we are now ready to surrender it to Jesus.

- **Choose** to forgive the person who let you down. Using the same process that we learned in forgiving a person for an act committed against us, we can also forgive the person who didn't meet our needs.

- **Accept** the person (even though you may still detest their behavior) and the circumstances that led to where you are today. Often people who neglected us were physically or emotionally unavailable to us because of their own painful issues, or even because of how they were raised by their own parents. This, in no way, justifies their action or inaction. However, it does help us realize that we cannot demand something from someone that they do not possess themselves. We must understand that when we forgive and accept someone, we stop trying to change that person. We stop trying to get our needs met through them. And we stop recreating similar dysfunctional patterns to get someone else to meet those needs.

- **Say goodbye.** If you are grieving the loss of a person, write that person a "no-send" letter to say goodbye. Explain in detail the pain of separation, but the desire to forgive and move on without them. Don't rush this process. Allow yourself to feel every word you write. Don't hold back your honest feelings. Remember, this is not a letter that is ever sent unless, at some point, you feel God is leading you to do so.

- **Ask God** to meet your unmet needs. While we are asked to let go of painful, unmet needs of our past, we must have the perspective and mindset that we have a God who is infinitely higher and greater than any need we have at any given time. Ask God to meet your needs through His perspective, and to give you the willingness and patience to wait on Him to do so. "Now all glory to God, who is able, through His mighty power at work within us, to accomplish infinitely more than we might ask or think" (Ephesians 3:20 NLT).

Prayer for the Grieving Process

Father God, I am so prone to now wanting to feel pain that even the thought of grieving scares me. I realize there were things in my life that I lost. Sometimes, I just couldn't face it. Other times, I resorted to anger and blame. I may have even blamed You for allowing this in my life. Lord, You know the barriers in my heart that have prevented me from healing. I ask that You please work in me and do for me what I can't do for myself. I ask, in exchange for my willingness to grieve and let go of losses, that You give me those things I really do need. I trust You, Lord. I know that You are able. In Jesus name I pray. Amen.

You Are Free to Be Accepted!

The journey toward healing is extraordinary! We may begin this journey bitter and angry toward others for the wrongs they committed against us. We may live our lives based on our perception of not measuring up, not being acceptable or worthy. We may have felt overwhelmed by our own shame and guilt. But through a journey of trust, surrender, and heart change, we find authentic acceptance. We also discover that wounded areas in our lives become gateways to new beginnings. The negative experiences don't go away, but they do become a part of our overall life experience.

> "Be thankful in all circumstances, for this is God's will for you who belong to Christ Jesus" (1 Thessalonians 5:18 NLT).

When we embrace forgiveness and benefit from its remedy, we can offer that same remedy to others. This means we are able to accept others too. Imagine spending the rest of your life feeling totally accepted exactly as you are! Imagine not having to worry about the flaws or the failures in your life. And no longer having to punish (even if only in your mind) those who added to them.

We are moving from our old experiences to a new place, from brokenness to wholeness. The entire process is meant to take away the damaging effects of sin and shame, those things that have attempted to disrupt God's plan and purpose for our lives.

> "The thief comes only to steal and kill and destroy; I have come that they may have life and have it to the full" (John 10:10 NIV).

> "For his anger lasts only a moment, but His favor lasts a lifetime! Weeping may last through the night, but joy comes in the morning" (Psalm 30:5 NLT).

If you are faithful in your desire to be set free, there is a new day on the horizon. The life of emotional and spiritual abundance isn't necessarily one that is problem free; it's one that is lived in Christ. God does not intend for you to stay tied to your past. He is waiting to pull you into safety and set you on a pathway of fulfillment and wholeness. King David described a moment such as this in his life:

> "I waited patiently for the Lord to help me, and he turned to me and heard my cry. He lifted me out of the pit of despair, out of the mud and the mire. He set my feet on solid ground and steadied me as I walked along. He has given me a new song to sing, a hymn of praise to our God. Many will see what he has done and be amazed. They will put their trust in the Lord" (Psalm 40:1-3 NLT).

Have you ever felt that you were in the pit? Have you ever hit rock bottom? Has God freed you from those dark places? **What He has done for others, He can and will do for you!**

Questions from Dr. Dave

For personal reflection or group discussion of Chapter 15

Emotional strongholds have their origins in strongly held false beliefs. In this chapter I expounded on five emotions that very commonly lead to emotional strongholds: anger, rejection, fear, loneliness, and powerlessness. One thing that these have in common is their dependence upon another human being. Ask God to show you whether it's these emotions that you're bound to, or could it be your shame-based expectations of others that gives these strongholds their energy.

Many of us find it difficult to forgive ourselves. This struggle is built entirely on a foundational false belief: People who fail deserve to be punished. Although the statement is true, we tend to overlook the fact that Jesus endured the punishment we deserved. We feel we need to continue to punish ourselves by holding on to condemnation. What areas of your life do you condemn yourself the most? What is keeping you from accepting God's free gift He paid for on the cross? Reflect what might look different in your life if this guilt and shame were removed.

The power of the cross and the resurrection separated "what we do" from "who we are" once and for all! God loves who we are as His children. But He hates the sin and selfishness in our lives. As followers of Christ, we are to see others in the very same way – hate their sinful behavior, yet fully love and accept the person for who they are. What parts of this are difficult for you to swallow? What might it cost if you were to see others through the eyes of Jesus rather than through the lens of what they've done or failed to do?

CHAPTER 16

Phase 4: N – Nurture Lasting Hope in Others

"Seldom set your foot in your neighbors' house – too much of you, and they will come to hate you"

Proverbs 25:17 NIV

BOUNDARIES

Turn Walls of Fear into
Healthy Boundaries

Introduction

As we embrace our authentic identity, we learn to value ourselves in God's eyes. We no longer desire to engage in the same unhealthy patterns of behavior that held our souls in bondage before. We will find that learning to live life in a healthy way can be enjoyable, meaningful, and fulfilling.

Even as our transformational journey continues, our old ways of thinking don't quickly die. Just because we've changed doesn't mean that the people in our lives have changed. In fact, we may become more aware than ever of unhealthy relationships and emotionally unhealthy people in our lives. This doesn't make us better than them. It makes us aware of their need for the hope we've found in Jesus.

- How can we find the freedom to be our authentic selves, yet at the same time protect ourselves from the effects of toxic people, places, and things? This lesson will help us learn to create boundaries to help us develop new, healthy ways of participating in relationships with others based on God's principles.

What Are Boundaries?

Boundaries are visible or invisible "fences" that define ownership, protect our rights, and set rules to determine what is acceptable and what is not acceptable within a relationship. Boundaries say, "I belong to me and you belong to you."

In their bestselling book, *Boundaries*, Christian psychologists Henry Cloud and John Townsend define a boundary in this way: "A boundary is a property line. We can easily understand this by thinking of one's property, which defines what is yours, and what is not yours. A boundary then simply defines ownership. Knowing the scope of ownership is important because whoever owns something controls it and is thereby responsible for it. In the material world boundaries are easily defined by such things as walls or fences, but in the immaterial world, such as human relationships, boundaries are harder to see."

Rather than merely separating, boundaries protect what we possess, are responsible for, and value, including the beauty of the life God gave us. Boundaries enable us to defend ourselves physically, emotionally, and spiritually against intrusive or unwanted risks or dangers. But the entire design and purpose of healthy boundaries is to create guidelines for mutual respect, consideration, protection, and safety in all areas of a relationship. Some of the parts of our lives that boundaries define and protect include:

- Our bodies
- Our emotions
- Our feelings
- Our family
- Our loved ones
- Our beliefs
- Our values
- Our identity
- Our time
- Our money
- Our responsibilities
- Our roles

- Our possessions
- Our freedoms

God's Boundary System

All of God's principles, laws, and promises rest on a perfect set of boundaries established through His word. These boundaries are specific for each area of our lives. In love, He established these to protect us and give us a safe environment in which to grow in our relationship with God and others.

God doesn't establish boundaries because He needs protection. He establishes them to offer His guiding principles for our lives – principles that, in fact, will protect us, sometimes even from ourselves and our own choices. With His boundaries in place, we learn how to thrive both in our relationship with Him and our relationships with one another.

Developing Healthy Boundary Systems

The establishment of boundary systems begins while we're small children. We learn the "rules' for life and family, and the concept of consequence for wrongful choices and behaviors. We are taught about the role of grace and forgiveness versus shame and punishment when we violate a boundary. The boundaries within each family are composed of individual family member's belief systems. Whether the boundary system is established fairly and under safe and healthy Biblical guidelines depends on how healthy or unhealthy those family members are emotionally and spiritually.

In a home where there is a lack of parental structure and a lack of Biblical morality being modeled to children, a child might not learn healthy boundaries. As a result, they will merely learn to survive and cope with the uncertainty, fear, and pain that surrounds them every day. When a child from this type of home becomes an adult, they will more than likely struggle to develop any type of healthy boundary system in their life, work, and relationships. For this to change, it will require a lengthy process of surrendering to God and His ways, identifying false beliefs and negative behaviors, and to develop a new belief system based on God's truth.

Conversely, in a home that is filled with love, grace, and safe, healthy boundaries, a child will learn that he or she has freedom to make choices – even if the choices are wrong – and still safely "be themselves." Wrong choices will carry consequences but shaming and rejecting are not among those consequences. This home also teaches the purpose of forgiveness, and other life-building virtues grounded in the word of God. A child raised in this type of family system will grow up to become an emotionally and spiritually healthy person, instilled with a sense of boundaries that were an inbred part of who he or she has become.

No matter how skewed our boundary system may have been, God's word provides the guidelines, answers, and specific boundaries we need to live life to the fullest. He not only teaches us these boundaries, but He also gives us the desire and ability to adhere to them.

Boundaries, Rights, and Responsibilities

In attempting to establish boundaries in our lives, we must consider two basic areas:

- **Rights.** Our God-given rights as human beings.
- **Responsibilities**. Our responsibilities in relationships versus those of God and of others.

One of the saddest misconceptions is that being a Christian means every single right is stripped from us, and we should always meet the needs and demands of others, all in the name of Christian love. The Christian life indeed requires that we surrender some rights, some comforts, some preferences, and some securities in sacrifice for the needs of others. Also, in standing up for God's truth and the foundational belief system surrounding Jesus Christ, we are willing to be persecuted for the cause if necessary.

But Christianity does not mean that we throw away our individuality and our right to think, feel, and act, based on our free will. And we certainly don't, as some describe it, become a "doormat." In surrendering ourselves to the Lord, we allow our individuality, thinking, feeling, and behaving to be molded into that of Jesus Christ.

As we learn to live our lives through Christ within us, situations in our lives that once may have caused us to feel denied or disadvantaged by others, will now be seen as opportunities for us to willingly deny ourselves in order to serve the needs of others. The behavior may not look much different to the unknowing observer. But the heart behind it will be radically different, as will the effect on the one being served. John 3:30 (NIV) says, "He must become greater; I must become less."

God-Given Freedoms

Each of us is given freedoms – by God and by society – which provide the foundation for our uniqueness to flourish.

It is important to remember that these freedoms should not, in any way, infringe on our ability to love others sacrificially and to die to self as God's word teaches. Therefore, if we begin to claim these as rights (entitlements) to justify what benefits us, we are misusing them and elevating self. This contradicts God's clear principles in His word and is very prideful.

Conversely, if we have not been allowed these freedoms in our lives, we will have no basis from which to perceive healthy boundaries for others or ourselves.

Early in this book I presented these five human freedoms from the perspective of their being absent in shame-based families. In this section, those same freedoms are presented in hopes of defining Christ-centered guidelines for creating healthy boundaries in our lives.

- **Perceive.** We are free to not condone or allow sinful behaviors and tendencies in our interactions with others, placing protections and consequences as necessary. God doesn't overlook sin. Just as God deals with sin through boundaries and consequences in our relationship with Him, so can we with others. We must seek His wisdom in each particular situation, so we don't overstep our boundaries with the other individual(s).
- **Think.** We are free to be the person God created us to be, even if it doesn't align with another person's expectations. We belong to God first and foremost. Other people's ideas of how they want us

to live life, including our parents, family members, spouses, and children, do not supersede God's vision for us.

- **Feel.** We are free to feel our feelings, even if someone else doesn't like what we feel or how we express it. However, if our emotions are sin-based, we must bring them to God, asking Him to deal with our hearts. We don't change our feeling merely to please another person. God did not authorize another human being to be in charge of our emotions, nor are we responsible for theirs.

- **Speak.** We are free to say "no" to something a person or persons requests from us when it opposes our own God-given conscience or God-given responsibilities. Just because people request things from us doesn't mean we automatically need to comply. We need God's discernment and judgment to do those things God asks us to do, not what we feel pressured to do in order to please others.

- **Ask.** We are free to pursue our dreams, to find joy, to live in peace, and to have balance in our relationships, despite what those close to us choose to do. We do not have to stay bound by toxic emotions, feelings of despair, and hopelessness. The revelation of God's word repeatedly reveals His plan for our lives. To think we should live in emotional pain contradicts God's heart for us and is never His will or desire for us.

- **Risk.** We are free to make our own free-will choices, based on facts and the guidance of the Holy Spirit. We do not have to live by what other people need, feel, desire, or want from us if it may cause us harm. We then have the choice to do things for others because of God's love and His leading, not from a basis of coercion, guilt, or obligation. We don't always have to "play it safe" as we may have been taught to do.

Discernment

Learning to discern where our personal God-given rights begin, end, and can be offered as an act of submission takes wisdom. We can start by asking ourselves these questions:

- According to God's word, do I have this freedom?
- Is my freedom infringing on or violating someone else's same freedom?
- Do I claim this freedom for myself but remain unwilling to give this same freedom to others?

Allowing Others Their Rights

Setting boundaries and establishing mutual basic rights in relationships becomes challenging when we confuse our "rights" to protect our own life with the "right" to control another person's behavior. While learning to embrace our rights can be a welcome relief, the challenge is that we must allow others the very same freedoms.

- We have no right to try to change how another person believes, thinks, feels, or behaves.
- We have no right to attempt to make a person into who we think they should be.

If we are dealing with emotionally or spiritually unhealthy people, this means we must allow them to make their own choices that might lead them to destructive and damaging consequences in their lives. It is important we give people the freedom to choose – whether it be right or wrong. People have that right.

If and when we attempt to stop, redirect, or fix another human being's choices and decisions, we are not only exhibiting shame-based behavior ourselves, but we are attempting to serve the role of the Holy Spirit in their lives.

Submission Versus Claiming Our Rights

God doesn't call us to be doormats, but He does call us to live submitted lives. Submission doesn't operate by someone else controlling us, or by us feeling obligated or guilted into doing something. Submission is a by-product of love and is built upon the respect and honor due to another person. In essence, when we submit, we give up our own rights and allow someone else to make a decision. This assumes we aren't compromising our core rights and beliefs in the process.

I often explain the concept of Biblical "submission" to my clients in this way: It is a gift we give another person, not something they take from us or force upon us. True submission does not place us under the authority of another person. No, true Biblical submission actually compels us to yield our needs in favor of the needs of another person so that they may experience the love and grace of Christ through us.

> "Do nothing out of selfish ambition or vain conceit. Rather, in humility value others above yourselves, not looking to your own interests but each of you to the interests of the others" (Philippians 2:3-4 NIV).

Submission in Christian Marriage

Submission does not seek to manipulate someone in order to get personal needs met or to control an outcome. Instead, as two people come together in love and submission, there should be compatibility, not compromise, and yielding, not manipulation.

We are able to submit to a person when we love God, ourselves, and others properly. If any of these are missing or lacking, submission will quickly become unhealthy and lead to either fear or identity dependence.

In the NLT version of the Bible, Ephesians 5:21 tells us to "Submit to one another out of reverence for Christ."

Responsibility in Relationships

Part of learning how to establish healthy, reasonable boundaries is to know where "I" end and "you" begin. To break this down, I've created a table that looks at three functions in a relationship:

Our responsibilities to God, self, and others	Our reasonable expectations of other people	God's responsibilities
We offer ourselves as complete human beings in relationships, not needing someone else to make us whole or to complete us.	We can expect people to be whole, complete human beings in relationships, not looking for us to make up for their deficiencies.	We learn to find sufficiency in Christ – He alone will make us whole and complete through Him.
We are able to offer forgiveness on a continual basis when others commit wrongdoing against us, offering a relationship pattern of grace.	We can expect people to offer forgiveness and grace when we fall short.	We know that all forgiveness comes from God. Where we fail each other, we find grace through Jesus Christ.
We are responsible for the changes we need to make in our life. We are not responsible for others.	We can allow people to be responsible for the changes they need to make in their lives. They are not responsible for ours.	God convicts us of those things we need to change, and then gives us the power only to change ourselves.
We take responsibility for our own emotions and don't attempt to make others responsible for our feelings and moods, whether good or bad.	We can expect people to take responsibility for their own emotions, not holding us accountable for their feelings and moods, whether good or bad.	We know that only God can help us identify our emotions and the root causes behind them.
We can offer our ideas, beliefs, and wishes in the relationship, no matter how different they might be from those of other people. We respect their differing views, but don't allow them to disrespect or compromise our core beliefs.	We can expect people to offer their ideas, beliefs, and wishes, and respect our views that may be different from theirs.	We ask God to take our ideas, beliefs, and wishes, and align them with His will.
We love others the best way we know how, understanding that, as human beings, our love cannot be perfect.	We can expect people to love us the best way they know how, understanding their love for us won't be perfect.	We know that only God loves us perfectly, and we allow our deepest need for love to be met by Him.

When problems occur, we take responsibility for our part and do not resort to blaming others or allowing ourselves to play the role of a victim.	When problems occur, we can expect others to take responsibility for their part and to not resort to blaming us or attempting to guilt us.	We ask God to resolve the issues in our life, and we seek the Word of God for answers, examples, and principles.
We commit to be faithful and honest to others.	We expect others to commit to being faithful and honest with us.	God is faithful by nature. It is impossible for Him to go against His own character of faithfulness; therefore, we can always trust Him and count on Him.

What to Do When Others Fail Us

So, what happens when we fulfill our responsibilities to others, but they don't fulfill theirs? If we are the recipients of a violation, we can set boundaries to protect ourselves from the violation recurring. But we can't change the other person's heart. Rather than attempting to balance an imbalanced relationship, we must be willing to simply let those gaps occur and ask God to fill in the missing pieces. If the relationship is extremely unhealthy or harmful, we may also need to withdraw from the relationship, temporarily or possibly even permanently.

Not only will we find that God can and will meet our needs when we do this, but when we don't manipulate the situation and simply focus on "keeping our own side of the street clean," God will also deal with the other person. In fact, it is often our own efforts to fix the situation that accelerates or worsens the problem. In our efforts to "fix," we can literally get in the way of what God wants to do in the other person's life.

Learning how to set boundaries in this way – allowing ourselves, others, and God to be responsible for their part in the relationship – requires the discipline of letting go and trusting God. Allowing God to change our heart in this area will lead to profound new levels of freedom, and ultimately, healthier, more well-balanced relationships. It will allow us greater sanity, as we are able to focus on the things we can change and learn to let go of the things we cannot change. When we learn to depend on God as our ultimate source, we no longer allow people to emotionally manipulate us, nor do we attempt to manipulate them. We come to understand that we are no longer dependent on what the other person has to offer, understanding that we have all our needs met through Jesus Christ. Just because others may be irresponsible, unhappy, unhealthy, or unloving doesn't mean we need to be or have to be!

Identify Where Boundaries Should Be Built

How can we begin to set boundaries in a difficult relationship? Here is a process that you might consider using in defining and carrying out healthy, clearly defined boundaries in relationships.

- **Identify** where you might compromise or allow wrongful behaviors in your life because you don't want to upset or lose the other person.
- **Write** a list of those behaviors along with the name of the person or persons each behavior involves.
  - "I cannot allow _____ (behavior) to continue in my life."
  - "If _____ (person) continues to engage in that behavior in my life, I have the right to impose a consequence upon them in order to protect myself from the harmful effects their behavior may cause me."
- **Apply** the consequence clearly and consistently.
  - "If this person continually breaks or disregards my boundary without sorrow or change, I am willing to follow through with the following consequence: _____."

In setting boundaries, we need to pray and seek God's wisdom. If we allow our emotions to lead us, we will not make wise decisions and can be hurt by relationships even more. If we are simply reacting in anger to punish someone, we are not actually creating a boundary, but overstepping one.

Evaluate the Motives of Our Heart

- Is my desire for the person to change their behavior valid? Or could it be selfish or prideful?
- Is their current behavior in clear violation of a healthy, safe relationship? Or could it actually be healthy and safe, and that makes me feel uncomfortable or undeserving?
- Are my personal preferences or emotional needs driving my actions? Or could it be some other motivation that I may be avoiding?
- Although I can refuse to allow the person's behavior in my life, do I understand it's not my responsibility to control their behavior?
- Why should I not allow this behavior in my life? What might be the result if I were to continue to allow it?
- What might happen if I set a boundary that opposes this behavior? Or if I don't? Am I willing to accept that outcome?

Remember, a boundary isn't used to exercise control over another person's behavior. It is used to protect our own lives, values, and wellbeing, from another person's choices.

Boundaries and Intimacy

While it seems as though living a life based on varying degrees of boundaries could cause separation, nothing is further from the truth. In reality, when two people learn healthy boundaries, they establish a safe environment characterized by mutual respect and honor. Their connection is based upon mutual choosing, not based upon neediness. It is in this environment that the relationship can thrive and grow, creating the atmosphere for true intimacy.

What is intimacy? Intimacy is the ability to fully see another person without the fear of rejection. It is a form of closeness based on vulnerability and honesty. It allows people to see us as we truly are, where we can reveal the deeper things that make us uniquely us. I often tell my clients that true intimacy is "being fully known and fully vulnerable, yet still being fully accepted and fully loved."

Prayer for Reconciliation and Intimacy

Father, as I see my boundary failures, I'm overwhelmed with where to begin. In one sense, I need to "take ownership" of myself again. But in another sense, I am actually setting the stage to love people more and love them more intimately. How these two realities intersect is difficult for me to comprehend; yet I know this is exactly how You operate within me. God, I ask You to change my heart, and I ask You to please intervene in my loved one's life so we can first experience intimacy with You, and ultimately experience honest, true intimacy with each other. Thank you that you created me to be in relationships that are fulfilling and meaningful. I pray that I would be able to experience that to the fullest. In Jesus name I pray, Amen.

"Yet to all who did receive Him, to those who believed in His name, He gave the right to become children of God"

John 1:12 NIV

IDENTITY

Turn Toward My True Identity in Christ

Introduction

As we learn to confront shame, we are given the opportunity to disengage its power. The removal of shame is both a process and a continual lifestyle. It is a choice we will be asked to make every day for the rest of our lives: Will I live my life based on the shame, fear, and the dysfunction in and around me? Or will I live my life on the basis of God's grace, mercy, forgiveness, and unconditional love toward me?

In Matthew 9:17 (NIV), Jesus explained a profound truth. He said, "And no one puts new wine into old wineskins. For the old skins would burst from the pressure, spilling the wine and ruining the skins. New wine is stored in new wineskins so that both are preserved." The effect of sin and shame in our lives, and our own efforts to overcome it, may have caused us to "burst," or to get to the end of ourselves. Even as Christians, we may have incorporated God's principles into an overall unhealthy belief system – a system infected by sin and shame, self-righteousness and false humility. We may have thought if we could just add some good things to our messy lives, somehow everything would be all right. But it didn't work.

- That's because in the spirit-led, authentic Christian life, change must occur at a foundational (heart) level, where entire mentalities, coping mechanisms, and belief systems are brought into alignment with God's truth. When this takes place, an entirely new world unfolds for us. The people and circumstances in our life may not change, but we are able to see them through an entirely different lens — the lens of God's grace! As this process occurs, there is perhaps nothing as healing and restoring as being able to embrace our new identity.

Who Am I, Really?

Identity simply is a perspective of how we see ourselves. We looked at this in great detail earlier in the book, but now I want us to personally wrestle with this question for ourselves: "Who am I, really?" When we were covered in layers of shame, our identity was concealed, damaged, or taken from us. We lived our lives based on lies — we believed what the people and experiences of our broken past had taught us. We believed that the measurements and standards of the world, and the approval of others who were just as human as we were, were the correct gauge of our self-worth and identity.

Here are some places where we may have tried to find our identity:

- **Our family role.** Within our family-of-origin, we functioned in a role that told us how to give and receive love, and how to see ourselves, others, and the world. If that family system was unhealthy or shaming, our sense of identity might have been based on outrageous lies, or it may have never been developed at all. We may have learned to take care of the needs of other family members, and in the process were never able to define our own personal needs, likes, preferences, goals, desires, beliefs, etc. Instead, we learned to adapt to whatever others needed or desired.
- **Our relationships.** We can become so enmeshed in our relationships that we feel unable to separate ourselves from a particular person. We might only feel secure when this person is around us, and continually focus on his or her needs and life issues. Because we don't have healthy boundaries in place, we have difficulty knowing where we end and they begin. Our entire

identity gets lost in this person. The word for this is "enmeshment," as we discussed a few chapters earlier. We can also bring unhealthy people into our lives that continually criticize and put us down, and we learn to believe what they're saying is true. In time, we become conditioned to view ourselves through that same filter.

- **Our appearance or sexuality.** We may have learned that our core value is in our physical appearance. We may have received validation when we outwardly made ourselves look good. We may have taken that to even more of an extreme and used our sexuality to gain power or attention from the opposite sex. Even in marriage we may continue to believe we are only as good as our appearance or sexuality. If our identity is wrapped tightly in how we look, a bad hair day can leave us feeling insecure and unworthy, and for some, we may be terrified of the changes that aging will bring. If we find our identity in our sexuality, our self-worth may plummet merely by failing to have an orgasm.

- **Our possessions or status.** We may have become attached to our material possessions or social status, using them to measure our personal worth. We can even reason that with enough "stuff" or success, we will one day find the security and confidence we need in life. We may have convinced ourselves that who we are is a reflection of what we have attained or achieved.

- **Our reputation.** We can strive hard to produce an outward reputation based on moral living, kindness, and other outward acts or goodness. We can find security in how we are viewed by others, including church members, co-workers, and others. That's not to say it may not align with our character, but often we can become obsessed with this reputation, fearing that if others really knew us, they might not approve of or accept us. If we ever entered into situations in life where this reputation appeared smudged or threatened, we could be devastated. We might come from dysfunctional family systems where those around us have negative reputations. We use our efforts to create a good reputation to overcome the shameful activities of other family members. This would be a clear example of the "Equal and Opposite Principle" we discussed earlier.

- **Our work.** Work is an important part of our life. We carry a title and a set of responsibilities related to the work we do. Some of us find our entire identity through our work. Furthermore, we become so consumed by our work, our entire sense of worth rests in our success or failure at that workplace. This was the type of family environment I grew up in. It seemed that regardless how important the life event – birthday, holiday, milestone – my dad could not be there. The answer was always the same: "He had to work." Others of us may have jobs or careers we chose out of obligation and need but find no joy whatsoever in the tasks. These jobs may stand in complete contrast with our temperament, skills, and talents. We feel chronically negative, detached, unsatisfied, and unmotivated as a result.

What is the common reality with all of these: our family roles, relationships, appearance, material possessions, reputation, and work? In truth, they don't offer identity – they actually steal our true identity. By becoming fixated and secure in any of these areas, we become fearful at the thought of losing or changing anything where our identity would stand a risk of being threatened. This means that when one of these areas fails, our entire world can seemingly fall apart.

My pastor, Kyle Idleman, said recently in a sermon, "We'll not fully discover our true identity in Christ until all of the idols in our lives have failed us."

Discovering Who We Are

If all of these are unhealthy methods of seeking identity, then what is the true method by which we should begin to discover who we are? Surely it can't mean we should stop relationships, live immorally, fail on purpose, let our appearance go, or quit our job? Of course not. Identity involves a much deeper perspective that may take some time to build. In reality, identity has little if anything to do with matters of the physical world, including the things on the list above. Collectively, chasing after these external pursuits is often referred to as being "externally defined."

Instead, identity is a core issue – being "internally defined." It is the very essence of our being – the intricate and detailed things that make us who we are. The only potential we have to truly capture our identity is to ask the one who designed and created us. By seeking His point of view, we are going to find who we are and the purpose for which we were created.

"I knew you before I formed you in your mother's womb.
Before you were born, I set you apart" (Jeremiah 1:5 NIV)

Gaining Identity

Everything we have done through the entire TURN process (as well as throughout this entire book) has led us to the place where we are finally ready to embrace our authentic identity. We have turned from toxic people, places, and things. And we have uncovered the shame, lies, and false beliefs. However, if our identity has been damaged or broken as a result of years and years of unresolved shame, rediscovering it won't happen immediately.

Many of us misunderstand the process of restoration (or sanctification). Forgiveness is a one-time event. But the consequences of our past may leave enough damage in our soul that we need time – possibly a lifetime – to regain what has been lost. Some of us have spent our entire childhood and much of our adulthood believing things that not only were untrue, but also were destructive to our identity, our self-worth, and our relationship with God. We have needed to reject the internalized shame in our lives and grow in forgiveness.

It will also be essential that we initiate the very process that would have naturally occurred through our childhood had we experienced an emotionally and spiritually healthy family system. We need to discover our gifts, unique talents, interests, skills, and passions in life. We need to step out in faith and try new things, discover new interests, and essentially learn who we really are on the inside. Although we need to be spiritually grounded, there is also a very practical element to finding our true identity. And this takes time, patience, prayer, community, and encouragement.

In order to move through this journey of discovery we need a guide to lead us. As we commit to claim our relationship with Jesus Christ and the truth of the word of God as the source of our identity, we begin to see ourselves as God's precious and valuable child.

From there, we naturally feel led to follow after our interests. Because the shame mask has been removed and the Holy Spirit has been given access to our lives, He is now in the process of redefining us – chipping away the layers to reveal the "angel" on the inside. He works within us – in ways unique to each of us – to unveil the true desires and gifts He has placed in our heart.

This journey will become exciting, I promise! As we begin to understand how connecting with our true identity is a privilege, and that the person God made us to be is fulfilling, we will find interests we would have never dreamed would be meaningful to us. And eventually we will find healthy, whole relationships with others that allow us to fulfill Jesus' words in John 13:34 (NIV): "As I have loved you, so you must love one another."

The struggle for identity first happens as a spiritual battle in the mind for the messages and beliefs we choose to receive and believe. Referring back to a metaphor I taught in an earlier chapter, just as a root springs up and produces fruit, when the messages of our heart come from God, they eventually produce wholeness and the expression of His will in our lives. **We no longer have to frantically search for life. We merely live it**. God begins to show us and places things directly into our heart and mind that align with His will for us.

> "For it is God who works in you to will and to act in order
> to fulfill His good purpose" (Philippians 2:13 NIV).

Who God Says We Are

God clearly describes our true identity in His word. Our true identity emerges as we see ourselves through the truth that we are called, loved, chosen, redeemed, and empowered by Him. There are many, many precious truths we can embrace that will guarantee us the ability to be transformed, restored, made whole, and set free to be the person God intended and created us to be.

But simply reading a portion of scripture doesn't mean that transformation will occur. We must receive God's promises and truth into our hearts. How does this occur? True change occurs at the belief level. We must allow the emotions of our heart to collide with the information in our mind.

- We must soften our heart, through faith, in order for the seed of God's principles and promises to have healthy soil in which to be planted.
- We must speak Biblical truth into our personal situations, even if our emotions tell us differently.
- We must hang on to those promises, even when things in this world don't appear to align with what God says.
- We must patiently wait to see the faithfulness of God translate His promises into reality.

Choosing to believe God's truth in our hearts (not just our minds) will allow us to see the world through His perspectives. It will defend us against the false, and potentially threatening, ways we formerly used to secure our identity. As we learn to anchor ourselves in how God loves us, no matter what happens, we will find security and peace in this knowledge. As we change at the very core of our being, we begin to see ourselves as precious. We begin to operate through the Holy Spirit, not our self-will or learned behaviors.

Where Our True Identity Begins

The entire Bible is a revelation of God's truth. But for it to become our own, we must continuously and repetitively connect ourselves to these truths. Here are a few fundamental ways we can become stabilized in our true identity and purpose in life.

- Pick out scriptures of your own that apply to your life situation and areas of struggle. These should be promises you need to personally receive into your life. Throughout this book, I have purposely included countless verses and passages from the Bible that I pray will connect to what your heart needs right now.

- Post the scriptures in places where you can access them throughout the day (for example, your phone background, bathroom mirror, car rearview mirror, desk at work).
- Speak the principles and promises of God's word aloud whenever possible.
- Pray for the faith to persevere until these truths become real and internalized within you.
- Make notes in your journal of how God made that scripture real in your life, and what parts He never wants you to forget.

Take Back What's Been Lost

The best gift God has given each of us is the true plan and purpose He created for our lives. There was a day somewhere in eternity past when He first thought of us. He determined our physical characteristics. He formed our family. He looked into our heart and implanted our temperament, our personality, our preferences, and our desires. Then He gave us a free will. So, despite how He created each of us uniquely, He left us space to make choices on our own.

For many of us, life got complicated along the way. Our survival mode caused us to lose focus and become distracted from our true identity, our true purpose, and our true self. When we begin to approach our search for authentic identity and significance, it may appear to others to be a selfish process, that we're only thinking of ourselves. Compared to how little we focused on ourselves in the past, any self-care might appear selfish to others (or feel selfish to us). However, when we see it in proper context, we find it is not self-focused, but God-focused – experiencing what He has prepared for us so that we can be a conduit of sharing God's best with others.

The formation of a healthy identity is a process of growth, not an immediate one-time event. We are now essentially asking God to take us on a journey that we may have bypassed (or missed entirely) in our youth. Grab hold of Him like a child and ask Him to show you and tell you what makes you uniquely you. He will not let you down or leave you!

Convergence Principle ©

In His conversation with a Jewish leader, Jesus clarified the purpose of life on this earth: "Love the Lord with all your heart, all your soul, all your mind, and all your strength. And love your neighbor as yourself. There is no greater commandment than these" (Mark 12:29-31 NIV).

In this simple but clear statement, Jesus brought into focus the mission He has created us to fulfill through the lives He's given us. I believe the real question we're asking is this: "How do I personally carry out my responsibility to love God with all of my being, and to learn to authentically love others with this same love?"

As three specific elements in our lives converge, they reveal a picture of how God intends for each of us to uniquely live out His purpose on this earth (convergence). For many years I have been teaching clients, groups, classes, and readers what I have entitled the **Convergence Principle.** The personal testimonials and positive responses this principle has received have legitimized its effectiveness. It provides a framework for men and women of all walks of life to build their life-purpose upon.

Not only has my own life-purpose been an unfolding of the paradox principles I've woven throughout this book, it also began to come into focus as I personally implemented this simple yet profound concept of convergence in my own life.

- **Body.** My life experiences and passions.
- **Soul.** My inborn, God-given temperament.
- **Spirit.** My God given spiritual gifts.

Life Experiences and Passions

This element of the principle identifies the "who" of our God-given life purpose. This will be the subgroup of people for whom our life experiences have developed a keen awareness of and compassion for.

Imagine walking down a hallway looking back on your life, noticing pictures on the wall. These pictures are like a photo album of all the events along the way. Some are large, framed pictures, representing the most significant experiences you've had so far. Some are good; some are not so good; some are happy; some are sad. What significant events from your life do you see that stand out? Is there a wedding? A birth? Are there family vacations or important sporting events pictured on the walls? Is there an achievement like a diploma or a degree or an award? Are there spiritual experiences like when you came to faith in Jesus, or a time when God especially touched your life?

Are there painful experiences — A divorce? Or the death of someone you really loved? A failure? Maybe a memory of having been abused? Or alcoholism, an eating disorder, a miscarriage, an abortion, or an addiction?

Realize that all these experiences have shaped who you are today. God didn't cause all these things to happen in your life, but He did allow them to happen so that He could continue to unfold His amazing story through you. God wants to use all of these experiences to grow you spiritually, to mold you into the likeness of Jesus, and to shape you for the unique purposes He has prepared just for you. **He doesn't want even one of your life experiences to be wasted**. God takes all of your life experiences— whether positive or painful, intentional or accidental, caused by you or by someone else – to shape you for His unique calling on your life. He turns your broken pieces into masterpieces!

> "We know that in all things God works for the good of those who love Him, who have been called according to His purpose" (Romans 8:28 NIV).

Your life experience is one of the most overlooked ways that God uses to shape you for the way He wants you to serve Him and others in this world. God is working in and through everything in your life — even your sins – to accomplish His purposes through you. God can take the messes in your life and bring a message out of them. He can take the tests in your life and create a testimony unlike any other. He can take a crisis and show Christ to others through it. 2 Corinthians 1:4 (NIV) tells us, "God comforts us in all our troubles, so that we can comfort those in any trouble with the comfort we ourselves receive from God."

When others are troubled in ways that resemble the troubles God has guided us through, we will be able to give them the same comfort God has given us. Our trouble can become the very instrument God will use to help other people – the basis of our credibility to speak hope into another human being.

Inborn, God-Given Temperament

Our unique temperament combination defines "how" we might most effectively utilize our life experiences and passions to bring hope, healing, and wholeness into the lives of others. In order to fully know our identity, we must know how we were created in God's image from the beginning. This inborn, God-given nature within each of us is called our "temperament."

In Chapter 8, I went into great detail about this topic. The most detailed temperament identification in the industry is provided through the Arno Profile System (APS) temperament profile. It accurately (with 95% reliability) identifies three separate human interactions:

- **Inclusion.** Our mind, and how it interacts in our surface relationships and environments.
- **Control.** Our will, and how it leads us to make decisions, perform tasks, seek competence, and respond to the will of others.
- **Affection.** Our emotions, and how they interact in deep relationships or situations that require feeling.

Historically, there have been four temperament types taught by other personality and temperament instruments:

- Melancholy
- Sanguine
- Choleric
- Phlegmatic

In the late 1970s, Drs. Richard and Phyllis Arno established the National Christian Counselors Association, and began seven years of research, with thousands of individuals in the Christian counseling setting. Their purpose was to develop a counseling model based on scripture. While researching the temperament models available, they identified a fifth temperament type: Supine. The Supine identification describes a person who, by their very nature, is a servant and feels that they have little or no value. They have a gentle spirit and can become very social or relational when they know they have been accepted.

The APS does not measure a person's behavior (like a personality test does), which can change throughout the person's life. Rather, it identifies a person's inborn temperament, individually placed in each of us by our Creator. Psalm 139 speaks of it as our "inmost being".

> "You made all the delicate, inner parts of my body, and knit me together in my mother's womb. Thank you for making me so wonderfully complex! Your workmanship is marvelous—how well I know it" (Psalm 139:13-14 NLT).

Who God created us to be (temperament) and who we've become through life experiences and learned behavior (personality), can be vastly different. From that comes great inter-/intra-personal conflict. We need to find out who God has created us to be "in our inmost being", and who we are in Christ, the new nature. By realizing who we are in Christ, we can learn to operate out of our God-given temperament strengths, and thereby overcome many of our temperament weaknesses. This is when God is most able to use our lives as a conduit to share His love and grace with others.

God-Given Spiritual Gifts

As we've already explored, our **life experiences and passions** define <u>who</u> in our lives we may have the greatest credibility and relevance to influence with the love of Jesus. Our **inborn, God-given** temperament paints a broad understanding of <u>how</u> we might interact with those God has prepared us to uniquely connect with. Now, let's look at **spiritual gifts** – the unique "God-talents" – that the Bible says God gives every one of His children for the purpose of fulfilling God's purposes through our lives. This (or these) gifts define <u>what</u> means God might likely use in our lives to make the greatest impact in the lives of others.

Spiritual gifts are supernatural enablers so we may serve God more effectively in the world and in the church through the power of the Holy

Spirit. Every Christian has at least one spiritual gift, and many have been given more than one. The various spiritual gifts are listed in Romans 12, Ephesians 4, 1 Corinthians 13-15, and elsewhere in God's word. I encourage you to read and study these scriptures to learn more.

It is very important to understand that our spiritual gifts may or may not complement what we believe to be our strengths. They are not based on our human capabilities, but on God's supernatural empowerment within us and through us. I've experienced many times when God made the most significant impact in others' lives or situations when I felt the most inadequate, underequipped, unprepared, or lacking competence. I think God often does this so that when amazing things happen, He gets the credit and praise! And I just sit back and marvel at how He takes my small contribution and multiplies it beyond my human understanding.

My favorite example from the Bible of Jesus taking a human being's small contribution and exponentially turning it into enough to meet the needs of others is the story known as "the fish and the bread," found in Matthew 14:15-21 (NIV):

> "As evening approached, the disciples came to him and said, 'This is a remote place, and it's already getting late. Send the crowds away, so they can go to the villages and buy themselves some food.' Jesus replied, 'They do not need to go away. You give them something to eat.' 'We have here only five loaves of bread and two fish,' they answered. 'Bring them here to me,' Jesus said. And he directed the people to sit down on the grass. Taking the five loaves and the two fish and looking up to heaven, He gave thanks and broke the loaves. Then He handed them to the disciples, and the disciples gave them to the people. They all ate and were satisfied, and the disciples picked up twelve basketfuls of broken pieces that were left over. The number of those who ate was about five thousand men, (plus a great number of) women, and children."

Passionately seek after an understanding of your spiritual gifts. All spiritual gifts are given for the betterment and building up of the Christian community, never for self-promotion. Ask God to reveal to you where and how He intends for your gifts to be used in accordance with His purposes.

There are multiple assessment tools available that help us discover the spiritual gifts God placed in our lives. I encourage you to seek guidance from a pastor, spiritual mentor, or trusted Christian friend.

When combined, an authentic acceptance of our life passions, an understanding of our inborn temperament, and an awareness of our God-given spiritual gifts, empowers us to carry out the purpose God has placed in our lives.

God Wants the <u>Real</u> You

The Bible isn't filled with people who are superheroes. They are ordinary people. People God chose, redeemed, and ignited with the Holy Spirit. They are people who messed up, failed, and didn't have anything of great value to offer the world – except Christ in them!

> "God chose things the world considers foolish in order to shame those who think they are wise. And He chose things that are powerless to shame those who are powerful. God chose things despised by the world; things counted as nothing at all and used them to bring to nothing what the world considers important. As a result, no one can ever boast in the presence of God" (1 Corinthians 1:27-29 NLT)

We must come to a place where no matter what we do or who we are, we know we are chosen only because of God's grace. If it is offensive for us to hear the truth that we aren't chosen based upon all our efforts, control, perfectionism, and accomplishments, then we aren't truly ready for this journey. God requires our true surrender – when we are willing to stop striving to earn or prove our worth through our own human efforts, and to let Him fill us with His truth and the power of His Spirit.

> "The eyes of the Lord search the whole earth in order to strengthen those whose hearts are fully submitted to Him." (2 Chronicles 16:9 NLT)

God needs you! No, not to because He can't accomplish His purposes without you. What He needs is the person He hand-created you to be, so He can use you in accordance with the experiences, temperament, gifts, and abilities He has already equipped you with. This will allow Him to build His kingdom in this generation and in the generations to come.

Prayer for Identity and Vision

Father God, thank you for claiming me as Your very own child. I stand in assurance of who I am based on Your grace, not based on anything I have done or how well or poorly I have done it. I reject the lies I have believed about who I've come to believe that I am. My identity isn't founded in anything or anyone else other than the truth of who You say I am.

Father, just as I have asked You to release me from the shame in my life, I now ask that You reveal and empower the authentic person You made me to be. Help me to find all that You have for me personally. Guide me to what I am to share with others. Give me Your vision so I am not confused about the future. Thank you for all that You have done for me. In Jesus name I pray, amen.

"And we know that God causes everything to work together for the good of those who love Him and are called according to His purpose for them."

Romans 8:28 NLT

PURPOSE

Turn from Confusion to Purpose

Introduction

We've been on a journey together. We may have begun this journey worn out and broken down, looking for answers as to why life wasn't working. We may have found some things we expected, but more than likely, we found many things we didn't anticipate.

In truth, the journey from brokenness to wholeness in Christ can be painful in our soul. Now that we have encountered the reality of the issues that we need to face, it can be extremely overwhelming to realize that the journey doesn't end here. It's really only beginning! It is a lifelong process. It requires rigorous honesty, fearless self-confrontation, daily surrender to God, and a willingness to live a life that reflects the nature of Jesus.

- What exactly is the end result of this process? If we are courageous enough to follow God's ways, we will embark on experiencing the fulfillment we've been seeking all along – a true, lasting inner peace and understanding of the love of God.

As we experience intimacy with Jesus Christ, we will be able to become the very person we were created to be. Even if human relationships at some point fail us, we will discover that we still have the capacity to experience the highest form of love possible – the agape love of Jesus.

Balancing Spiritual and Practical

There are two sides to the process of life transformation. The first is spiritual. It rests in the unseen things and the battle we are engaged in for our entire system of living – our beliefs, thoughts, feelings, and behaviors. To grow and become strong spiritually, we need to develop a lifestyle of spiritual discipline. This comes down to nurturing an intimate relationship with Jesus. It means being saturated in His truth and finding deep connections with others who personally know and have experienced God's love. It does not mean legalistically attempting to "do" the Christian life. **It means immersing ourselves in God's Son, God's word, and God's people!**

The other side to authentic transformation is the practical side. Since we live in a physical world and deal in physical-world situations, we need to learn to apply Biblical, spiritual principles to tangible life events. In other words, we need to make God's truth sensible and real to others! If we over-spiritualize our lives to the point that we are absorbed by scripture referencing and concepts, yet don't know how to effectively apply them in loving others, we will have little effect in reaching others with the saving, transforming message of Jesus. The broken world we live in wants to experience a real and relatable Jesus through us. Not one that is pious, intellectualized, religious, and unreachable.

The transformation process occurs as God changes us spiritually and brings that change into reality in our practical day-to-day situations of life. We cannot compartmentalize the Christian life. Our jobs or family or hobbies are not independent of our spiritual life. In fact, our lives in their entirety fall under one of two systems:

- Self-effort
- Christ-dependency

Where We are Headed

Jesus taught a parable of two men: a priest and a despised tax collector. If we were to retell this story in today's culture, the story might take place between a righteous, religions person and someone who the world may consider an outcast. Here's my version of how Jesus' parable might read today:

> "The righteous, religious person stood by themself and prayed this prayer: 'I thank you, God, that I am not a sinner like all these others. I don't cheat; I don't steal; I don't commit adultery; I've never killed anyone; I live by the Ten Commandments; and I've always been a good Christian. I'm certainly not like that dirty, addicted person I saw standing outside the church doors this morning, begging for money! I lead my family in prayer before meals; I give ten percent of my income to the church, and I try to be a decent person.' But the addict stood at a distance, afraid to draw near, and dared not even lift his eyes to heaven as he prayed to God. Instead, he beat his chest in sorrow, saying, 'O God, be merciful to me, for I am a sinner. Nothing about me is good. I've made a mess of my life. I've been addicted, divorced, imprisoned, and homeless.' Jesus said to them, 'I tell you, this sinner, not the righteous, religious person, returned home justified (made right) before God. For those who celebrate themselves will be humbled, and those who humble themselves will be celebrated by Me!" (Based on Luke 18:11-14).

We often look at the "righteous," "religious" person as the model for life in America – a man or woman who has it all together. Maybe a great marriage and family; successful well-behaved kids; a great job and career; money in the bank; a home in the suburbs; and a future that looks bright. We measure our progress in the Christian life by how we are attaining to what we believe is God's "checklist." Yet, in truth, God isn't interested in all that. In fact, quite the opposite. **The Bible tells us that those who think they've got it, haven't really got it at all!**

God desires our humble admission of our weaknesses. We are justified – made right before God – as we humbly admit from our heart where we fall short. In this transaction, we are given access to the Holy Spirit. The Holy

Spirit causes our lives to change from the inside out, through the inward reality of Christ living in us.

So how can we actually measure our progress in this journey from brokenness to wholeness, and in the Christian life in general? It's safe to say it's more than merely setting boundaries, learning new rules, or even walking in obedience to God's word while refraining from evil. The measurement of a changed life is someone who seeks to live by the principles that reveal the heart of God: walking by grace, thankfulness, and unconditional love. As more and more of our life comes under the authority of God's word and principles, we will produce more and more fruit in our relationships with others.

Setting Priorities

Life is all about priorities. We have only so much time in a day to accomplish things. We only have so much room in our hearts to carry things. We only have so much energy to focus on things that need to be done. That is why the structure of our priorities will determine the order of all practical functions of our lives. For example, if we're compelled to please people, our activities and the balance of our lives will be built around that priority. If we're driven to success, all of our activities will move us toward that objective. **Every aspect of our lives will submit to what or who we choose to put at the top of our list of priorities!**

Healthy, Godly Priorities

Relationship Priorities

In an identity dependent life, our relationship priorities got skewed. We took upon ourselves the needs of others, based on our own compulsions, shame, and guilt. We believed we needed to focus on others, more than on ourselves. But these misplaced priorities led to numerous problems. Rather than attempting to change everything in our life that isn't working in our physical-world circumstances, we need to choose to live each day based upon God's priorities.

- **We must seek an intimate relationship with Jesus Christ first and foremost, above everything and everyone**. This will be the entire goal of our days and the entire purpose of our lives.
- **We must open our heart to allow God's truth to enter into our life**. That means our heart must be able to receive the gifts He gives, and we must get rid of our selfish and prideful tendencies.
- **We must learn to serve and love people in the way God asks us to serve and love**. We no longer feel obligated to react to others, but we allow the Spirit of God in us to lead us to respond to situations in Biblical, Christ-like ways.

The nature of our relationships won't necessarily change right away. **One of the most difficult lessons to learn in life is that we can't change other people.** But God does give us the ability to change ourselves as we submit to Him. He transforms us through His love and grace and teaches us to live by His relationship principles. These become the foundation for building healthy relationships in our lives. Working these principles into our daily lives by first experiencing them with God, and then transferring them into our relationships with others may take some time. It is a maturing and growing process. By understanding these principles and encountering Jesus at the heart level, we have the opportunity to apply these same principles to every relationship we encounter.

- **Love.** The basis of God's relationship with us is based on unconditional, agape love (see 1 Corinthians 13). We learn to give away the same love to others. We don't love people based on whether they are lovable or not or whether they deserve it or not. We love them because God first loved us.
- **Holiness.** The basis of God's relationship with us is His holiness. We should never condone or allow sinful behaviors. We can learn to hate negative, destructive behaviors in our relationships with others, and realize we don't need to allow them into our life. We do have the choice of saying no.
- **Freedom.** The basis of God's relationship with us is free will. He doesn't ever operate by controlling us in order to force us to surrender our will to His. Likewise, in our own life,

we honor the free will of others and avoid the tendency to attempt to control their behaviors. If their choices could harm us personally, we can set boundaries that protect us and impose consequences on them.

- **Grace and mercy.** The basis of God's relationship with us is grace and mercy. Grace is receiving the things we don't deserve. Mercy is not receiving the consequences we do deserve. As we receive these amazing gifts from God, we offer them in our relationships with others.

- **Discipline.** God loves us enough to discipline us when we do things that take us away from His best. His discipline is evidence of His love (see Hebrews 12:6). We apply godly discipline to our relationships where we stand in a position of authority or leadership, using the same form or loving discipline that we have experienced from God.

- **Forgiveness and reconciliation**. God reconciles us to Himself through forgiveness. Forgiveness is the bridge that continually gives us access to enjoying God's intimacy, peace, and love. Our relationships are reconciled and restored through that same forgiveness. Sometimes we need to forgive ourselves. Sometimes we need to forgive others.

- **Personal development**. God seeks to build us into a vision He has for our life. This means everything He offers in our relationship with Him is to nurture us to become like Jesus and to fulfill His purposes in and through our lives. In the same way, we must learn to offer others the freedom to become the people God created and intended them to be. We don't interfere or attempt to make others into our own idea of what or who we think they should be.

- **Intimacy.** The highest desire of God's heart is that we experience continual intimacy with Him through our relationship with Jesus Christ. This is closeness where we deeply know Him, and we allow Him to deeply know us. The highest desire in our close relationships is this same intimacy. When we learn to be authentic, vulnerable, and honest, we have the potential to grow close to others who reciprocate and honor that intimacy.

Prayer To Apply God's Relationship Principles

Father God, this list overwhelms me! I'm amazed by how You love me, respect me, and care for me in our relationship. I don't even know how to receive it entirely, much less offer it to others. I pray that as I grow in my relationship with You, I will become more and more like You. And that I would learn how to give these same gifts to others through the gift of unconditional love that You have given me. I thank you for who You are. In Jesus name I pray. Amen.

Practical Priorities

We may have lived much of our lives feeling drained by the pressures and expectations placed upon us. So much of our focus was spent on doing things that we weren't even intended or supposed to do. We took on everyone else's priorities and needs, often at the neglect of our own. As we face this new chapter in our lives, we need to take our schedules, commitments, and goals, and allow God to sift through them.

But how can we know where to begin? Or what to keep and what to let go of? First, we need God's wisdom, which is why our relationship with Him must remain at the forefront of our priority list and daily schedule. Through His perspective, we need to wisely manage our time, resources, and gifts. We might consider the following questions as we evaluate the practical priorities in our life:

- Why am I doing this? What are my motives?
- Has Jesus asked, called, or moved me to do this? How do I know?
- Who or what other than Jesus might be motivating this choice?
- Is there any emotion that is affecting this? Is it a negative feeling, such as guilt, shame, or fear?
- Who will be pleased if I do this? God? Myself? Or someone else?
- By saying yes to this, who or what will I be saying no to?
- If I'm taking on multiple things at one time, which responsibility should have the greater priority? Why?

This understanding – when combined with an authentic acceptance of our life passions and an understanding of our God-given spiritual gifts – empowers us to carry out the calling God has placed in our lives.

Prayer for Practical Priorities

Father God, I realize that sometimes I am being governed by the needs and urgency of the moment rather than being led by You. Please help me understand what You would have me do in each situation. I feel unable to separate my priorities and responsibilities from those You would prefer I choose. I pray that as I step out in faith, You will guide and direct me from this day forward. In Jesus' name I pray, amen.

A Balancing Act

If we look at all the concepts we have learned throughout this book, we are able to see two opposing paths:

- God's way
- Our survival strategies

Many times, we have the tendency to attempt to externally change our behaviors and move to the opposite of whatever negative behavior we're dealing with. That sounds like a logical thing to do. Without true heart change though, we may externally do the opposite thing, but the unhealthy, shame-based root is still what is driving the behavior. Author John Bradshaw states, in his book *Bradshaw: On the Family:* "The opposite of dysfunctional is just as dysfunctional. Both extremes are driven by the same shame messages." We explored this idea at length in an earlier chapter, as I presented the "Equal and Opposite" model. It may be worth your revisiting this in order to get a deeper appreciation for this concept now that you're personally digging into the shame messages in your life.

When the Holy Spirit enters our lives in an experiential sense, He gives us the ability to take the many facets of our life, and perfectly balance and align them in accordance with His truth. He deals with the root and applies the remedy, causing our behaviors to come into balance with our heart. A change that only occurs **from the inside out!**

Here are some examples of how we may become imbalanced during the early (immature) parts of our transformational journey, assuming that the opposite of our old, dysfunctional patterns must necessarily be better.

- **We become independent.** We realize that we were needy in relationships, therefore we cut ourselves off from others and seek to become independent and self-sufficient.
- **We become irresponsible.** We see that we have been finding our security in our job performance, so we become lazy, apathetic, or stop trying altogether, causing us to become unproductive and irresponsible.
- **We become insensitive.** We see how we've been enabling another individual, so we completely cut them off without notice, leaving them to fend for themselves.

In order to deal with the core of our dysfunctions, it is often hard to know where to begin. Here are some primary root issues we might initially focus on to help us find a more balanced approach to heart change:

- **Balance truth with love.** If we just focus on the truth of what we have learned in this journey, we could become self-righteous, insensitive, and critical. We must remember, we're not better than others; we're just better than we were. Truth is a marvelous gift – it ultimately sets us free. However, if we use truth as the standard by which we evaluate others and ourselves, we have negated the need of balancing truth with love. In fact, 1 Corinthians 13:1-2 reminds us that all gifts we possess, including knowledge and understanding, are meaningless without love.
- **Balance our ability to see flaws in ourselves and others with our ability to give and receive grace.** When God begins to reveal the areas in our lives that need to change, that doesn't mean He expects us to change everything immediately or perfectly. God may show us our selfish or ungodly tendencies continually in our daily life experience. He uses this exposure of our behavior to

allow us to confess, repent, and ask Him to change us, knowing that in most things, our nature can't "just stop." As we continually confess and ask God to change us, we gradually move away from our unhealthy tendencies and learn to adopt a system of freedom and grace in our life and relationships.

- **Balance acceptance of people with the intolerance of sin.** Through healthy boundaries, we gradually begin to learn how to reject and discourage sinful behaviors yet love people right where they are. If people are sinning and committing acts of violation against us, we must set whatever boundaries we need to protect ourselves from those effects. Sometimes these boundaries will have little to do with the person but will empower us to respond differently to negative situations. If we are just becoming aware that we have allowed toxic people and negative situations into our lives, we could be prone to begin to "throw people out," and maybe become rude, judgmental, or self-righteous in our approach – looking down at others for the very same attitudes or behaviors we ourselves had just a short time ago. While we can defend and protect ourselves from spiritually and emotionally unhealthy people and their choices, we must remember that they too need to experience grace, mercy, and forgiveness, just like we did (and do). Our focus should always be to pray for them. As we grow in Christ, our heart should be loving and compassionate despite their behavior. We will begin to see them through the lens of Jesus.

- **Balance our need to detach with the ability to be intimate.** We may need to detach ourselves from toxic people or unhealthy relationship bonds. These bonds were established on our sinful, need-based system of "love." Detachment may occur for a season but doesn't mean we need to totally isolate ourselves from people. Instead, detachment means we are removing the harmful way we are bonded in relationships. These bonds were actually based on identity dependency, not genuine love. Once we detach from toxic and unhealthy relationships, we can prepare our hearts for healthy attachments that will ultimately give us the opportunity to be emotionally intimate – possibly in healthier ways than ever before. Our journey with Christ prepares our hearts to properly give and receive love.

Prayer for Balance

Father God, as I learn these new principles, and understand how I may have been unhealthy in my relationships, please give me the grace to change slowly and in alignment with Your spirit working within me. I can't do it all right away. I can't fix it instantly. I know that You already know that; help me be convinced of it myself. Help me to learn balance in my life. In Jesus name, amen.

Completing the TURN

As our twelve-lesson TURN journey comes to a close, it culminates with us prayerfully identifying individuals in our lives who need to encounter the very healing and transformation we have been blessed to experience through this book and the TURN process.

Jesus, in what is referred to as the "Great Commandment," succinctly described the life purpose of every one of us who choose to follow Him. Although I have referred to this passage in many places throughout this book, none of my references are as exhilarating as my use of it right now.

> "One of the teachers of the law came and heard them debating. Noticing that Jesus had given them a good answer, he asked Jesus, 'Of all the (613) commandments, which is the most important?' 'The most important one is this:' answered Jesus, 'Hear, O Israel: The Lord our God, the Lord is one. Love the Lord your God with all your heart and with all your soul and with all your mind and with all your strength. The second is this: 'Love your neighbor as yourself. There is no commandment greater than these'" (Mark 12:28-31 NIV).

As our relationship with Jesus grows and matures, so should our commitment to sharing the blessings of knowing Him with others. Our mission as Christians is to share the love of Jesus with people in our everyday lives – those who are very much like us, as well as those we share little in common.

409

Pursue a Timothy in Your Life

In the Bible, the apostle Paul invested in a young man by the name of Timothy. Timothy was younger in his faith and less disciplined in his walk with God than Paul was. Paul took it as his personal responsibility to mentor, encourage, and be present with Timothy along his transformational journey with God. We are all called to move beyond being a "Timothy" (a receiver of Christ-like love, guidance, and support) to being a Paul (a giver of Christ-like love, guidance, and support) for others.

Commit in your heart to pray for and pursue an individual who might need you to be a "Paul" in their life – someone who is experiencing similar wounds as you have, but who has yet to find healing through their personal relationship with Jesus. Take the initiative to reach out to them. Communicate with them every week. Stay in touch with them when you know they're going through important times in their life. Share with them the hope, healing, and wholeness you have found in Jesus Christ. At the same time, though, be cautious to not neglect your own continued growth and restoration along the way.

Dr. Dave's Personal Challenge to You

As you finish reading this book and continue working through the twelve aspects of TURN, I encourage you to consider this challenge from the final phase of our TURN journey together: **N - Nurture Lasting Hope in Others.**

Nurture

To nurture means to be attentive to; to meet the needs of; and to assure the growth of. As you pray about who might be the Timothy (or Timothies) that God is urging you to reach out to and mentor, allow yourself to nurture them in their young faith development.

Lasting

The word "lasting" carries with it the connotation of something that is enduring, persevering, resilient, and unwavering. God does not desire for us to be like a seed planted in shallow soil, that dries up and blows away at the first sign of difficulty. He calls each of us to be like trees whose roots are planted deeply into healthy soil and drawing life from the infinite spring of living water, Jesus. As we pour into the lives of the Timothies we encounter, we must be intentional to cultivate good soil in them and introduce them to the water that will allow them to never thirst again.

Hope

Hope in Christ is not merely wishful thinking, like rubbing a lucky rabbit's foot, hoping that something good will happen. No, true hope is placing our trust in the absolute promises of a loving God and the person Jesus Christ. He alone is our hope! Be an agent of hope in the lives of others, particularly your Timothy. Use your words and your life to lift them up.

In

Oftentimes when the Bible uses the word "in", it means "intimate with" or "connected to." We are instructed to be "in Christ" (2 Corinthians 5:17 NIV), meaning an intimate relationship with Him – fully known yet still fully accepted. We are also to connect with others in the world around us in a similar way. We must allow ourselves to build a connected relationship with our Timothy. We can't let fear stand in our way. And we can't worry whether they will reject us or abandon us. Our hope is in the reality that Christ, whose spirit lives within us, says He will never reject us or abandon us. That's sufficient.

Others

Who are "others?" When Jesus was asked a similar question in the Parable of the Good Samaritan, "Who is my neighbor," He answered in a way the religious leaders least expected. He described their (our) neighbor as anyone we encounter along our life path who is in need, or who may feel they least deserve God's love, or who may least expect someone to love them and invest in them.

We live among a world of people who need to experience the unconditional, life-changing love of Jesus Christ through us. As followers of Jesus, we must be the ones who turn from our comfort zones and turn toward those whom Jesus wants to touch through us!

**Our world, our nation, our state, our community,
our neighborhood, our street, maybe even our own
home – is filled with Timothies. Jesus is ready to turn their
broken pieces into masterpieces, just as He is ours!**

Questions from Dr. Dave

For personal reflection or group discussion of Chapter 16

How have you found it difficult to create and maintain healthy boundaries in the past? I've found that the effectiveness of healthy boundaries in life and relationships are a reflection of our commitment to honor the boundaries God lays out for us in scripture. Consider how this may be true for you. Do you allow others to rob you of your inborn freedoms? Are there any ways you rob others of theirs?

Our identity is much like the story I shared of "the angel in the marble.". Our true self is layered over by the guilt and shame of sin. In what ways has reading this book given you the courage to begin to chip away at some of those layers? What baby steps do you feel God is wanting you to take? Personalize how your story converges with your inborn temperament and God-given spiritual gifts to create your one-of-a-kind purpose. Take a few moments to put that into words. God wants the "real" you, not a man-made version. Are you ready for Him to expose what needs to be removed in order to expose the person He created you to be?

As Christ-followers in the twenty-first century, it may be more critical than ever that we balance the spiritual truths of our faith in Christ with the practical realities of being in the world but not of the world. People are longing for a real and relevant encounter with Jesus. In what ways has this book inspired you to nurture lasting hope in others? What might be the first step? I encourage you to ask God to put a "Timothy" in your life, someone who He wants to love through you.

ACKNOWLEDGEMENTS

I've had the itch to author a book for who knows how long. But I just couldn't land on the right theme. I knew for sure that I wanted to celebrate Jesus' amazing work in my life. I also sensed that I had a distinctive (maybe inspiring) personal story to tell. I believed I had a responsibility to point others to the authentic soul work and spiritual growth I had discovered. And I certainly didn't want to leave out snippets of my incredible twenty-five-year career in high profile college sports.

Finally, it came – the answer, and the passion to go with it. My first book would meld all of these and many other elements together into one sincere, heartfelt message that would be meaningful and relevant across the gamut of people in the diverse world we live in.

I've come to realize there are so many individuals who had a hand in the writing of my story, that there aren't enough pages in this book to acknowledge them all. I only have time and space to shine light on the high places. The remainder of you, please accept my unspoken debt of gratitude. You all know who you are.

First, I must acknowledge how God has been so faithful and loving to me, even when I least realized it and certainly least deserved it. In His prevenience, He has protected me from myself. In His tenderness, He has knelt beside me as I've picked up the broken pieces on more occasions than I can recount. In His grace and mercy, He has transformed my heart in the midst of the lowest, most vulnerable times in my life. In His unconditional love, He has filled me with Himself, and led me on the path of sharing His unending, undeserved, sometimes uncomfortable love with others.

The number of people I've encountered in my life is far too vast to comprehend. Left to myself, there would have been very little redemptive value to many of those encounters. In looking back, it's apparent how God chose to incorporate many of the most nondescript people, places, and things into my life to make some of the most profound differences. Although some individuals may have been more present, all were equally important.

My passion for genealogy has allowed me to identify nearly every human being in every direction with whom I share DNA. Growing up, I often felt that I had been short-changed by being a member of the family I came from. Now, in retrospect, I would not change that for anything in the world. I would not be who I am, being with the people I'm with, doing the things I'm doing, having the influence I'm having, writing the book I'm writing, for the purpose I'm writing it, had my past not been exactly what it was. I thank God for that.

The storyline of my life has been much like scenes in a captivating stage play – every one with a different subplot and change in characters. Those who moved in and out of my life when I was a kid whose dreams had been dashed by my parents' divorce. Those who carried me through my teen years after I moved to live with new parents, in a new house, in a new town, in a new state, attending a new school, with all new peers. Those who were patient and caring when I was a clumsy young husband, father, and Christian. Those who gave me a chance to rise in my career to the pinnacle of my profession. Those who wrapped their loving arms around me as everything crumbled at my feet. Those who gave me a second chance. Those who encouraged my calling as a pastor, teacher, and counselor. Those who believed that what God placed in my heart deserved to be written about and shared. And those who were with me through it all. Thank you.

I would be remis to not specifically acknowledge those who are and have always been in the "inner circle" of my life. My wife Ann. My kids, step-kids, and grandkids. My parents who are now deceased. My sisters and brother. And Jesus. Each of you has helped make me who I am today. Please accept the content of this book as my gift back to you.

CONTRIBUTORS

TURN Content Contributor
Stephanie Tucker, DMin, CATC, MDAAC

Special Editor
Judy Kercheval

Guest Reviewers
Rachael Craig
Jamie Curtis
Steven Hammond
Wendy Hammond
Bill Roitsch
Lisa Roitsch
Mike Shanks
Tracy Shanks
Bob White
Judy White
Joyce Wood

NOTES

Introduction

1 Bradshaw, John E. 1988. *Bradshaw on: The Family: A New Way of Creating Solid Self-Esteem.* Health Communications.

2 McGee, Robert. 2003. *The Search for Significance: Seeing Your True Worth through God's Eyes.* Nashville, TN: Thomas Nelson.

3 Campbell, Joseph. (2019) *If the Path Before You Is Clear, You're Probably on Someone Else's.* Independently Published.

4 Newton, Sir Isaac. 1687. *Third Law of Motion.*

5 Tyndale (Trans.). (2018). *NLT New Living Translation Bible: Revised edition.* American Bible Society.

6 Zondervan Publishing. (2002). *Zondervan NIV Study Bible.* Grand Rapids, MI: Zondervan.

Chapter 1

1 Scazzero, Peter. (2017). *Emotionally Healthy Spirituality: It's Impossible to Be Spiritually Mature, While Remaining Emotionally Immature.* Grand Rapids, MI: Zondervan.

2 Merriam-Webster. 2006. *Merriam-Webster's Collegiate Dictionary.* 11th ed. Merriam-Webster.

3 Trumbull, H. C. (2012). *Practical Paradoxes.* Charleston, SC: Nabu Press.

4 Zondervan Publishing. (2013). *Amplified Bible.* Grand Rapids, MI: Zondervan.

Chapter 2

1 Idleman, Kyle. 2011. *not a fan: Becoming a Completely Committed Follower of Jesus.* Grand Rapids, MI: Zondervan.

2 *US Among Most Depressed Countries in the World – China Leads in Various Categories Tracked by the World Health Organization.* By Deidre McPhillips.

419

3   Black, Claudia. 1987. *It Will Never Happen to Me.* New York, NY: Ballantine Books.

4   Dobbs, Troy. 2020. *The Blessed Life: That No One Really Wants.* Tristan Publishing.

5   Idleman, Kyle. *God's Will for Your Life.* Sermon, October 25, 2018. Southeast Christian Church.

Chapter 3

1   Warren, Rick. 2019. "Knowing God Helps You Know Yourself - Pastor Rick's Daily Hope." Pastorrick.com. December 26, 2019. https://pastorrick.com/knowing-god-helps-you-know-yourself/.

2   Beattie, Melody. 1987. *Codependent No More: How to Stop Controlling Others and Start Caring for Yourself.* London, England: HarperSanFrancisco.

3   Tucker, S. (2013). *The Christian Codependence Recovery Workbook: From Surviving to Significance.* Spirit of Life Recovery Resources.

4   Beattie, Melody. 2010. *The New Codependency: Help and Guidance for Today's Generation.* Thorndike Press.

5   Melero, Angela. 2018. "This Common Habit Is Actually A Sign of Codependency." Thezoereport.Com. The Zoe Report. October 19, 2018. https://www.thezoereport.com/p/what-codependent-behavior-looks-like-these-days-how-to-change-it-12618132.

6   Co-Dependents Anonymous, Inc. 2011. *Recovery Patterns of Codependence.*

Chapter 4

1   Roitsch, Lisa. (2017). *Dear Shame, Let's Break Up! How to Stay Present Inside of God's Truth and Be Set Free from the Torture of False Beliefs.* CreateSpace Independent Publishing Platform.

2   Graham, Billy. 2009. "Billy Graham: Does the Holy Spirit Live in You?" Decisionmagazine.Com. April 30, 2009. https://decisionmagazine.com/does-the-holy-spirit-live-in-you/.

3   Peterson, Eugene H. 2012. *The Message.* Colorado Springs, CO: NavPress Publishing Group.

4   Bradshaw, John. 2006. *Healing the Shame That Binds You.* Deerfield Beach, FL: Health Communications.

5   Burgo, Joseph. 2018. *Shame: Free Yourself, Find Joy, and Build True Self-Esteem.* St. Martin's Essentials.

Chapter 5

1   Vinopal, Lauren. 2019. "Parent Shaming: Why It Hurts so Bad and Can't Be Avoided." Fatherly.Com. Fatherly. June 18, 2019. https://www.fatherly.com/health-science/why-parent-shaming-is-so-hurtful/.

2   Brown, Brene. 2015. *Daring Greatly: How the Courage to Be Vulnerable Transforms the Way We Live, Love, Parent, and Lead.* London, England: Penguin Life.

3   "Virginia Satir's 5 Freedoms to Strengthen Self-Esteem." 2018. Exploringyourmind.Com. July 12, 2018. https://exploringyourmind.com/virginia-satirs-5-freedoms-to-strengthen-self-esteem/.

4   "'Good' Children - at What Price? The Secret Cost of Shame." n.d. Naturalchild. Org. Accessed January 11, 2021. https://www.naturalchild.org/articles/robin_grille/good_children.html.

Chapter 6

1   Max-Planck-Gesellschaft. 2008. "Decision-Making May Be Surprisingly Unconscious Activity." *Science Daily*, April 15, 2008. https://www.sciencedaily.com/releases/2008/04/080414145705.htm.

2   "The Iliad – Homer – Poem: Story, Summary, & Analysis." Ancient Literature. April 24, 2020. Accessed January 24, 2021. https://www.ancient-literature.com/greece_homer_iliad.html.

3   Dove, Lynn. 2018. "Most Misinterpreted Scripture Verses – 1 Corinthians 10:13." Lynndove.Com. September 28, 2018. https://lynndove.com/2018/09/28/most-misinterpreted-scripture-verses-1-corinthians-1013.

4   Compulsive Behavior. n.d. Wikipedia.Org. Accessed October 3, 2020. https://en.wikipedia.org/wiki/Compulsive_behavior/.

5   Berlinger, Joe, dir. *Conversations with a Killer: The Ted Bundy Tapes.* Netflix, 2019. https://www.netflix.com/title/80226612

6   "R Zaccharias." n.d. Goodreads.Com. Accessed October 20, 2020. https://www.goodreads.com/author/show/6977444.R_Zaccharias.

7   Spurgeon, C. H. (2019). *Faith's Checkbook.* Independently Published.

Chapter 7

1   Steele, Lauren. 2018. "How Child Discipline Has Changed: A Brief History." Fatherly.Com. Fatherly. January 26, 2018. https://www.fatherly.com/parenting/how-child-discipline-has-changed-a-brief-history/.

2   Mulvey, Stephen. 2019. "The Long Echo of WW2 Trauma." *BBC*, June 7, 2019. https://www.bbc.com/news/stories-48528841.

3   Their War Ended 70 Years Ago. Their Trauma Didn't. (2015, September 11). *Washington Post (Washington, D.C.: 1974)*. Retrieved from https://www.washingtonpost.com/opinions/the-greatest-generations-forgotten-trauma/2015/09/11/8978d3b0-46b0-11e5-8ab4-c73967a143d3_story.html

4   Brokaw, Tom. 2002. *The Greatest Generation*. New York, NY: Bantam Doubleday Dell Publishing Group.

5   "PTSD: National Center for PTSD." n.d. Ptsd.va.Gov. Accessed March 18, 2021. https://www.ptsd.va.gov/professional/treat/specific/ptsd_family.asp.

6   Carlson, Eve, and Ruzek, Joseph. *Effects of PTSD On Families*. US Department of Veterans Affairs National Center for PTSD.

Chapter 8

1   Carruth, Hayden. 1968. "Tabula Rasa." *The Hudson Review* 21 (1): 83.

2   Arno, Richard Gene, and Phyllis Jean Arno. 1993. *Creation Therapy: A Biblically Based Model for Christian Counseling*. Sarasota Academy of Christian Counseling.

3   "A Quote by Albert Einstein." n.d. Goodreads.Com. Accessed September 12, 2020. https://www.goodreads.com/quotes/8136665-everybody-is-a-genius-but-if-you-judge-a-fish.

4   Arno, Richard Gene, and Phyllis Jean Arno. 2009. *Created in God's Image*. Peppertree Press.

Chapter 9

1   Vaughan, J. (2015, October 17). The Tale of the Two Seas: The Secret of Those Who Give. Retrieved January 18, 2021, from Blueshirtproject.com website: http://www.blueshirtproject.com/the-tale-of-the-two-seas-the-secret-of-those-who-give/

2   Lewis, C.S. 1989. *The Case for Christianity*. London, England: Prentice Hall & IBD.

Chapter 10

1   Boyle, Marjorie O'Rourke. 2005. "Broken Hearts: The Violation of Biblical Law." *Journal of the American Academy of Religion. American Academy of Religion* 73 (3): 731–57.

2   Darabont, F. 1994. *The Shawshank Redemption. Columbia Pictures.*

3   Nelsonword. 1993. *Bible: New King James Bible*. Nashville, TN: Thomas Nelson.

4   Watson, T., Jr. (2012). *Discourses On Important and Interesting Subjects (volume 1); Being the Select Works of Thomas Watson*. General Books.

5   Niebuhr, Reinhold. 1932. *Serenity Prayer*.

Chapter 11

1   Hillsong Music. "Oceans (Where Feet May Fail). iTunes audio, 8:55. 2013. https://music.apple.com/us/album/oceans-where-feet-may-fail/720105570?i=720106050

2   TerKeurst, L. (2016). *Uninvited: Living Loved When You Feel Less than, Left Out, and Lonely*. Nashville, TN: Thomas Nelson.

3   "Quotes & Inspiration - National and State Organizations." n.d. Google.Com. Accessed February 1, 2021. https://sites.google.com/a/celebratethechildren.org/national-and-state-organizations/quotes-inspiration.

4   Crabb, Lawrence J. 2006. *Inside Out*. Colorado Springs, CO: NavPress.

Chapter 12

1   Parker, Nils. 2013. "The Angel in the Marble." Medium. July 9, 2013. https://nilsaparker.medium.com/the-angel-in-the-marble-f7aa43f333dc.

2   Harvest House Publishers. 1999. *Bible: New American Standard Bible*. Eugene, OR: Harvest House.

Chapter 13

1   www.facebook.com/steppesoffaith. 2020. "The 7 Types of Love in the Bible." Steppesoffaith.Com. February 14, 2020. http://www.steppesoffaith.com/faith/7-types-love-bibl

Chapter 14

1   The Editors of Encyclopedia Britannica. (2019). Oedipus Rex. In *Encyclopedia Britannica*.

2   Gaultiere, Bill. 2016. "Inventory of Emotional Wounds from Your Mother or Father." Soulshepherding.Org. January 10, 2016. https://www.soulshepherding.org/inventory-of-emotional-wounds-from-your-mother-or-father/.

Chapter 15

1   Chery, Fritz. 2021. "20 Reasons Why God Allows Trials and Tribulations." Biblereasons.Com. March 1, 2021. https://biblereasons.com/reasons-for-trials/.

Chapter 16

1   Cloud, Henry, and John Townsend. 1996. *Boundaries: When to Say Yes, When to Say No to Take Control of Your Life.* Grand Rapids, MI: Zondervan.

ABOUT THE AUTHOR

David Ralston, PhD, is the founder and director of Life Training Ministries in Louisville, Kentucky, a leading provider of Christ-centered counseling and mentoring for metro-Louisville as well as online globally. His counsel and guidance have become highly sought after, especially in the areas of shame, brokenness, identity dependence, and soul work.

Dr. Dave is a gifted presenter, teacher, and counselor, and has spoken to groups and audiences of all sizes, both close to home and across the country. In addition to writing his weekly blog, *Training for Life*, he is the author of numerous curricula, articles, and seminar resources, including *TURN: Turn from Brokenness to Wholeness in Christ, Marriage Foundations: Seven Pillars of a Well-Built Marriage*, and his highly recognized article, "Am I Spiritually Hydrated?"

He holds an earned doctoral degree from Colorado Theological Seminary in Clinical Christian Counseling with board certification in Marriage & Family therapy. He is credentialed as an Advanced Licensed Christian Counselor and Certified Temperament Counselor by the National Christian Counselors Association.

David Ralston's nearly four-decade-long journey of personal spiritual formation has been forged through his commitment to his local church, complemented by his experiences as part of the Walk to Emmaus, Promise Keepers Men's Ministry, Fellowship of Christian Athletes, and the Liminal Unknown weekend.

Dave's full-time ministry began in Owensboro, Kentucky over a decade ago, when he and his wife Ann founded Life Training Ministries, a nonprofit ministry focused on addressing the soul wounds of the hurting, broken, and marginalized in that community. After a fruitful season in western Kentucky, he and his wife joined the staff at a thriving megachurch in north Houston, Texas, where Dave served as Pastor for Counseling &

Restoration, seeing God use the unique TURN approach to transform hundreds of lives, marriages, and families. Currently he serves as president and director of Life Training Christian Counseling in Louisville, Kentucky, a division of Life Training Ministries. Dr. Ralston and his wife Ann have four children and four grandchildren.

Made in the USA
Monee, IL
06 January 2022

88104707R00267